Sarah Coakley and the Future of Systematic Theology

Sarah Coakley and the Future of Systematic Theology

Janice McRandal, editor

Fortress Press
Minneapolis

SARAH COAKLEY AND THE FUTURE OF SYSTEMATIC THEOLOGY

Cover image: Many Rooms©Jan Richardson

Cover design: Laurie Ingram

Library of Congress Cataloging-in-Publication Data

Print ISBN: 978-1-5064-1072-2

eBook ISBN: 978-1-5064-0806-4

Manufactured in the U.S.A.

This book was produced using Pressbooks.com, and PDF rendering was done by PrinceXML.

Contents

Being George Eliot: An Impossible Standpoint?

Janice McRandal

"Coakley is the George Eliot of Theologians."[1]

This claim, made by Mark Oppenheimer, has sat uncomfortably in my memory for many years now, punctuated by a perpetual question mark. Oppenheimer was most likely referring to the way prose operated in Coakley's work, but the ambiguity, or rather the irony, of this analogy has stuck. Eliot, of course, chose to conceal her gender. It was a means to an end, a way to penetrate the literary community of the Victorian era; a choice she felt would allow her work to be taken seriously and shield her from the puritanical gaze. It was a successful strategy for Mary Ann Evans: George Eliot's legacy is secure alongside the great writers of Western literature. But this is hardly an uncomplicated ascription, perhaps demonstrated by the lasting confusion surrounding Virginia Woolf's famous declaring of Eliot's *Middlemarch* to be "one of the few English novels written for grown-up people."[2] In Coakley's case, writing systematic theology as a woman

---

1. Mark Oppenheimer, "Prayerful Vulnerability," *Christian Century* 120, no. 13 (2003): 26.
2. Virginia Woolf, "George Eliot," *The Times Literary Supplement*, 20 November 1919. Regarding the

has become an identity marker, a way in which her work is praised and critiqued. She has been celebrated for her "erudite, challenging and eirenic theological voice,"[3] her work being described as a "connoisseur's piece,"[4] while simultaneously being critiqued for her academic *Fachsprache*,[5] an ongoing issue of concern for feminists debating the use of exclusive language in the field.[6]

Much of this evaluation seems to depend on assumptions regarding what constitutes a serious systematician, or a solemn feminist. Why would a feminist even bother pursuing the systematic field, upholding the center at the cost of voices from the margins? Can't Coakley see that this is simply reifying an oppressive ideology of "theology proper"? In some sense the Oppenheimer quote is fitting. Does Oppenheimer praise Coakley because she has penetrated the "men's club"? Is her prose duly admirable, her scholarship rigorous enough for her to escape the easy dismissal often afforded so-called "contextual" theologians? The ambiguity around Coakley's work, especially upon the publication of the first volume of her systematic theology, creates an intersection of competing standpoints. And while Coakley's work is gaining a wider audience in some pockets of the theological world, it also points to a collision of disciplinary trajectories. In gathering such a broad range of theoretical concerns, and naming them theological issues (*théologie totale*), Coakley remains vulnerable to the critique of failing to execute any approach "rightly." In this collection of essays, scholars explore Coakley's multifaceted contribution to contemporary theology, and explore the many questions her work raises within and beyond the systematic field. It is hardly surprising that Coakley's work—traversing sociology, anthropology, science, medicine, philosophy, spirituality, and liturgical studies—has found itself to be a dialogue partner in a variety of academic conversations. And yet Sarah

debate around Eliot's status as a feminist, see June Szirotny, *George Eliot's Feminism: The Right to Rebellion* (New York: Palgrave Macmillan, 2015).

3. Gavin D'Costa, "Book Review of 'Powers and Submissions: Spirituality, Philosophy and Gender,'" *International Journal of Systematic Theology* 6, no. 2 (2004): 330.

4. Esther Reed, "Christ Without Absolutes (Book Review)," *Biblical Interpretation* 7, no. 2 (1999).

5. David Louth, "Book Reviews," *Heythrop Journal* 45, no. 3 (2004).

6. Marcella Althaus-Reid and Lisa Isherwood, *Controversies in Feminist Theology*, Controversies in Contextual Theology (London: SCM, 2007), 132.

Coakley is a systematic theologian. It is precisely her conception of systematic theology—*théologie totale*—that causes this interdisciplinary collision.

For Coakley, then, systematic theology is the integration of those theoretical concerns that are often considered outside the purview of the systematic theologian:

> However briefly, or lengthily, it is explicated (and the shorter versions, have, in Christian tradition, often been as elegant, effective and enduring as the longer ones), systematic theology attempts to provide a coherent and alluring unfolding of the connected parts of its vision.[7]

It is the "allure" of this proposal that strikes the reader with a sense of Coakley's magnetic understanding of structure. Coakley recognizes the inherent pull of life's matter(s) into the larger Christian scheme, clearly demonstrated in the breadth of sources she appeals to, her provocative methodology, and her defense of systematic theology in the face of contemporary dismissal.

Contemporary theology often finds itself engaged in the debates of continental theory (or more specifically psychoanalytic/ psycholinguistic theory). However, Coakley has taken the unusual step of promoting an ongoing relationship with analytic philosophy of religion, while simultaneously prompting a return to patristic theology and what she describes as the "contemplative matrix."[8]

> If it be objected that this strategy is so objectionably taking up the master's tools, I can only reply that these tools are so powerful and significant already that the demands of Realpolitik drive me to handle, redirect, and imaginatively negotiate their usage.[9]

To medicine, anthropology, art criticism, and the sociological

---

7. Sarah Coakley, "Is There a Future for Gender and Theology? On Gender, Contemplation, and the Systematic Task," *Criterion* 47, no. 1 (2009): 4.
8. A title that Coakley ascribes to Part II of her essay collection; see A. Denise Starkey, "Powers and Submissions: Spirituality, Philosophy and Gender (Book)," *Anglican Theological Review* 86, no. 4 (2004).
9. Sarah Coakley, "Feminism and Analytic Philosophy of Religion," in William J. Wainwright, *The Oxford Handbook of Philosophy of Religion*, Oxford Handbooks in Philosophy (New York and Oxford: Oxford University Press, 2005), 517.

fieldwork that is significantly developed in volume one of the systematics, we see an astonishing range of sources engaged by the theologian. Already in Coakley's early treatment of Ernst Troeltsch, she utilized Basil Mitchell's definition of the "cumulative case" argument;[10] the idea that a theological thesis arises from accumulated points and not from isolated "knockdown" ideas. Against the backdrop of Coakley's entire corpus, we see a similar picture emerging.

And yet this leads to a particular, and certainly polarizing, methodology.[11] The contemplative position assumed by Coakley is considered to be the proper subjective stance for all theologians, regardless of contextual priority. This is not to suggest that Coakley sidesteps so-called contextual agenda. Rather she places gender and race[12] (most prominently) firmly at the center and refuses simply to accept the tag of "context" placed on similar fields of study. Coakley's unique stance is to assert that theology begins with contemplation and not the contextual experience, a point of significant distinction, suggests Rachel Muers.[13] Coakley's bold assertion is that contemplative practices are truly transformative and empowering, and therefore give rise to the prophetic voice and act.[14]

Coakley's endeavors have always been, after all, pointing toward the systematic process. As we point to the individual strategies and achievements of her *théologie totale*, we must recognize that such features find their place only in relation to the larger systematic project. This project, as a coherent and alluring scheme, is itself the real goal toward which she has been working. Thus whatever isolated

---

10. Sarah Coakley, *Christ without Absolutes: A Study of the Christology of Ernst Troeltsch* (Oxford: Oxford University Press, 1988), 103. Max Stackhouse commends Coakley in this regard. Max L. Stackhouse, "Christ without Absolutes (Book Review)," *Theological Studies* 50, no. 4 (1989).

11. This approach is noted and welcomed by Andrew Louth who laments the "Balkanizing" of much Christian theology. Of Coakley's status as a feminist, Louth says: "Coakley writes as a feminist, but what she has to say deserves a much wider audience, just as her reading extends much more widely." Louth, "Book Reviews," 367.

12. This distinction is made in anticipation of *Divine Darkness and Epistemic Justification: An Essay "On the Contemplative Life,"* volume 2 of her systematic theology; an essay that will focus on race as a fundamentally epistemological category.

13. Ibid., 122. Rachel Meurs, "Book Reviews," *Theology & Sexuality: The Journal of the Institute for the Study of Christianity & Sexuality* 9, no. 1 (2002): 123.

14. Margaret Daphne Hampson, *Swallowing a Fishbone?: Feminist Theologians Debate Christianity* (London: SPCK, 1996), 110, 11.

contributions the scholar believes Coakley might offer are already enmeshed in this frequently denounced project of systematics. In short, Coakley's most important prophetic contribution to theology/theory of any kind is nothing else than the renewal of systematic theology.

***

How Coakley's work will be received and appraised is yet to be seen, especially as we await a further three volumes of her systematic theology. It is a dauntless enterprise, one in which Coakley assumes no easy position. But this is, of course, the challenge of theological writing. Or as George Eliot suggested in her first publication: "Religious ideas have the fate of melodies, which, once set afloat in the world, are taken up by all sorts of instruments, some of them woefully coarse, feeble, or out of tune, until people are in danger of crying out that the melody itself is detestable."[15]

---

15. George Eliot, *Scenes of Clerical Life* (London: Penguin Books, 1998), 258.

1

Exegetical Mysticism: Scripture, *Paideia*, and the Spiritual Senses

Benjamin Myers

A retrieval of the tradition of the spiritual senses—the idea that there is a spiritual apparatus of perception analogous to the five physical senses—has been a major part of Sarah Coakley's theological project.[1] Coakley's explorations of this tradition have opened up new avenues in contemporary theology. Many of her deepest preoccupations converge around this theme: her commitment to doctrinal *ressourcement* through a rereading of patristic sources; her emphasis on contemplative

---

1. See especially Sarah Coakley, "Gregory of Nyssa," in *The Spiritual Senses: Perceiving God in Western Christianity*, ed. Sarah Coakley and Paul L. Gavrilyuk (Cambridge: Cambridge University Press, 2012), 36–55; idem, "The Resurrection and the 'Spiritual Senses,'" in *Powers and Submissions: Spirituality, Philosophy, and Gender* (Oxford: Blackwell, 2002), 131–52; idem, "The Identity of the Risen Jesus," in *Seeking the Identity of Jesus*, ed. Beverly Gaventa and Richard Hays (Grand Rapids: Eerdmans, 2008), 301–19.

practice; her understanding of embodiment and of the role of the body in knowing; her concern to identify more fluid "feminine" modes of knowing not reducible to the logocentric discourse; and her interest in the epistemological problems identified in the tradition of analytic philosophy of religion. The patristic sources are fundamental to Coakley's work in this area. In this paper I will explore the roots of the spiritual senses tradition in the writing of Origen of Alexandria, before making some suggestions about how Origen's teaching might inform a contemporary retrieval of the spiritual senses.

There is substantive research on Origen's teaching on the spiritual senses, building on the pioneering work of Karl Rahner.[2] One of the most significant recent studies appears in the volume on the spiritual senses co-edited by Sarah Coakley.[3] Origen plays an important role in Coakley's own reflections on the spiritual senses, even though it is Gregory of Nyssa whom Coakley regards as the exemplary representative of the spiritual senses tradition. In this chapter I will take a closer look at Origen's teaching on the spiritual senses, and I will argue that his language about the spiritual senses is intimately linked to his understanding of the spiritual interpretation of scripture. I will try to demonstrate that, for Origen, scriptural exegesis is the main context in which the spiritual senses are developed. This will lead to some critical questions about whether Coakley has adopted Origen's mystical outlook without preserving its connection to Origen's commitment to the practice of biblical exegesis. If there is to be a contemporary retrieval of the Origenist tradition of the spiritual senses, then we will need more than an account of contemplative silence; we will need an account also of contemplative reading and of the mysticism of exegesis.

---

2. Karl Rahner, "The 'Spiritual Senses' according to Origen," in *Theological Investigations*, vol. 16, trans. David Morland (New York: Seabury, 1979).

3. Mark J. McInroy, "Origen of Alexandria," in *The Spiritual Senses: Perceiving God in Western Christianity*, ed. Sarah Coakley and Paul L. Gavrilyuk (Cambridge: Cambridge University Press, 2012), 20–35. For a broad account of the Origenist tradition, see also the monograph by the same author, *Balthasar on the Spiritual Senses: Perceiving Splendour* (Oxford: Oxford University Press, 2014), chapter 1.

Spiritual Senses and Scriptural Exegesis in Origen

Origen's commentary on the Song of Songs explores the rich sensual language of the Song, and argues that each of the five senses has a corresponding spiritual sense. When the divine Logos encounters believers, he "takes possession of their hearing, their sight, their touch, and their taste as well, and offers excellences from himself that match each single sense according to its natural capacity."[4] Having caught a glimpse of Christ's glory, our eyes desire to see nothing else but him. Having heard his word of life, our ears desire to hear nothing else. Having handled the Word of life in our hands, we yearn to take hold of him and to touch him more than any other thing. "Because he tastes so sweet and so delightful, all other flavors will now seem harsh and bitter compared to him."[5]

Origen is not referring to a spiritual capacity that is activated in one moment, but about an extended process of growth. The senses need to be exercised and educated. They can be cultivated through practice. The perfect, Origen says, "have their senses trained." The spiritual senses "are acquired by training" so that the believer comes to apprehend spiritual realities "with more acute perception."[6] The Christian life is an education in spiritual perception. As our desire for Christ grows, so our perception becomes ever more refined and more receptive to divine realities. "Only those who with their whole intention and with all their love hold the divine Logos in their heart will be able to perceive the odor of his fragrance and his sweetness."[7]

Considering such passages from Origen's commentary in their immediate contexts, it is possible to advance two hypotheses about the way the spiritual senses relate to the wider structures of Origen's thought. First, the cultivation of the spiritual senses belongs to *paideia*, the educative process by which Christ transforms the believer. Second, the spiritual senses are activated specifically in the interpretation of

---

4. Origen, *Commentary on the Song of Songs* 1.4; English translation in Origen, *The Song of Songs: Commentary and Homilies*, trans. R. P. Lawson, ACW 26 (New York: Newman, 1956).
5. Origen, *Commentary on the Song of Songs* 1.4.
6. Ibid.
7. Ibid., 2.10.

scripture, which is itself the principal instrument of Christ's *paideia*. Let me try to substantiate both these hypotheses.

In the passages already quoted, Origen does not only describe the spiritual senses and their cultivation, he also explains how the spiritual senses operate. He states that a reader will not be able to understand the commentary that is before them unless their senses have been trained. The "sensual man," Origen says, will not be able to "perceive and understand" when he hears "these matters so interpreted."[8] Because his senses are dull, he will judge Origen's exegesis as "foolish and empty"; he will hear without hearing, and the sweet aroma of the Song of Songs will be for him an unpleasant odor, "the odor of death" as Origen says quoting St. Paul (2 Cor. 2:15-16). By contrast, those who bring to the commentary a "subtle spiritual sense" will embrace "this kind of interpretation" of the Song[9]—that is, the spiritual or anagogical interpretation that Origen is presenting.

It is not simply that Origen uses scriptural passages to explain the function of the spiritual senses. He connects spiritual senses with the practice of scriptural reading itself. It is as one reads and interprets scripture anagogically that one perceives Christ, the Logos, with the eyes and ears and nose and mouth and hands of the heart.

One of the most peculiar things about Origen's exegetical practice is the fact that the real subject-matter of his commentaries is so often the practice of exegesis itself. He writes commentaries about the process of writing a commentary. The spiritual realities that Origen finds in the scriptural writings turn out to be these writings themselves as instruments of divine *paideia*. This is because spiritual exegesis is, for Origen, always about encountering the Logos who speaks in the text. When readers ascend anagogically through the text, they are brought into the presence of Christ the Teacher. The passage in which the bridegroom is said to come leaping on the mountains and bounding over the hills (Song 2:8)[10] is taken by Origen to refer to Christ leaping toward humanity over the mountains and hills of the prophets and

8. Ibid., 1.4.
9. Ibid.
10. Old Testament references and quotations are from the Septuagint (NETS edition).

apostles.[11] And Origen explains this interpretation by referring to the experience of scriptural reading:

> Now every soul . . . if at any time it is in the thick of an argument about some passage—and everyone knows from his experience how when one gets into a tight corner like this, one gets shut up in the straits of propositions and enquiries—if at any time some riddles or obscure sayings of the Law or the Prophets hem in the soul, if then she [this soul] should chance to perceive Him [the Word] to be present, and from afar should catch the sound of His voice, immediately she is uplifted. And, when he has begun more and more to draw near to her senses and to illuminate the things that are obscure, then she sees him "leaping over the mountains and the hills"; that is to say, then he suggests to her interpretations of a high and lofty sort, so that this soul can rightly say: "Behold, he comes leaping upon the mountains, skipping over the hills."[12]

What Origen describes here is simply the experience of a patient, contemplative reading of the Bible. Laboring over a difficult passage, the reader suddenly catches a glimpse of the divine Logos and "perceives him to be present" in the text. As Christ "draws near to [the] senses" he "illuminates the things that are obscure," so that the soul sees him clearly. He "leaps" over the text toward the expectant soul.

For Origen, then, scriptural exegesis is not a convenient method for uncovering certain facts about Christ. The practice of exegesis is itself the means by which spiritual transformation, including the refinement of the spiritual senses, takes place. What the Bible turns out to be *about* is Bible-reading—as long as one remembers that "Bible-reading" for Origen refers to the whole economy in which the divine Logos communicates itself and imparts itself to the believer, drawing the believer into an unceasing process of growth and transformation.

Because the subject-matter of scripture is divine *paideia*, and because scripture is the instrument of that *paideia*, Origen finds scripture filled with references to exegetical practice. The planks of Noah's ark refer analogically to the "divine library" of the prophets and apostles; and the soul should likewise become a library containing these writings.[13]

---

11. Origen, *Commentary on the Song of Songs* 3.11.
12. Ibid.

The lamb eaten by the Israelites is analogically related not, as one might expect, to Christ's sacrifice but to Christ's teaching through scripture. Commenting on the command that the Israelites were to "eat the meat this night, roasted in fire" (Exod. 12:8), Origen says that the lamb is the text of scripture: "If the lamb is Christ and Christ is the Logos, what is the flesh of the divine words if not the divine scriptures?"[14] And the roasting with fire refers to the work of the Holy Spirit who uses the text of scripture to induct the reader into spiritual realities: "For the words are changed by such fire."[15]

The same tendency to interpret scripture as a book *about* scriptural reading is very pronounced in Origen's Song of Songs commentary. When the bridegroom is portrayed as peering through the lattice (Song 2:9), Origen comments that the lattice represents the text of scripture. The sensitive reader perceives Christ himself peering through the letters of the text, and calling the reader to come away with him. Thus the reader's "spiritual senses" are linked to what is usually called the figural or "spiritual sense" of the text. Not all readers can perceive Christ in scripture. It takes a reader whose senses have been properly trained and educated. Origen writes: "For the Word of God . . . does not appear as set in public places where everyone can see. . . . Rather he is found when he is sought for, and found, as we said, not in the open courtyard but covered over and as it were hiding behind the wall."[16]

Origen makes much of the "wound of love" referred to in the Septuagint version of Song 2:5. In one of his surviving homilies on the Song, he explains that it is scriptural interpretation that inflicts this wound on the soul of the hearer. "How beautiful, how fitting it is to receive a wound from Love! . . . If anyone is wounded by this homily, if any is wounded by the teaching of the divine scripture," then that person has shared the experience of the disciples on the road to Emmaus [Luke 24:32], who said, "Were not our hearts burning within

---

13. Origen, *Homilies on Exodus* 2; English translation in Origen, *Homilies on Genesis and Exodus*, trans. Ronald E. Heine, FC 71 (Washington, DC: Catholic University Press of America, 1981).

14. Origen, *Peri Pascha* 26; English translation in Origen, *Treatise on the Passover and Dialogue of Origen with Heraclides*, trans. Robert J. Daly, ACW 54 (New York: Paulist, 1992).

15. Origen, *Peri Pascha* 27.

16. Origen, *Commentary on the Song of Songs* 3.13.

us while he was talking to us on the road, while he was opening the scriptures to us?"[17]

The close connection between exegesis and the spiritual senses also explains Origen's warnings against the debasement of the spiritual senses. In a homily on Exodus, he suggests that "eye for eye, tooth for tooth" (Exod. 21:24) refers to the removal of false teachers from the church:

> Let [the false teacher] also surrender an eye for an eye if he injured the eye of [another] soul, that is, if he disturbed its understanding. Let his own eye be removed by him who presides over the church, and let that turbulent and fierce intellect of him who produces a stumbling block be cut off. But also if he injured a tooth of the hearer with which he had been accustomed, when receiving the food of the Word, to crush or grind it with his molars in order to transmit the subtle meaning from these words to the stomach of his soul; if that man damaged and tore out this tooth so that ... the soul cannot receive the Word of God subtly and spiritually, let the tooth of that man who did not crush well and divide the foods of the scriptures be removed. Indeed, perhaps it is for this reason that it is said elsewhere about the Lord: You have broken the teeth of sinners [Ps. 3:8].[18]

Heterodox interpretation of scripture injures the spiritual eye so that it cannot see and damages the spiritual tooth so that scripture can no longer be chewed and digested. Scriptural interpretation is what the spiritual senses are *for*. Heresy dulls or distorts the senses so that believers can no longer properly discern the presence of the Logos in scripture.

Elsewhere Origen uses sensory language to describe the difference between mature and immature believers. In a homily on Genesis, he tells a spiritually inept congregation that their own immaturity has placed limits on what the preacher is able to tell them:

> And you, if you should not still be "a little child" and in need of "milk," but should bring your "senses exercised" [Heb. 5:12-14] and should come more capable to an understanding of the Word of God after very much instruction has been set before you, there will also be a great feast for you.

---

17. Origen, *Homilies on the Song of Songs* 2.8; English translation in *The Song of Songs: Commentary and Homilies*, trans. R. P. Lawson.
18. Origen, *Homilies on Exodus* 10.4.

> The vegetables of the weak will not be prepared for you as food, nor will you be nourished with milk by which "little children" are nourished, but the servant of the Word will make a great feast for you. He will speak to you the wisdom which is offered among the perfect. . . . He will reveal Christ to you.[19]

The feast of the Word, Origen continues, is "for those who know how to hear more perfectly, and bring their senses instructed and exercised for hearing the Word of God."[20] Here spiritual purification is depicted as the cultivation of the senses for the sake of a rich spiritual interpretation of scripture.

Origen even suggests that the same Logos will taste different to each individual hearer of a homily. In a homily on the manna in the wilderness (Exodus 16), Origen remarks that we become capable of digesting the "solid food" of the Word only once we have been perfected through "long exercises." He refers to the rabbinic tradition according to which the manna in the wilderness tasted like whatever each person desired.[21] Manna "imparts the kind of taste to each mouth that each one wishes," so that "if you receive the Word of God which is preached in the church with complete faith and devotion, that word will become whatever you desire."[22] The same scriptural passage can communicate different truths and different degrees of truth. The Logos who speaks in scripture is lovingly adapted to the individual need and capacity of each listener.

Origen's extensive use of sensory language finds its place within the overarching structure of his conception of spiritual *paideia*. The refinement or debasement of the spiritual senses is a gauge of the soul's level of purification through divine teaching. The perception of believers undergoes a continuing transformation as they come under

---

19. Origen, *Homilies on Genesis* 14.3; English translation in *Homilies on Genesis and Exodus*, trans. Ronald E. Heine.
20. Origen, *Homilies on Genesis* 14.3.
21. Cf. the Exodus midrashim on the manna: "It had all sorts of flavors, the Israelites tasting in it each what they desired" (Exodus Rabbah 25:3); "the manna descended with a taste varying according to the needs of each individual Israelite. The young men, eating it as bread, . . . the old, as wafers made with honey, . . . [while] to the babes it tasted like the milk from their mothers' breasts" (Exodus Rabbah 5:9).
22. Origen, *Homilies on Exodus* 7.8.

the influence of Christ's *paideia*. And the main instrument of this educative process is holy scripture.

Sarah Coakley's Interpretation of Origen and Gregory of Nyssa

Sarah Coakley's theological explorations of the spiritual senses are inspired more by Gregory of Nyssa than by Origen. Coakley regards Gregory as an advance on Origen in two ways. First, she understands Gregory to be advocating a form of wordless mysticism; and second, she believes Origen advances a dualism between the "inner" and "outer" senses, while Gregory sees the spiritual senses as the transformation of ordinary perception. On both these points, however, I believe Coakley has underestimated the depth of Gregory's indebtedness to Origen.

In the first place, Gregory shares with Origen an educational picture of the economy of salvation in which human beings are progressively transformed through the agency of the divine Logos. It is against this wider backdrop of *paideia* that Gregory's use of mystical language has to be assessed. While Gregory's homilies on the Song of Songs reiterate Origen's theology of the spiritual senses, the same homilies also contain echoes of the Origenist conception of exegesis as a means of spiritual transformation. In his third homily, Gregory remarks that the opening verses of the Song of Songs "have the power that belongs to means of purification and illumination; by their agency souls that have been purified are prepared for the divine." These opening verses (Song 1:1-8) are thus a necessary "preface" to the Song. They provide the spiritual purification that is required before one can hear the speech of the bridegroom that follows in Song 1:9-14. Of this speech, Gregory says: "The words of the present passage are a participation in divinity itself, since the divine Logos in his own voice confers on the hearer a fellowship with the undefiled power."[23] Gregory's homilies are themselves a means of *paideia* and transformation, since they lead the hearer by progressive stages into the mysteries of union with Christ.

---

23. Gregory of Nyssa, *Homilies on the Song of Songs*, homily 3; English translation in Gregory of Nyssa, *Homilies on the Song of Songs*, trans. Richard A. Norris (Atlanta: SBL, 2012).

Looking back on the first two homilies of the series, Gregory tells his audience: "The insight into the prefatory parts of the Song of Songs that we achieved in our earlier homilies on the preceding two days has been of profit to the extent that the sense contained in the words has washed and scrubbed us from the filth of the flesh. But today . . . God the Logos himself will be manifested to those who have been purified."[24] The scriptural text itself is the path that leads to ever-greater degrees of participation in God. There is no question that this exegetical motif is much more prominent in Origen than in Gregory; but there is nonetheless strong continuity between the two, and Gregory's own mystical theology cannot fully be appreciated until it is set within a tradition of the practice of spiritual exegesis.

Second, Coakley has often stated that Gregory of Nyssa took a decisive step beyond Origen's stark division between "inner" and "outer" modes of perception.[25] In contrast to Origen's Platonic squeamishness about bodily life, Gregory's "subtly adjusted views seem to allow for some significant point of continuity or development from the physical to the spiritual in the spectrum of purgation of the senses."[26] Coakley bases this interpretation on Gregory's remark that his homilies on the Song of Songs are for "the more fleshly-minded"[27]—an apparent contrast with Origen's claim that his commentary on the Song of Songs was written for the spiritually advanced. There is, however, no theological difference between Gregory and Origen on this point. It is no more than a difference of genre. It was Origen's view that homilies are "milk" while commentaries are "meat"; they are modes of exegesis adapted to two different kinds of believers.[28] Jerome reiterated this view when, translating Origen's two homilies on the Song of Songs, he observed that the homilies, by contrast to the commentary, are "not strong

---

24. Gregory of Nyssa, *Homilies on the Song of Songs*, homily 3.
25. Coakley, "The Resurrection and the 'Spiritual Senses,'" 136–39; idem, "The Identity of the Risen Jesus," 313–14; idem, "Gregory of Nyssa," 43–44.
26. Coakley, "Resurrection," 137–38.
27. Gregory of Nyssa, *Homilies on the Song of Songs*, preface.
28. See Éric Junod, "Wodurch unterscheiden sich die Homilien des Origenes von seinen Kommentaren?" in *Predigt in der Alten Kirche*, ed. E. Mühlenberg and J. von Oort (Kampen: Kok Pharos, 1994), 50–81.

meat" but only "treatises which [Origen] composed for babes and sucklings."[29] Here Jerome alludes to Origen's own preface to the commentary on the Song, in which he warned the "children" to stay away from the strong meat of this commentary.[30] Because Gregory of Nyssa is presenting homilies and not a commentary, he follows Origen in addressing himself to the immature or "fleshly-minded" believers. The difference is one of genre, not of theological substance.

The reason homilies are presented to the immature is that the homily itself is a means of their purification. One of Origen's homilies on Genesis begins by roundly rebuking the congregation for their lack of spiritual seriousness. They are unable to receive the meat of the Word. But a homily adapted to their level will itself be the means of their purification and advancement in the spiritual life. The spiritually sluggish believer can be raised from sensuality to "the union of the soul with the divine Logos." But this can occur only through scriptural interpretation: "It is certain that this union of the soul with the Logos cannot come about otherwise than through instruction in the divine books."[31] It is through scripture that believers are drawn more deeply into mystical union with God. It is as believers inquire more deeply into the scriptural books that Christ himself will "take you up and unite you with himself, that you may be made one spirit with him."[32] That is why Origen's homilies often proceed not by logical steps only but by gradations of purification.

Gregory of Nyssa stands squarely within this Origenist tradition. His homilies on the Song of Songs begin by charging his hearers to receive the proclaimed word in a way that will lead to their purification. "I testify," he tells them, "as one who is about to treat the mystical vision contained in the Song of Songs. For by what is written there, the soul is in a certain manner led as a bride toward an incorporeal and spiritual and undefiled marriage with God." Gregory's hearers are to ascend toward God as they listen to the preacher's words. Through

---

29. Jerome, prologue to Origen's *Homilies on the Song of Songs.*
30. Origen, *Commentary on the Song of Songs*, prologue 1.
31. Origen, *Homilies on Genesis* 10.4.
32. Ibid.

their attention to the exposition of the Song, they will be purified and will "journey to the inner shrine of the mysteries manifested in this book." As the hearers attend to "this book" they will be "changed into something more divine by the Lord's instruction."[33] Gregory follows Origen in seeing scriptural interpretation as an instrument of spiritual purification. The ascent of the soul is not a flight into wordless mysticism but an ascent into the mysteries "manifested in this book."

What of Coakley's claim that Origen dualistically divorces the "inner" (spiritual) senses from the "outer" (physical) senses?

In Origen's homilies on the Song of Songs, one finds an explicit connection between the spiritual senses and the incarnation. Explaining the verse in which the bridegroom looks out through the "lattices" or "nets" (Song 2:9), Origen says it is the incarnation that has disentangled us from the "nets" of the devil in which we were ensnared. The Logos has come and peered through the nets of our human nature. He did this by becoming incarnate: "he came to the nets when he assumed a human body that was held in the snares of the hostile powers." Now the Logos looks out through our nature. Further, Origen suggests that the "windows" (Song 2:9) refer to the senses. "One window is one of our senses; the Bridegroom looks out through it. Another window is another sense; through it he gazes with solicitude. For what senses are there through which the Word of God does not look out?"[34] In the incarnation, Christ assumes the senses and sanctifies them, "looking out" through each one with a pure perception.

If the "windows" are the five senses, then Origen adds that death also enters through these windows—for example, when a man looks lustfully on a woman. But when a person "perceives the creator of all in the beauty of his creatures and marvels at his works and praises their Maker, to this soul life enters through the windows of the eyes."[35] Similarly, when a person "listens to the Word of God and takes delight in the reasonings of his wisdom and knowledge," life enters through the ears.[36] There is a connection then between the bodily senses and

---

33. Gregory of Nyssa, *Homilies on the Song of Songs*, homily 1.
34. Origen, *Homilies on the Song of Songs* 2.12.
35. Origen, *Commentary on the Song of Songs* 3.13.

the spiritual senses. Bodily sight is a gateway to spiritual vision. Bodily hearing can become a means of spiritual listening—especially in the case of listening to the preacher's scriptural exposition. Hans Urs von Balthasar was correct to observe that Origen's understanding of the spiritual senses is not dualistic. The "fleshly" senses and the "spiritual" senses are on the opposite ends of a continuum of perception. "It is the same senses which first are earthly and then become heavenly."[37]

Conclusion

We tend to think of scriptural reading and mystical contemplation as two quite different kinds of activities—a dichotomy that is perhaps reinforced in Sarah Coakley's reflections on the priority of "wordless" contemplation. Origen is of particular significance here, since he is the principal founder of the Christian exegetical tradition and the Christian mystical tradition alike. These are not two different parts of his work but only two different (anachronistic) ways of describing a single cohesive vision of the economy of divine *paideia*. The spiritual practice that corresponds to this vision is what might be called exegetical mysticism. Origen uses the language of the spiritual senses to describe a practice of contemplative scriptural reading. In this practice, the spiritual interpretation of scripture serves as a means of *paideia* and *morphosis*. In Origen—and in Gregory of Nyssa after him—an extensive repertoire of sensual and mystical language serves not to evoke an experience of wordless mysticism but to depict the accommodation of the Logos to our senses in a way that awakens our desire and leads us ever deeper into participation in divine reality. Our perception is refined as we learn to encounter the Logos who speaks and acts in scripture. Christ "draws near to our senses,"[38] delighting and enrapturing the soul as it contemplates his *logoi*. In the disciplined contemplative reading of scripture, "the hand of the interior soul" reaches out and touches the living Word.[39]

36. Origen, *Commentary on the Song of Songs* 3.13.
37. Hans Urs von Balthasar, *The Glory of the Lord*, vol. 1 (San Francisco: Ignatius, 1982), 370–71.
38. Origen, *Commentary on the Song of Songs* 3.11.
39. Ibid., 2.9.

There is, I believe, great promise in Sarah Coakley's rehabilitation of the spiritual senses tradition. But this tradition can be fully recovered only in a theological epistemology that takes account of not only contemplative silence but also contemplative reading; not only word-less mysticism but also exegetical mysticism. An integrative theology of this kind would, I believe, be able to develop the kind of dynamic, transformative, pedagogical vision that Coakley is aiming at when she describes her project as *théologie totale*—a contemporary version of what the Alexandrian tradition called *paideia*.

2

———

The "How" of Transformation in Levinas and Coakley

Annette Pierdziwol

To all appearances, Levinas's philosophical project seems driven by a vision of ethical transformation—of the possibility, as one commentator puts it, of "a capacity for responsiveness to the sufferings and needs of the other that is seemingly almost beyond the extent of the human."[1] Indeed, it often seems as if Levinas refuses to set any limits at all on the prospects of such transformation: responsibility is a matter of being ready to respond prior to establishing the domain of one's duties; it is infinite and "irrecusable."[2] Moreover, he implies that this is the truth he would have each of us incarnate in our everyday,

1. David Michael Kleinberg-Levin, *Before the Voice of Reason: Echoes of Responsibility in Merleau-Ponty's Ecology and Levinas's Ethics* (Albany: State University of New York Press, 2008), 231.
2. Emmanuel Levinas, *Totality and Infinity: An Essay on Exteriority*, trans. Alphonso Lingis, Martinus Nijhoff (Pittsburgh: Duquesne University Press, 1969), 201.

even banal, interactions with one another. For certain critics, however, such visions seem eminently unsuited to philosophy. Perhaps the most blunt critique along these lines has come from Alain Badiou, who contends that much recent continental moral philosophy, especially the "ethics of difference" (which often claims the influence of Levinas), really amounts to nothing more than "a dog's dinner . . . a pious discourse without piety"[3]—ultimately empty and hypocritical.

For Badiou, the simple solution here is that neither pious discourse nor piety belongs in philosophical ethics, but for Levinasians, perhaps attracted precisely by what Badiou disparagingly labels the "pious" tone of Levinas's philosophy (or, what might more positively be designated, its moral seriousness, its refusal of excuse and proviso, its demandingness), this remains a serious question. Does Levinas offer merely a "pious discourse without piety"? And is this charge exacerbated even further in his case by the use of hyperbole, a pious discourse that seems to reach fever pitch?[4] We are exhorted to an infinitely demanding responsibility to all and for all that exceeds our capacities. But the more epic this vision of ethical transformation becomes, the greater the worry grows concerning what all this talk amounts to in everyday practice. Are we given any account of how it might be achieved and what it would look like in terms of an everyday pattern of action: a real-life "piety"?

A somewhat similar concern is expressed by Sarah Coakley. While she has not as yet engaged at length with continental ethics in her published work, from the vantage of her own project she offers the following succinct critique of a certain omission evident in this field. She contends that "there is much talk of the problem of attending to the otherness of the other in contemporary post-Kantian ethics and post-colonial theory . . . there is very little about the intentional and

---

3. Alain Badiou, *Ethics: An Essay on the Understanding of Evil*, trans. Peter Hallward (London and New York: Verso, 2002), 23.
4. As Kevin Hart puts it, "The language of this philosophy becomes increasingly exorbitant: Levinas speaks of the 'I' as the *hostage* of the other person, as being *obsessed* with the other, and as being *persecuted* by him or her. We have a new philosophy of the subject that in its very presentation is methodologically committed to exorbitance" (Kevin Hart, "Introduction: Levinas the Exorbitant," in *The Exorbitant: Emmanuel Levinas Between Jews and Christians*, ed. Kevin Hart and Michael A. Signer [New York: Fordham University Press, 2010], 11–12).

embodied practices that might enable such attention."[5] Here again then we have the worry about "pious discourse" and empty rhetoric, but we also have a hint toward a fuller synopsis of the missing element in the implied need for an account of how this kind of ethical attentiveness might be cultivated; of the pragmatic means by which it is enabled and sustained over time.

For Coakley, as will be explored in this chapter, this "how" can only be answered in terms of practice. Indeed, she is an unrepentant pessimist about the power of ideas (whether philosophical or theological) or of declarations of intent by mere *fiat* to effect change in and of themselves.[6] Yet, she also repeatedly warns against the opposite extreme, namely, the "dangers of a busy pragmatism" that assumes it can "leap to the supposedly clear-cut goal of 'justice' without delicate training in *attending* to the 'other.'"[7] It is Coakley's writings on the nature of such training, found in her reading of "older, theistically-oriented traditions of personal transformation,"[8] and in particular of the patristic "spiritual senses" tradition with its depiction of such transformation as attained only progressively through the lifelong effort of repeated bodily practices, that this chapter will explore and seek to bring into conversation with Levinas's ethics.

However, before turning to stage this engagement, it must first be asked whether Coakley's diagnosis of this certain weakness in post-Kantian ethics really counts as a fair critique with regard to Levinas. After all, as many of his commentators point out, he is engaged in a highly distinctive ethical project that has little to do with the kind of philosophical ethics that seeks to construct a set of normative guidelines or practices. His focus, rather, is on elucidating "the pre-ontological condition for any ethical activity at all."[9] More recently,

5. Sarah Coakley, "Is There a Future for Gender and Theology?: On Gender, Contemplation, and the Systematic Task," *Criterion* 47, no. 1 (2009): 6.
6. See Sarah Coakley, "Why Gift? Gift, Gender and Trinitarian Relations in Milbank and Tanner," *Scottish Journal of Theology* 61, no. 2: 228–29; Sarah Coakley, *Powers and Submissions: Spirituality, Philosophy and Gender* (Malden, MA: Blackwell, 2002), xx, 159; Coakley, "Is There a Future for Gender and Theology?": 6–7, 11n2.
7. Coakley, *Powers and Submissions*, xvii.
8. Ibid., 157.
9. Claire Elise Katz, "Education East of Eden: Levinas, the Psychopath, and the Paradox of

however, a number of Levinasian scholars, themselves deeply sympathetic to the unique nature of his project, have nonetheless begun to articulate some criticisms in terms not dissimilar to those employed by Coakley above. They too highlight a certain omission or sidelining of questions of moral growth that needs to be redressed. For example, Claire Katz argues that we can see there is something missing in Levinas's account if we consider how the question of failure remains ambiguous in his project.

> Emmanuel Levinas's conception of ethical subjectivity emphasizes an obligation that is not chosen and from which we cannot recuse ourselves. It emphasizes our obligation and response to the Other, which cannot be discussed in terms of failure—we are already obligated. But in spite of this claim, certainly it is the case that this obligation to others is violated, betrayed, and ignored. Not only do we often fail in our response to the Other, it is also unclear how this response occurs or why it fails.[10]

Now Levinas is certainly aware of this everyday failure of ethical response and its disastrous consequences. Indeed, it seems to constitute the prime motivation for his project: his writings seek to aid us in overcoming the pervasive moral unresponsiveness with which they diagnose us.[11] They aim to "refashion the way we perceive the human condition"[12] and to impact "on our approach to concrete situations so that we come to see them as ethical."[13] In this sense we

---

Responsibility," in *Radicalizing Levinas*, ed. Peter Atterton and Matthew Calarco (Albany: State University of New York Press, 2010), 172. Levinas's commentators frequently emphasize that his chief concern is to elucidate the meaning of ethics and its conditions of possibility, in short, to describe the constitution of subjectivity as inherently responsible in the first place. For further on this see, for example, Derrida's well-known claim that Levinas is interested in "not simply some region of ethics" but in "ethicity itself, the whole and the principle of ethics" (Jacques Derrida, *Adieu to Emmanuel Levinas*, trans. Pascale-Anne Brault and Michael Naas [Stanford: Stanford University Press, 1999], 50).

10. Claire Elise Katz, "'The Presence of the Other Is a Presence That Teaches': Levinas, Pragmatism, and Pedagogy," *Journal of Jewish Thought and Philosophy* 14, no. 1–2 (2006): 92.

11. As Kleinberg-Levin writes: "the whole point of the philosopher's written work assumes that the address, the appeal, of his thought could alter our investments in the ego's egoism, its imperial disregard for the other" (Kleinberg-Levin, *Before the Voice of Reason*, 220).

12. Bettina G. Bergo, "Levinas's Project: An Interpretative Phenomenology of Sensibility and Intersubjectivity," in *Continental Philosophy and Philosophy of Religion*, ed. Morny Joy (Dordrecht: Springer, 2011), 80.

13. Robert Bernasconi, "What Is the Question to Which 'Substitution' Is the Answer?," in *The Cambridge Companion to Levinas*, ed. Simon Critchley and Robert Bernasconi (Cambridge: Cambridge University Press, 2002), 250.

could say that his writings offer us a certain "vision" or orientation; they invite us into a different way of seeing and responding, into "a certain form of economic life."[14] In short then, Levinas's frequent focus on transcendental questions concerning the constitution of responsible subjectivity should not mislead us into overlooking the fact that his writings remain thoroughly invested in our ethical transformation at the empirical, concrete level of our everyday interactions with other persons.[15]

However, if this is the case, then Katz's contention is that Levinas ought rightly to have said more about the causes of this failure of ethical response and how it might be overcome. As such, she argues that the widespread reality of "[t]he failure to respond to the other ethically requires us to ask if Levinas's project needs . . . a model of moral cultivation to supplement it."[16] That is, an account of the pragmatic contours of how exactly one might increasingly come to respond to others ethically. It is this diachronic process of moral growth that, for Katz, Levinas fails to elaborate upon sufficiently in his ethical works.[17] As another critic sums up the charge, "his phenomenology of ethical experience has nothing to say about the formation or development of a moral consciousness, a moral sensibility"; about the diachronic "stages in moral maturation . . . ethical life as an ongoing practice."[18] In other words, despite his seeming investment in our moral transformation and awakening to

---

14. Emmanuel Levinas, *Totality and Infinity*, 172. This "vision," orientation, or way of life is variously titled: the "dimension and perspective of transcendence," "the 'vision' of the face as face" (ibid., 301, 172), the singularity of the other, the infinity of responsibility, "the perspective of holiness," "the ethical perspective," "the interhuman perspective of *my* responsibility for the other," and so on (Emmanuel Levinas, *Entre Nous: Thinking-of-the-Other*, trans. Michael B. Smith and Barbara Harshav [London: Continuum, 2006], vii, 81, 87).

15. On this tension between "transcendental" and "empirical" readings of Levinas's methodology, see Robert Bernasconi, "Rereading Levinas," in *The Question of the Other: Essays in Contemporary Continental Philosophy*, ed. Charles Scott and Arleen Dallery (Albany: State University of New York Press, 1989), 23–34. I comment further on this issue below in section one.

16. Katz, "'The Presence of the Other Is a Presence That Teaches,'" 91. See also ibid., 92.

17. Katz, however, goes on to argue that there are resources in other parts of Levinas's philosophy for developing this supplement, particularly in his writings on Jewish moral education. I consider these sources later in section three.

18. Kleinberg-Levin, *Before the Voice of Reason*, 230, 212.

responsibility, Levinas in fact says relatively little about the "how" of such thoroughgoing transformation.

There are then it seems some commentators who would agree that the question of the "how" of transformation is a fair one to pose to Levinas. No doubt, in response to this challenge, there are multiple avenues that could be pursued in order to construct the sort of developmental supplement needed. For example, one might explore other parts of Levinas's oeuvre outside his strictly ethical works for resources and/or one might seek to bring his work into conversation with other writers who do focus on these questions. While I will address the former approach in section three, the chapter as a whole principally attempts a conversation of the latter kind by exploring what if anything Coakley's analysis of the key insights of writings on the "spiritual senses" might have to offer to Levinas—and, indeed, by extension, to moral philosophers of any stripe who find themselves thin on details when it comes to the "how" question.

The first section of the chapter begins by offering a brief introductory orientation to Coakley's interest in the "spiritual senses" tradition. Despite the seemingly vast differences between the focus of this tradition and that of Levinas's ethics, I identify some basic structural similarities between the two accounts that suggest bringing them into conversation may prove fruitful. Following this in section two I lay out the key insights concerning the "how" of transformation that Coakley finds in certain "spiritual senses" writers, particularly Gregory of Nyssa. In the third section I use these insights as a guide in reapproaching Levinas's texts to see what resources they might harbor for thinking about moral cultivation. Lastly, in the fourth section, I consider a final challenge from Coakley stemming from her attention to the dangers involved in advocating certain types of cultivation practice and highlight the methodological lesson this affords to all thinkers interested in assessing and defending the merits of certain practices for ethical life.

I. A few structural similarities between writings on the "spiritual senses" and Levinas's ethics

To enter upon the main task of this section it is first necessary to offer a brief introduction to Coakley's writings on the "spiritual senses." To date, her published work has taken a keen interest in this topic and she has also indicated it will be a continuing emphasis in the second volume of her systematic theology.[19] What then is meant by spiritual sensation or perception and what is Coakley's particular interest with regard to it? In the Introduction to her collection *The Spiritual Senses: Perceiving God in Western Christianity*, coedited with Paul L. Gavrilyuk, the following working definition is offered: "we use the expression 'spiritual senses' to designate non-physical human perception."[20] That is, the idea that there is some "special form of perception that makes direct human contact with God possible."[21] Such an approach is evident in authors where the use of sensory language to describe the encounter with God is not merely metaphorical (that is, just used "figuratively to refer to ordinary mental acts")[22] but where it denotes a unique mode of spiritual perception and where an analogy with (at least one of) the five physical senses is intended in order to understand its workings. That is, where "the operation of the spiritual senses is described in terms akin to the operation of physical sensation."[23]

19. For this indication see Sarah Coakley, "Gregory of Nyssa," in *The Spiritual Senses: Perceiving God in Western Christianity*, ed. Paul L. Gavrilyuk and Sarah Coakley (Cambridge: Cambridge University Press, 2012), 55n63. Coakley's key texts on the topic of the "spiritual senses" include the chapter just noted (Coakley, "Gregory of Nyssa," 36–55), as well as the following earlier essays: "The Resurrection and the 'Spiritual Senses': On Wittgenstein, Epistemology and the Risen Christ," in Coakley, *Powers and Submissions*, 130–52 (this chapter can also be found published as Sarah Coakley, "The Resurrection: The Grammar of 'Raised,'" in *Biblical Concepts and Our World*, ed. D. Z. Phillips and Mario von der Ruhr [Basingstoke, UK: Palgrave, 2004], 169–89); and "The Identity of the Risen Jesus: Finding Jesus Christ in the Poor," in *Seeking the Identity of Jesus: A Pilgrimage*, ed. Beverly Roberts Gaventa and Richard B. Hays (Grand Rapids: Eerdmans, 2008), 301–19. Related reflections can also be found in, Sarah Coakley, "Deepening Practices: Perspectives from Ascetical and Mystical Theology," in *Practicing Theology: Beliefs and Practices in Christian Life*, ed. Miroslav Volf and Dorothy C. Bass (Grand Rapids: Eerdmans, 2002), 78–93.
20. Paul L. Gavrilyuk and Sarah Coakley, "Introduction," in *The Spiritual Senses*, ed. Gavrilyuk and Coakley, 4.
21. Ibid., 1.
22. Ibid., 6.
23. Ibid. Summarizing this connection between physical and spiritual sensation, Coakley and Gavrilyuk write that they will use the term "'spiritual senses' as an umbrella term covering a variety of overlapping, yet distinct, expressions in which 'sense' in general or a particular sensory

However, at the same time, Gavrilyuk and Coakley highlight that "[t]he Christian vocabulary of non-physical perception is extremely fluid, sometimes exasperatingly so."[24] As such, they argue that "we look in vain for any systematic, or ordered, development of these traditions; we should speak rather of a series of overlapping 'family resemblances' between them."[25] In this spirit then any reference in this chapter to the "spiritual senses" tradition must be taken as reference to a very broad and diverse set of traditions, which will require further specification (this will be pursued in section two).

In their "Introduction" Gavrilyuk and Coakley also highlight that these various discussions relating to some notion of spiritual perception face a host of issues. In particular, as a first hurdle, "the claim that God could be perceived by special senses seems to violate notions of divine transcendence and immateriality."[26] It seems unclear "how the invisible God, whose theophany was potentially lethal to human beings, could manifest Godself in a visible form."[27] The fundamental shift that makes such discussion possible is, as Gavrilyuk and Coakley point out, the incarnation: "The Johannine emphasis that it is the incarnate Word who had made the knowledge of the Father possible provided a crucial epistemic clue for dealing with this problem."[28] Incarnation, resurrection, and the Spirit were thus often central themes in any discussion of spiritual perception (particularly when it was viewed as premised on transformed physical perception, a position I will elaborate on in section two). Given this, one key biblical locus for such reflections were the highly suggestive "post-

---

modality . . . is typically qualified by reference to spirit . . . , heart . . . , soul . . . , mind or intellect . . . , inner [man] . . . or faith" (ibid., 2).

24. Ibid., 2. Gavrilyuk and Coakley canvass the historical reasons behind this fluidity of vocabulary. First, they highlight that "the Bible as such offers no 'doctrine of the spiritual senses'" (ibid., 12). It is only with the Latin translation of the works of Origen that the expression "spiritual senses" is first used and that they come "to occupy a distinct place in [his] theological anthropology" (ibid.). However, in patristic authors, discussion around the notion of something like spiritual perception often occurred as part of largely nonsystematic reflections. It is only in "Western medieval theology [that] the concept of the spiritual sense(s) came to be used more systematically" (ibid., 2).

25. Ibid., 18.

26. Ibid., 1.

27. Ibid., 10.

28. Ibid., 10–11.

resurrection recognition scenes, such as the *Noli me tangere* (John 20:17) or the opening of the disciples' eyes during the supper at Emmaus (Luke 24:30-1)."[29] These are suggestive, Coakley explains, because they seem to indicate "the possibility of being with the risen Jesus and *not* recognizing him, for instance; having to go through a personal process of change or of particular ritual acts in order to 'see' him."[30]

It is these scenes that have so far formed the main focal point of Coakley's writings on the "spiritual senses," particularly of those essays where she attempts to assess what such teachings have to offer "as a live philosophical and theological option for today."[31] Her engagement takes shape as a reflection on what would be involved in recognizing Christ "if his hypostatic identity qua second divine person is to be properly intuited and responded to."[32] That is, she turns to this tradition for help in addressing an epistemological dilemma in theology concerning whether and how (under what conditions) it can be said that contemporary believers recognize and respond to the risen Christ.[33] I will address why Coakley turns to this tradition, and to certain writers in particular such as Gregory of Nyssa, in section two where I examine in detail the specific insights she finds in their writings. In this section, however, I first outline what if anything this tradition might have in common with Levinas's concerns—a question to which at first glance there hardly seems an obvious answer.

Despite incredible gulfs of dissimilarity between writings on the "spiritual senses" and Levinas's ethics—most obviously that they are concerned with entirely different "others": the former with the risen Jesus and the latter with the other person—there do nonetheless seem to be a few structural similarities in the issues that both confront.

---

29. Ibid., 11.
30. Coakley, "The Identity of the Risen Jesus," 315.
31. Coakley, "Gregory of Nyssa," 55.
32. Coakley, "The Identity of the Risen Jesus," 313.
33. As she summarizes it: the aim was "to explicate the possible conditions for contemporary 'seeing' of the resurrected Jesus by reference to the patristic 'spiritual senses' tradition" (Coakley, "The Identity of the Risen Jesus," 313). In the chapter "The Resurrection and the 'Spiritual Senses': On Wittgenstein, Epistemology and the Risen Christ," Coakley situates this theological question as caught in an impasse in modernity between two opposed options: a "Lockean" approach and a "Barthian" one, one emphasizing the resurrection as a historical event, and the other as an ahistorical event. See Coakley, *Powers and Submissions*, 132–35.

Firstly, both are concerned with a type of recognition or acknowledgment that, while occurring within the everyday empirical world, nonetheless goes beyond it in some sense: neither the risen Christ for writers on the "spiritual senses" nor the other for Levinas are straightforwardly available to normal perception and sensory response. For Coakley, this point is evident with regard to Christ from the above-noted New Testament accounts of post-resurrection sightings in which, although certain people see, hear, or touch Jesus, there is nonetheless a failure of recognition. Ordinary physical perception does not enable them to see and respond appropriately; rather there seems to be some sort of blockage in the capacity to see and respond when it comes to recognizing the risen Christ.

Turning to Levinas, he too makes clear that ordinary sense perception does not allow one to recognize and respond to the other. Indeed, he rigorously insists throughout his ethical writings that the face of the other "cannot be comprehended, that is, encompassed. It is neither seen nor touched," rather it "determine[s] a relationship different from that which characterizes all our sensible experience."[34] Levinas thus eschews the language of sensation principally due to its association (via Husserl) with the grasping movement of intentional consciousness. For him, normal sense perception offers no access to the face of the other and its summons to responsibility.[35]

Many of Levinas's commentators have taken this to suggest that it is therefore a kind of category mistake for a Levinasian to ask about recognizing and responding to the other within experience; instead they argue that all Levinas's talk of the other must be interpreted transcendentally and so as describing events prior to experience. For

---

34. Emmanuel Levinas, *Totality and Infinity*, 194, 187. According to Levinas, one does not approach the other via intentionality but rather the encounter with the other registers passively via sensibility, which is "'anterior' to the crystallization of consciousness" (ibid., 188). For an in-depth phenomenological analysis of Levinas's descriptions of "pre- or semi-conscious sensibility" and their evolutions throughout his oeuvre, see Bergo, "Levinas's Project," 61–88.

35. Shaw explains this well: "The relation to the other cannot be represented, [Levinas] seems to argue, in the 'meaning structures' that define our standard spatiotemporal mode of experiencing the world. The other is not, as he puts it in a 1965 essay, a 'phenomenon' but an 'enigma'" (Joshua James Shaw, *Emmanuel Levinas on the Priority of Ethics: Putting Ethics First* [Amherst, NY: Cambria, 2008], 136).

other commentators, however, this ignores the fact that there is also much evidence in Levinas's texts for an alternate "empirical" reading of his methodology.[36] Without entering into the full debate here, the basic point is that there are places in Levinas's analysis where, as Bernasconi puts it, he speaks of the face-to-face encounter "as a concrete experience that we can recognize in our lives."[37] Moreover, he "seems to imply that at various moments in our lives, we can do a better or worse job of recognizing the other and our responsibility for her."[38] Indeed, as briefly noted in the introduction, Levinas's project as a whole seems premised on the judgment that for the most part we do a worse job: our lives exhibit a pervasive failure to respond to the other, with disastrous consequences. In this sense then it seems as if Levinas too thinks we suffer from some sort of blockage in our capacity to see and respond when it comes to other persons. Our ordinary perceptual capacities do not enable us to respond appropriately to the vulnerability of the face and its summons to responsibility. Yet, if overcoming this failure of response is the prime motivation for Levinas's ethical project, then *contra* the assumptions of some commentators, it is not a mistake to ask about the possibility of recognizing the face of the other in everyday experience—it is in fact Levinas's central concern (even if, as we will see, for certain very important reasons, he will avoid perceptual language to articulate this).

However, conundrums still remain. Even if the empirical reading convinces us that "[t]he other's face and voice . . . are thoroughly empirical and relative," they nonetheless remain highly unique sorts of empirical things in that "they are the bearers of something transworldly and absolute, namely, an unconditional call to moral responsibility."[39] Interestingly, in seeking to explicate this claim,

---

36. As noted earlier, see Bernasconi, "Rereading Levinas," 23–34 for an account of the "transcendental" vs. "empirical" readings of Levinas.

37. Ibid., 23.

38. Shaw, *Emmanuel Levinas on the Priority of Ethics*, 139. Shaw concludes that "[t]he empirical view seems to be correct, therefore, in its claim that the relation to the other is a concrete experience that we can recognize in our lives, or, alternatively, that can be stifled or absent from them under certain political regimes."

Westphal draws an analogy with the problem addressed in the Nicene Creed concerning Jesus and, as Coakley had it, "his hypostatic identity qua second divine person." Westphal explains, "The Nicene Creed, 325 A.D., affirms that Jesus is and was fully human but also fully divine. . . . The face and the voice of the other in Levinas embody a similar unity of the empirical and transempirical."[40] There is then a structural similarity in that both seem to be grappling with the notion of recognizing and responding to something (or rather, someone), which is only accessible within experience (thoroughly empirical) and yet which goes beyond it in some crucial sense.

For the writers Coakley examines, this conundrum about the possibility of such recognition beyond ordinary sense perception prompts them to inquire into the possibility of "senses" beyond senses, of "experience" that exceeds normal sensory experience with its usual demands and criteria, that is, into the possibility of what they term "spiritual perception" of some kind.[41] Now, we might expect Levinas to make a similar move, for example, to invoke the possibility of some sort of "ethical perception" in order to account for our ability to recognize the face of the other even as it exceeds ordinary perceptual recognition. However, he never takes this route and remains extremely wary of employing any terms to do with perception, recognition, seeing, knowing, or the like to speak of the ethical relation, even at the everyday level.

Does this then invalidate any similarities between the two positions already outlined? It certainly indicates a deep divergence over the appropriate language to be used but perhaps not an entirely opposed position if we consider that Levinas's rigorous avoidance of this language is often aimed at preventing us from falling into the trap of assuming that recognizing another person is in any way fundamentally like our ordinary acts of perception and cognition. Levinas's key point

---

39. Merold Westphal, "The Second Great Revolution in Phenomenology," *Journal of Speculative Philosophy* 26, no. 2 (2012): 336.
40. Ibid., 345n8.
41. It is important to note, however, that such "spiritual senses" can be conceived as either discontinuous with (and so separate from) or as continuous with (and so a transformation of) ordinary sense perception. I discuss Coakley's preference for the latter view in section two.

is to encourage us to see that acknowledging the face of the other is entirely unique. How so? Quite simply in that "it requires a practical response";[42] as Levinas famously put it, "no face can be approached with empty hands."[43] The relation to the other and its everyday enactment then is not primarily one of comprehension, as is characteristic of ordinary perception, it is rather an ethical act. As such, for Levinas, it could be said that to "see" the face, to "hear" the voice of the other summoning one to responsibility or to "recognize" the otherness of the other is to respond—to offer help in concrete, practical actions. In this sense then he is certainly interested in whether we can recognize the other in our everyday lives, but he seeks to highlight that this recognition is of a peculiar sort compared to all other perceptual acts: it demands a practical response, enacted as a way of life.

Taking this into account we are perhaps not too far from the sorts of concerns writers on spiritual perception are grappling with in that even if they retain the language of perception and sensation more explicitly, they are nonetheless also seeking to account for an entirely unique variety of it. As Coakley puts it, they are trying to "indicate a particular sort of knowing that is alone *appropriate* to the mystery of the identity of Jesus."[44] But again here the uniqueness of this recognition seems to lie in the fact that it must be practical: the one who "sees" the risen Christ is the one who responds in certain ways, who embodies a certain way of life. As Coakley explains then, there is something similar at stake in both recognizing Christ and recognizing another person that fundamentally distinguishes both from all recognition of objects, namely, "the possibility of relationship: I do not only grasp but am also grasped by the living mystery of the 'other,'"[45]

42. Shaw, *Emmanuel Levinas on the Priority of Ethics*, 19.

43. Levinas, *Totality and Infinity*, 172.

44. Coakley, "The Identity of the Risen Jesus," 315. Or, as Coakley also puts it, in speaking of recognizing and responding to the risen Jesus one is dealing with "a profound *possibility* of a paradoxical and 'apophatic' sort—one that intrinsically undercuts my natural longings to control and predict the epistemic outcome."

45. Ibid., 312. Note: while highlighting this similarity, Coakley also emphasizes the way in which "acknowledging the identity of Jesus is different from any other such identifying of persons" (313). This has principally to do with her claim that it must necessarily involve "my first being

which demands a response from me. For Coakley too then the question of seeing, identifying, or recognizing translates ultimately into a question of response. To recognize the risen Jesus is, as she puts it, "to respond to the identity of Jesus in those whom they serve. Jesus is found precisely in the incarnational *physicality* of these poor and destitute whom they have given their acknowledgement and aid; Jesus is ignored, unrecognized, despised, by those who fail so to will and act."[46]

II. Coakley on the key insights of writings on the "spiritual senses," especially Gregory of Nyssa

Drawing on Coakley's various analyses of writings on the "spiritual senses," this section seeks to distill what she takes to be the novel achievements and key insights of this tradition, focusing in particular on what it has to say about the "how" of transformation. The first novel move can be seen in the way that for writers in this tradition the question of the possibility of recognizing the divine—and all the metaphysical and epistemological conundrums this poses—prompts them to engage in an extensive investigation into the *conditions* for such recognition and how these might be attained.[47] Their inquiry into the possibility of "spiritual senses" is thus an attempt to "to probe the conditions of the divine-human encounter"; to specify "the cognitive equipment enabling such a communication."[48] Furthermore, Coakley argues that in undertaking these investigations, such writers arrive at insightful claims about these conditions; most significantly, they

---

grasped, not just by the living mystery of the other person of Jesus himself, but by that in God (what Christians call the Spirit) that so *dispossesses* me that I can truly 'see' Jesus." For further on these motifs of interruptive dispossession and destabilization, see ibid., 313–14. It is interesting to note, however, that parallels remain here with Levinas's depiction of the face-to-face encounter with another person: he too emphasizes the interruptive, destabilizing effect the other has on the I.

46. Ibid., 317.

47. Of course, as Gavrilyuk and Coakley note, these conundrums need not lead this way: other traditions such as modern rationalism and empiricism might feel themselves compelled to give up the possibility of encountering the divine altogether, or others might "emphasize that God in his self-communication brings it about that humans receive divine revelation without specifying the cognitive equipment enabling such a communication" (Gavrilyuk and Coakley, "Introduction," 2).

48. Ibid.

contend that sensing or recognizing the risen Christ requires "a *process of change*"[49] in which our ordinary physical senses and perceptual capacities (what Coakley will designate under the broad heading of "epistemic" capacities[50]) must undergo transformation in order to achieve such recognition. In short, the claim is that spiritual transformation requires "epistemic" transformation, that is, "*transformation* of normal sense perception."[51]

In order to make sense of this proposal regarding the possibility of spiritual perception it will be helpful at this point to outline a key division among writers in the broad and diverse "spiritual senses" tradition. Drawing on an article by Mariette Canévet, Coakley points out that there is an "ambiguity in the Christian spiritual senses tradition between those who posit a 'discontinuité' between corporeal and interior senses and those who urge the possibility of a 'transfiguration' of the 'sens corporels.'"[52] Thus, for the former, including for example Origen, there is a disjunction between bodily and divine sense and so the rather Platonic notion of "utterly separate sets of cognitive faculties parallel to, and infinitely better than, the bodily ones."[53] By contrast, for the latter group, what is at stake in speaking of "spiritual senses" is precisely "the transfigured workings of ordinary perception."[54] It is this line of thought, with its emphasis on "a malleability in the faculties' capacity to respond,"[55] which most interests Coakley.[56] While she notes that hints of this approach can be

---

49. Coakley, *Powers and Submissions*, 139.
50. It is crucial to note here that Coakley employs the term "epistemic" very broadly in a deliberate move that stems from her rigorous insistence on the impossibility of neatly separating off the noetic from the affective/erotic (see ibid., 140). Thus, where she speaks alternatively of "epistemic capacities," "perceptual capacities," or "epistemic sensibilities" (ibid., 140, 146, 131), she has in view "all the faculties and senses (intellect, feeling, will, imagination, aesthetic sensibility)"; the entire range of "the apparatuses of one's own thinking, desiring and seeing." Sarah Coakley, *God, Sexuality and the Self: An Essay 'On the Trinity'* (Cambridge: Cambridge University Press, forthcoming).
51. Coakley, *Powers and Submissions*, 152.
52. Coakley, "Gregory of Nyssa," 43.
53. Ibid., 48.
54. Ibid.
55. Coakley, *Powers and Submissions*, 131n3.
56. Coakley's standard definition of the patristic "spiritual senses" tradition thus emphasizes this aspect: she writes that it "charts in some detail the proposed capacity of our gross physical senses to undergo profound transformative change, or sharpening, in the Spirit, in order to come

found in Origen,[57] it is with Gregory of Nyssa that it becomes more developed and so it is to him that Coakley's analyses often turn. For her, the above-noted insight that spiritual transformation requires "epistemic" transformation is essentially a Nyssan one. Summing up this reading of his oeuvre, she writes:

> I propose that Gregory's works, from the time of his *De anima* on, go well beyond Origen's approach; for they set out a developing and systematic account of how ordinary perception and the gross physical senses are capable of a progressive transformation in this life into spiritual senses via a purgative process of "death" and regeneration.[58]

It is this Nyssan emphasis on the "transfiguration of the bodily sense"[59] and so on "the possibility of a human continuum of epistemic transformation,"[60] allowing it would seem "for some significant point of *continuity* or development from the physical to the spiritual"[61] that Coakley considers the crucial insight. She contends that the difference in the epistemological implications stemming from these two views are "non-trivial . . . since on Nyssa's view the toehold for spiritual perception is precisely *in* the physical."[62] In short, the Nyssan view insists "that our perceptual capacities have labile and transformative possibilities."[63] Thus, for Gregory, if any spiritual transformation—any sensing and recognizing of Christ—is to come, then it is precisely our ordinary "epistemic" capacities of physical sensory perception and response that will need to be changed and stretched in order to make it possible.

It is now clearer how Nyssa's writings in particular shape Coakley's view of the first key insight of the "spiritual senses" tradition. For her, it lies in their awareness of "how seeking and recognizing the resurrected Christ require a *process* of change,"[64] one that involves not

---

ultimately into desired recognition of, and union with, the risen Jesus" (Coakley, "The Identity of the Risen Jesus," 313–14).

57. See Gavrilyuk and Coakley, "Introduction," 12.
58. Coakley, "Gregory of Nyssa," 42.
59. Ibid., 44.
60. Ibid., 47. See also ibid., 45.
61. Coakley, *Powers and Submissions*, 137–38.
62. Ibid., 138.
63. Coakley, "Gregory of Nyssa," 48.

only "some prior, interruptive undoing of epistemic blockage"[65] but also "some actual change in the perceptual capacities."[66] On Coakley's reading then, the "how" of spiritual transformation "cannot finally be explained except by an account of a transformation of the believer's actual epistemic *apparatus*";[67] by a change in one's very capacity to see and respond.

Two implications stemming from this are worth mentioning here. First, this reading confronts us with the deep-seated, thoroughgoing nature of the transformation involved. Recall that if, as noted above, ordinary perception is incapable of recognizing and responding to the risen Christ (if it suffers from a sort of pervasive blindness on this front), then overcoming this such that one might come to see and respond will require not simply minor adjustments and improvements in the usual operations of our perceptual capacities but rather a fundamental transformation or restructuring of those capacities themselves and their usual *modus operandi*. Secondly, there is also a question about the nature of this transformation—what kind of deep-seated change in the structure of ordinary sense perception is required? Coakley uses a variety of terms with regard to this, sometimes speaking of cleansing, purifying, and purging, also of destabilizing and breaking, while at other times emphasizing growth metaphors of stretching and enlarging, or appealing to the idea of refining: of sensory operations becoming sharper and more subtle. Although there is not space to enter into this issue here, it is worth highlighting that as a general rule the transformation of ordinary perceptual capacities at stake seems to proceed in the direction of unmastery and attentiveness to the other. In this sense the blockage in our ordinary capacity to see and respond is depicted as having to do with its tendency to grasp and master, "to control and predict the epistemic outcome,"[68] to know in advance what to expect, what can

---

64. Coakley, *Powers and Submissions*, 139.
65. Coakley, "The Identity of the Risen Jesus," 313.
66. Coakley, *Powers and Submissions*, 146.
67. Ibid., 131.
68. Coakley, "The Identity of the Risen Jesus," 315.

be seen, and so to encounter just that: simply seeing one's own face.[69] The required transformation thus seems to principally involve a shift toward receptivity.[70]

Thus far I have suggested that the first crucial insight Coakley finds in the Nyssan discussion of the problematic surrounding recognition of the risen Christ is its move to enquire into its *conditions* and in particular to suggest that the condition of such recognition is "epistemic" transformation, that is, the "*transformation* of normal sense perception."[71] The second key insight flows out of this, namely, that for these writers the pressing question then becomes the need to address how such deep-seated "epistemic" transformation occurs, that is, "*how* does the transfiguration of the bodily sense occur?"[72] And it is in what Nyssa and others have to say on this question that Coakley finds perhaps the most challenging insights to arise for modern approaches. As she sums it up, what they emphasize is "that the spiritual or epistemic conditions for the recognition of the risen Jesus . . . demand a cumulative tangle of *practices*—meditative, sacramental, but also moral—in order to sustain this paradoxical form of unknowing/knowing."[73] In short, the answer to the "how" of transformation is practice.

In another essay, Coakley discusses the wide variety of such practices to be found in the Christian tradition, ranging from the seemingly mundane through to the rigors of contemplation.[74] Beginning with examples such as those of the "disciplines of scriptural mediation, sacramental observance, . . . pastoral care," psalm-singing, welcoming strangers, and "endurance in community living,"[75] Coakley notes that believers were exhorted to undertake such practices "in order that, over a lifetime, there may be a habituating of love."[76]

69. Ibid., 313.
70. As Coakley puts it, "a very particular, and normally undiscussed, form of epistemic receptivity is here required of us, which is spiritually transformative" (ibid., 312n21).
71. Coakley, *Powers and Submissions*, 152.
72. Coakley, "Gregory of Nyssa," 44.
73. Coakley, "The Identity of the Risen Jesus," 315–16.
74. See Coakley, "Deepening Practices," 78–93.
75. Ibid., 83, 86, 87.
76. Ibid., 86.

Implied is the suggestion that such practices could stretch and extend one's capacity to see: "that they will cause us to find Christ, for instance in new and unexpected places"[77]—"in the entirely unromantic other, in the exhausting poverty of my neighbor, in the nuisance of the beggar at my gate."[78] Similarly, elsewhere Coakley argues that the repeated practice of contemplation over the long haul "precisely *inculcates* mental patterns of un-mastery . . . [and] opens up a radical attention to the other."[79]

Coakley thus draws attention to the way such claims made in these Christian traditions, advocating a host of seemingly banal practices, provoke

> reflection on the almost subliminal and unconscious way in which spiritual re-modulation and transformation may occur over a lifetime *through repeated practices*. It is not obvious, for instance, why the daily and reiterated recitation in choir of psalmody should be either meritorious or life-changing . . . ; boredom might be the more predictable outcome. . . . This alerts us to the importance of *disciplined repetition* in the fruitful interaction of belief and practice.[80]

A central plank of their approach is thus an emphasis on the way repeated bodily practices serve to habituate, train, and cultivate us in certain ways.[81] They highlight, as Coakley puts it, the way in which "bodily acts of worship and attention (even if the mind is distracted) have their own integrity and effect."[82] As such, they insist that any

---

77. Ibid.
78. Coakley, "The Identity of the Risen Jesus," 316.
79. Coakley, "Is There a Future for Gender and Theology?," 5 (emphasis added). It is on this ascetical practice of contemplation that Coakley mainly focuses in her work, since it is here she claims we see the clearest example of the way a repeated bodily practice can wreak the most profound level of the kind of "epistemic" transformation discussed above. I return to discuss Coakley's defense of this practice in the final section of this chapter.
80. Coakley, "Deepening Practices," 86–87 (emphasis added).
81. Of course, most writers also emphasize the "graced" nature of these practices as crucial, of their being more a matter of God's practice in us than simply busy activity on our part. They thus frequently appeal to the Holy Spirit as playing a vital role in the breaking and reshaping of ordinary perceptual capacities effected by such practices (see, for example, Coakley's comment on spiritual and "epistemic" transformation "involving crucially . . . a radical dispossession to the Spirit," in Coakley, "The Identity of the Risen Jesus," 316). However, this does not amount simply to an invocation of supernatural intervention that mysteriously and instantly takes effect. Rather, since the Spirit works through these natural processes of habituation, the original insight remains crucial regarding the way various bodily practices serve to train and cultivate us in certain ways.
82. Coakley, "Deepening Practices," 87.

deep-seated restructuring of our perceptual apparatus can never be an achievement of thought and will alone—it is not the product of a one-off decision or moment of insight—but rather happens only via a patient disciplining of the self that cannot circumvent the body. As Coakley sums up the prime lesson for all philosophers interested in the possibilities and paths of personal transformation: "change cannot occur by mere thought, but is precisely the product of arduous exercise."[83] It is only via committed repetition that such practice can begin to progressively remodulate our capacities and inculcate habitual dispositions of deeper attentiveness. There is then no short cut around the time and effort this will involve: deep-seated "transformation of one's actual epistemic capacities" cannot be "achieved at speed"[84] but only "over a lifetime of maturation";[85] it requires embarking on "a complete lifetime's *epistemological* programme."[86]

Moreover, the language this tradition employs to describe ongoing ethico-spiritual transformation is all "about a *diachronic* spectrum of possibilities in human responses to God."[87] Its acknowledgment of these differing and more advanced capacities of perception and response[88] requires that spiritual transformation be seen not as a one-off moment but as a "progressive *transformation* of the self's response to the divine through a lifetime of practice, purgation and prayer."[89]

---

83. Coakley, *Powers and Submissions*, 159.
84. Ibid., 140.
85. Gavrilyuk and Coakley, "Introduction," 13. As Coakley elsewhere puts it, it will "involve long years of moral and spiritual preparation, [and] prolonged *practice* in 'sensing' and responding to the divine" (Coakley, *Powers and Submissions*, 139).
86. Ibid., 139.
87. Gavrilyuk and Coakley, "Introduction," 13.
88. For Coakley, to have recourse to the language of sensation and perception is *ipso facto* to employ a language of degrees, which requires us to acknowledge that "[w]e perceive at different 'levels'" with differing depths (Coakley, *Powers and Submissions*, 145). Thus, as she summarizes the key insight here (one that she thinks Wittgenstein also sees and furthers in his own way, see ibid., 141–48), it is the claim that "there are distinct and different levels of perception, depending on one's spiritual maturity and (concomitant) epistemological capacity" (ibid., 139). Hence, the resulting implication is the treatment of spiritual transformation as a *progressive* process of "ascent" through these multiple levels. Coakley notes that this suggestion has often been charged with implying a kind of dangerous spiritual elitism (see ibid., 139 and Coakley, "Deepening Practices," 91–92). Nonetheless, she argues that if one remains vigilant against this danger, then the explanatory benefits gained via this language are indispensible (see Coakley, *Powers and Submissions*, 132).

For Coakley, it is this "subtle *multi-levelled* aspect of the pre-modern spiritual senses tradition"[90] which serves to constantly foreground the inherent "diachronic complication"[91] that inevitably translates every vision of personal transformation into a program of progressive transformation: an invitation, as noted above, to an ongoing, lifelong task.

III. Returning to Levinas

Do the insights outlined above have anything to offer Levinas and his problem of needing to offer some account of how it is that we might increasingly come to recognize and respond ethically to others in our everyday lives? What might such insights suggest? Firstly, they prompt the question of whether the sort of ethical transformation Levinas envisions might likewise be premised on a deep-seated "epistemic" transformation of our normal capacity to see and respond. After all, if Levinas does think that our ordinary patterns of perceptual response to the world (those that typically render us blind and unresponsive to the other) can be changed such that we might increasingly come to do a better job of recognizing and responding to the face of the other in concrete experience, and if furthermore he refuses to appeal to any extra, separate faculties that could accomplish this perception for us over and above our ordinary senses and faculties (for example, some special moral sense faculty), then perhaps for him too it is our ordinary perceptual capacities that will have to be changed if there is to be any chance of ethical growth into increasing recognition of and response to the other. Moreover, here too, it seems that, given Levinas's portrayal of the pervasive default failure of our ordinary perceptual and responsive capacities on this front, what will be needed is a similarly deep-level change: a transformative restructuring of those very capacities. And, once again, the type of "epistemic" transformation needed seems to lie principally in a shift to receptivity.

---

89. Coakley, *Powers and Submissions*, 136.
90. Coakley, *Powers and Submissions*, 139.
91. Coakley, "Is There a Future for Gender and Theology?," 11n10.

What is at stake is a profound change in these capacities of the sort that would alter their usual grasping, controlling *modus operandi*, which constantly reduces the other to the same and so fails to respond to the face and its summons to responsibility.

This then suggests that the question of how Levinas's vision of ethical responsibility can be unfolded in everyday life translates into the question of how this sort of deep-seated transformation of our ordinary capacity to see and respond can occur. It is here that the second insight highlighted by Coakley from writings on the "spiritual senses" might enter in, namely, their claim that change of this sort—change that alters the fundamental structures and *modus operandi* of our perceptual equipment, our very way of seeing and responding —can occur only via the effort of repeated practice, thus foregrounding ethical transformation as a progressive, diachronic task of continued development through various levels of recognition and response over the course of a lifetime. This emphasis on bodily practice as the chief means for effecting profound change in our perceptual capacities thus certainly offers one clear avenue that might be pursued for addressing the problem we saw Levinas faced in the introduction, namely, his need to offer an answer concerning the "how" of the sort of ethical transformation his project seems deeply invested in. That avenue is, as Coakley worded the challenge, to specify "the intentional and bodily practices that might enable such attention" to the otherness of the other.

What would be the result of taking this insight as a cue? Firstly, it could offer a new lens through which to reapproach Levinas's texts. Having an eye toward the question of practices might prompt one to search the margins of his ethical texts for hints in this regard or to search outside these texts altogether in other areas of his oeuvre.[92]

92. The first option of rereading Levinas's ethical works in the light of this question is one fascinating angle to pursue. While there is not space to develop this here, I think there is scope to read Levinas's account of the infinity of responsibility as premised on a similar sort of intuition about the significance of repeated, lived bodily practice for stretching one's capacity to see and respond. Recall, in particular, that Levinas defines this infinity on many occasions by saying that responsibility is the kind of thing that increases as it is assumed (Levinas, *Totality and Infinity*, 100–101, 244; Emmanuel Levinas, *Otherwise than Being, or, Beyond Essence* [Pittsburgh: Duquesne University Press, 1998], 12, 93–94, 139–40, 142). One way of interpreting this definition is to see it

Alternatively, one might conclude that pursuing this question will require constructing a new supplement to Levinas's ethics that draws on resources external to his project, for example, on other thinkers or traditions that devote more sustained attention to questions of moral cultivation and offer more detailed analyses and defenses of the moral potential of specific practices. In the remainder of this section I will make some comments about the former approach and then in the last section I consider a final methodological insight from Coakley on how the latter task of navigating discourse on the moral potential of various practices might need to proceed.

Interestingly, some commentators have suggested that Levinas himself recognizes something like the need for an appeal to ritual or practice in some of his writings outside his major works on ethics. Katz, for instance, argues that to identify the account of moral cultivation implicitly assumed in Levinas's ethical works "means making the necessary turn to his writings on Judaism and to the implicit role Judaism plays in his philosophical project."[93] In doing so, some hints can be found of Levinas considering the ethical import of certain religious practices. For example, in the essay "A Religion for Adults" he states that "[t]he ritual law of Judaism constitutes the austere discipline that strives to achieve this justice. *Only this law can recognize the face of the Other* which has managed to impose an austere role on its true nature."[94] Here Levinas seems to suggest that the "effort," "discipline," and "daily fidelity" of such practices, as Morgan puts it, "trains the Jew to greater attentiveness and greater sensitivity to others. . . . Indeed, it may do so in an especially effective way."[95]

as exhorting us toward a lived practice of assuming responsibility—even in banal circumstances, even when we don't feel like it. Perhaps for Levinas such attempts at taking responsibility might be the prime sort of intentional, bodily practice he would advocate for moral cultivation. As he suggests on one occasion, "This is the original and incontestable meaning of the Greek word *liturgy*," namely, a "ritualism" of devoted, concrete, daily service to the other (Emmanuel Levinas, *Difficult Freedom: Essays on Judaism*, trans. Seán Hand [Baltimore: Johns Hopkins University Press, 1997], xiv).

93. Katz, "'The Presence of the Other Is a Presence That Teaches,'" 100. I will comment briefly on Katz's own constructive project in this regard in the final section.

94. Emmanuel Levinas, *Difficult Freedom*, 18 (emphasis added).

95. Michael L. Morgan, *Discovering Levinas* (Cambridge: Cambridge University Press, 2007), 377. On interpreting these passages see also Morgan's article "Levinas and Judaism," *Levinas Studies* 1 (2005): 1–17. Pages 6–11 contain a careful examination of these comments on ritual and assess

Perhaps Levinas can be read here as "interpreting Jewish ritual . . . as training for being receptive to the other, as a kind of training in passivity."[96] On this reading, as Morgan puts it:

> ritual is not solely about motivation and obedience. It is also about *awareness or recognition* of the face as a commanding presence, and indeed in a precise way. Operating within theological territory, ritual points beyond nature and totality; in this way, ritual prepares the Jew for an encounter with the other's vulnerability and hence for an awareness of his or her ethical responsibilities. Ritual, that is, expresses or trains the Jew to see what lies hidden in concrete, everyday life, a dimension of responsibility, purpose, and meaning often neglected or obscured or wholly occluded.[97]

To take a specific example of Jewish ritual, one could consider Levinas's extended treatment of prayer in his essay "Prayer without Demand,"[98] where he offers a reading of "the prayer of the just man, prayer which conforms . . . to Jewish piety."[99] Here he portrays prayer as an affirmation or expression of one's responsibility for the other and in this sense as a step on the way to the full culmination of this expression in which one responds concretely to the other in ethical action.[100] Prayer then could be seen as in some sense expressing and cultivating ethical action.[101] However, neither in this discussion nor in the above comments on ritual does Levinas elaborate explicitly at any length on how exactly practices such as these might be conducive to moral life.

---

different interpretations offered by Edith Wyshogrod and Tamra Wright, as well as offering Morgan's own complementary interpretation.

96. Morgan, "Levinas and Judaism," 9. This comment is Morgan's gloss on one side of Wyschogrod's interpretation of this passage. See also the additional evidence Morgan provides in support of this view from Levinas's essay "Revelation in the Jewish Tradition" (ibid., 9–11). Morgan draws on this essay to explain how it is that ritual acts provide this training in receptivity, namely, they "do so by occurring in nature and by setting up a 'distance' between the Jew and nature, on the one hand, and God, on the other" (10). For further in Levinas's early work on this notion of ritual creating distance with regard to nature and on its being "a suspension of a natural attitude," see Joëlle Hansel, "Beyond Phenomenology: Levinas's Early Jewish Writings," *Levinas Studies* 5 (2010): 5–17 and Emmanuel Levinas, "The Meaning of Religious Practice," trans. Peter Atterton, Matthew Calarco, Joëlle Hansel, *Levinas Studies* 5 (2010): 1–4.

97. Morgan, "Levinas and Judaism," 10 (emphasis added).

98. Emmanuel Levinas, "Prayer without Demand," trans. Sarah Richmond, in *The Levinas Reader*, ed. Seán Hand (Malden, MA: Blackwell, 2000), 227–34.

99. Ibid., 232.

100. Morgan, "Levinas and Judaism," 15.

101. See ibid., 11–15.

In short, as Morgan sums up the verdict: "his account of how ritual contributes is neither complete nor precise enough."[102]

Moreover, even if Levinas is motivated when addressing a Jewish audience to inquire into the ethical significance that various Jewish practices and rituals might hold for the Jewish community, as Putnam notes, "he never attempts to tell gentiles what their equivalent to the 'ritual and the heart-felt generosity' of traditional Judaism, their equivalent to 'the particular type of intellectual life known as study of the Torah.' might be."[103] The "way of living" through which recognition of and responsibility to the other might be "acquired and held," the particular "training" it might take, remains unspecified—a seemingly rather problematic omission if Levinas's ethics is supposed to be applicable to everyone.[104]

As such, it appears as if Levinas neither wants to recommend and defend certain specifically Jewish practices to a wider audience as the key to the ethical transformation his works advocate, nor does he offer an account of other "equivalent" practices in their place. Perhaps this is because he assumes that multiple efficacious avenues might be pursued in this regard or perhaps it is because he thinks there is a kind of universal core to these practices that can be abstracted out and reapplied independently of their specific context—after all, this is how Levinas often depicts the project of his philosophy: as a distillation of the ethical core of Judaism. Something like this latter approach seems suggested in Levinas's comments in "Prayer without Demand," where in considering the particular spiritual practice of Jewish prayer

---

102. Morgan, *Discovering Levinas*, 379.

103. Hilary Putnam, "Levinas and Judaism," in *The Cambridge Companion to Levinas*, ed. Robert Bernasconi and Simon Critchley (Cambridge: Cambridge University Press, 2002), 52–53. The quote from Levinas on which this comment is based is taken from his essay "Judaism and the Present" and concerns how the "essential content" of Judaism can be learned, in response to which Levinas writes: "It is acquired through a way of living that is a ritual and a heart-felt generosity wherein a human fraternity and an attention to the present are reconciled with an eternal distance in relation to the contemporary world. It is an asceticism, like the training of a fighter. It is acquired and held, finally, in the particular type of intellectual life known as study of the Torah" (Levinas, *Difficult Freedom*, 213).

104. As Katz sums up the problem, if Levinas's ethical philosophy is supposed to be applicable to everyone and "if his conception of response can or needs to be cultivated, then do we not need a conception of that cultivation that is also universally applicable?" (Katz, "'The Presence of the Other Is a Presence That Teaches,'" 92–93).

he provides a candid glimpse into his methodology. He states that his aim is to "try to isolate certain strands of thought which, in our view, take us beyond the categories and colours of the particularism—the narrowness of focus—which forms their context."[105] To be fair, Levinas adds some important nuances to this project of appropriation.[106] Nonetheless, ultimately his own emphasis still falls on the attempt to "try here to free our discourse from it."[107]

But will this sort of methodological approach suffice when it comes to the question of recommending and defending the significance of certain practices for moral life? Indeed, it is precisely this sort of "abstracting" move that motivated Badiou's complaint considered at the start of this chapter against Levinas's "pious" ethical discourse. For Badiou, the attempt to distill an ethical lesson and praxis that is universally applicable ultimately remains formal and empty.[108] Badiou has his own reasons for registering this complaint; here though we are particularly concerned with the potential of this approach for addressing the unavoidable (or, so it has been argued) question of "which practices?" In the closing section of this chapter, I examine as a final insight from Coakley the way in which her own approach to this question suggests that any attempt to address it must take shape more as a wide-ranging, complex process of debate among particular religious and secular traditions of practices rather than any easy process of abstracting a universal praxis regardless of context.

---

105. Levinas, "Prayer without Demand," 229.
106. For example, Levinas admits that to completely neglect the "entire tradition" ("built upon a Talmudic and Kabbalistic framework") would impoverish his account of the ethical significance of prayer. Moreover, he argues that such a context is "worthy of respect, since it is probably the only way in which these ideas could first be formulated" and, furthermore, he admits the ultimate impossibility of fully escaping such context—the "echoes" of its particularism and "singularity" cannot be completely silenced (ibid., 229).
107. Ibid., 229.
108. As Badiou puts it, "What then becomes of this category if we claim to suppress, or mask, its religious character, all the while preserving the abstract arrangement of its apparent constitution ('recognition of the other.' etc.)? The answer is obvious: a dog's dinner. . . . We are left with a pious discourse without piety" (Badiou, Ethics, 23). Regardless of whether one agrees with Badiou's assumption about the essentially religious sources of Levinas's ethics, one might still share his concern over its apparent formality or contextlessness.

IV. Which practices?: Coakley on the significance of context

This section examines a particular practice that Coakley herself is willing to defend and recommend to others as vital to moral life, namely, her contention that contemplative prayer is able to provide the deepest "epistemic" transformation into radical attentiveness to the other.[109] Firstly, though, I consider the significance of the serious warnings she offers about the dangers of advocating practices of this sort. Following this, I highlight the unique way she thus proceeds to defend the transformative potential of this practice and argue that her approach contains a crucial methodological insight for others interested in assessing and recommending various bodily practices for the sake of moral cultivation.

While Coakley certainly agrees that a whole range of practices from various sources may prove effective in moral cultivation,[110] she also makes the provocative suggestion that the very deepest level of transformative change in our capacity to see and respond, the most profound breaking and stretching of our "moral antennae,"[111] can be attained only via the practice of contemplative prayer. Returning to her original criticism of post-Kantian ethics about the need to specify "the intentional and embodied practices that might enable such attention," her own answer is that

---

109. As noted throughout, Coakley's interest, writing as a theologian analyzing certain Christian traditions of personal transformation, is of course primarily on spiritual transformation (one's coming to recognize and respond to the risen Christ). However, according to her, it is a crucial feature of such spiritual transformation that it begins with and indeed never takes its leave from a profound moral transformation in which a believer's life becomes increasingly centered on love and service of others. As such, we might fairly expect there to be insights in Coakley's analyses of such traditions and the practices they advocate which would be applicable to any attempt—whether religious or secular—to offer a vision of "personal transformation beyond normal human expectations and restrictions" (Coakley, *Powers and Submissions*, 161).

110. As Simone Weil highlights in an essay on attention, practices of more mundane sorts—even ones that may seem morally and spiritually irrelevant, such as attending to "a Latin prose or a geometry problem"—can bear fruit in a deeper capacity of attentiveness to the suffering other (Simone Weil, *Waiting for God*, Harper Perennial Modern Classics edition (New York: HarperCollins, 2009), 65.) In an interview, Coakley comments on the early attraction and profound impact this essay of Weil's had on her; see Rupert Shortt, *God's Advocates: Christian Thinkers in Conversation* (Grand Rapids: Eerdmans, 2005), 67–68.

111. Coakley, "The Identity of the Risen Jesus," 316.

[t]he moral and epistemic stripping that is endemic to the act of contemplation is a vital key here: its practiced self-emptying inculcates an attentiveness that is beyond merely good political intentions. Its practice is more discomforting, more destabilizing to settled presumptions, than a simple intentional *design* on empathy.[112]

For Coakley then, "the ascetic practices of contemplation are themselves indispensible means of a *true* attentiveness to the despised and marginalized other"[113] and ones that moral philosophy "ignores or derides at its peril."[114] Her claim is that this practice of "willed passivity"[115] harbors the most radical potential for personal and political transformation and empowerment. Contemplation, as the "regular, patient attempt to attend to God in prayer"[116] simplified "into an empty waiting on God"[117] is, according to Coakley, a "spiritual practice of attention"[118] that is alone capable of producing the most profound changes in the degree and depth of our attentiveness to others.

However, at the same time, Coakley draws attention to the serious dangers of advocating such a practice of vulnerability designed to inculcate mental patterns of unmastery and radical attentiveness to God and others. As Coakley sums up the charges, for many it seems "that such practice encourages societal 'submissiveness,' disassociated introversion, apolitical anaesthesia, or the silencing of 'woman.'"[119] Prayer, contemplation, and the like are practices that smack of the unpopular and worrying tropes "of 'heteronomy'—of submission, dependency or vulnerability."[120] Rather than constituting an essentially transformative ingredient within moral life, they appear, if anything, dangerously counterproductive to it: more likely to entrench oppression than to produce transformative social effects. Interestingly,

---

112. Coakley, "Is There a Future for Gender and Theology?," 6–7.
113. Ibid., 6.
114. Coakley, *Powers and Submissions*, xvii. Note: in its original context this quote is directed at "the feminist movement" but the point seems generalizable.
115. Ibid., 37.
116. Coakley, *God, Sexuality and the Self: An Essay 'On the Trinity.'*
117. Coakley, "Deepening Practices," 92–93.
118. Coakley, "Is There a Future for Gender and Theology?," 4.
119. Coakley, *Powers and Submissions*, xvii.
120. Ibid., xiv.

similar sorts of critiques have also been aimed at Levinas, particularly by feminist interpreters who raise concerns about his emphasis on heteronomy, passivity, and a vulnerable submission to the command of the other. How can we judge whether cultivating these types of self-emptying and radically attentive modes of perception and response (which Levinas often describes in very extreme terms such as persecution or trauma) will lead to the transformative increase of one's ethical capacity for response or in fact to the crushing of it? These are serious questions for any moral philosophers who see the cultivation of something like receptivity, vulnerability, and attentiveness to others as vital to ethical life.

How then does Coakley answer this critique? Most significantly, in contrast to the above-noted emphasis in Levinas on abstracting from particular context,[121] Coakley's own discourse seems saturated with it as she constantly highlights the crucial role such context plays in her own reasons for commending the transformative potential of contemplative prayer. Perhaps surprisingly then, if we examine the texts where Coakley offers more extended arguments in support of this contention, we in fact never find her attempting to defend the general *form* of contemplation in and of itself.[122] Indeed, as far as its basic structure goes, Coakley would side with feminist concerns about

---

121. Another example of a very different thinker who seeks to commend the transformative potential of prayer-practice for ethical life independently of its religious context is the secular moral philosopher Iris Murdoch. She contends that "whatever one thinks of its theological context, it does seem that prayer can actually induce a better quality of consciousness and provide an energy for good action which would not otherwise be available" (Iris Murdoch, *The Sovereignty of Good* [New York: Routledge, 2001], 81).

122. Note: Coakley does occasionally make claims about the common features shared by different specific practices of prayer, contemplation, and meditation. For example, she claims that they all seem to have not only individual but also societal effects, thus for each of them it would be false to suggest "that 'contemplative practice' is narrowly introverted or apolitical" (Coakley, *Powers and Submissions*, xix). Crucially however, for Coakley, this claim is not reached by abstracting from the specific context of each of these practices to see what they all have in common but rather is arrived at only on the basis of a "close examination" of each particular practice in the context of its own specific tradition. Thus, in making the above comparative claim, Coakley relies on studies that engage in a "close examination of the theories of the social—as well as individual—effects of 'mediation' practice in Buddhism, Daoism, Sikhism, Zoroastrianism and modern Japanese religion" (ibid., xix n. 31). Toward the end of the chapter, I will return to the significance of this "careful attention to context," which alone can "form a *preparatio* for the infinitely complex task of 'comparative' study" between the practices of different traditions (Sarah Coakley, "Introduction: Religion and the Body," in *Religion and the Body*, ed. Sarah Coakley [Cambridge: Cambridge University Press, 1997], 9).

the dangers of promoting practices that, according to most distillations of their form, involve risky and undesirable states (for example, those of passivity, vulnerability, submission, and so on). For Coakley, there is nothing self-evident in the abstract arrangement of attentiveness to the divine (or to the transcendent, the other, the good, etc.) that would make it immune from the warranted critical concern that it might undermine ethical life, let alone anything to convince us of the much stronger claim that it might be essential to it and provide a vital path toward increasing one's capacity for moral responsiveness.

What we find in Coakley's more extended writings on contemplative prayer then is that rather than seeking to make a case for the benefits of something like attention to the divine in general, she instead affirms and attempts to defend the transformative potential of one *specific* form of this practice embedded in the context of a specific tradition, namely, in her case, a specifically Christian form of contemplative prayer-practice. Moreover, Coakley commends this practice to us not independently of or in spite of its particular context but rather because of it. Thus, for example, she argues that it is certain key theological assumptions about "how divine 'power' is construed in relation to the human"[123] in the Christian tradition that enables it to coherently sustain an account of how this practice of attention can indeed "be a graced means of human empowerment in the divine."[124] Since contemplative prayer is defined here as an act of attending to God—of "silent waiting on the divine" where "we cease to set the agenda [and] 'make space' for God to be God" and so as "a regular and willed *practice* of ceding and responding to the divine"—then everything about the specific form it takes hinges on the nature of this divine power.[125] If, as Coakley notes, the touchstone for construing divine power in the Christian tradition comes from its "primary commitment to the given *narrative* of the New Testament, and especially the gospel accounts of Jesus' life,"[126] then, as she seeks to show, this should lead to a

123. Coakley, *Powers and Submissions*, 15.
124. Ibid., xvii.
125. Ibid., 34.
126. Ibid., 24.

profoundly unique form of power, fundamentally at odds with what is normally meant by worldly power. It is, as Coakley puts it at different points, "the power of the cross and resurrection," a "non-abusive divine power," "the subtle but enabling presence of a God who neither shouts nor forces, let alone 'obliterates'"; in short, "authentic divine power, itself 'made perfect in weakness.'"[127]

For Coakley, then, it is this Christian form of divine power (Trinitarian, incarnational, kenotic, and so on) that makes the specific practice of vulnerability involved in contemplative prayer a locus of human empowerment. Once again, this is not praise for vulnerability in general (which, as Coakley notes, is "often a dangerous or regrettable state") but only the commendation of "a *special* form of human 'vulnerability'" that gets its distinctive shape from the Christian narrative.[128] In this context, Coakley claims, such practices can bear fruit in "personal empowerment, prophetic resistance [and] courage in the face of oppression" because "if our fundamental and *practiced* dependency is on God, there is the fulcrum from which our (often necessary) dependencies on others may be assessed with critical discernment."[129] Thus while this "form of waiting" on the divine may well involve great personal commitment and risk, often bringing bewilderment and pain, it is a practice of attention that, *when embedded in this context*, Coakley is also willing to affirm as one that is "transformative and empowering."[130]

One contribution of Coakley's own writings on contemplative prayer then is to offer a sustained explication of how the Christian theological context suggests and coherently sustains an account of the transformative potential of this practice. Now, of course, others will no doubt want to offer defenses of other specific forms of this practice or indeed of other practices altogether, embedded in different contexts —some of which may well be incompatible with one another. But, for

---

127. Ibid., 33, 34, 35, 38.
128. Ibid., 33, 32. For further on the "Christic" shape of "the *special* self-effacement of this gentle space-making," see ibid., 35.
129. Ibid., xx; see also xviii.
130. Ibid., 35, 39.

Coakley, this would be a welcome development since it is precisely at this level of full particular context that the debate over the transformative potential or dangers of various practices for ethical life must take place. Something of Coakley's own efforts at trying to foster this kind of detailed comparative work—with its "careful attention to context" rather than attempt to abstract from it—can be seen in her edited collection *Religion and the Body*.[131] In the introduction to this collection, Coakley sums up the crucial challenge that these kinds of "careful exegetical and phenomenological accounts" pose, namely, they

> give *pause* to the idea that "bodily" practices from other religious and ritual contexts can be taken over merely for the purposes of undemanding relaxation and restoration [and here, we might add, for the purposes of cultivating moral attentiveness in the most effective way]. Particular bodily practices imply (no less particular) metaphysical and cultural commitments, and may indeed finally induce them.[132]

Returning one last time to Levinas and his commentators, the above analysis has sought to foreground the way in which Coakley's distinctive methodological approach to the question of "which practices"—her sensitivity to particular context and so her concerted effort to develop and promote local defenses of the moral significance of certain practices—may well offer an instructive model for those Levinasians who have likewise become convinced of their need to address the "how" question. Indeed, some examples of this type of sensitivity to context can already be found, for instance, in Katz's own proposal regarding how Levinasians should go about constructing an account of moral cultivation to supplement his ethics. For her, the recommended practices and a defense of them ought to be found in the Jewish sources of Levinas's thought.[133] In particular, she advocates

---

131. Coakley, "Introduction: Religion and the Body," 9.
132. Ibid., 9, 8.
133. However, Katz writes, "This is not to say that other religions should be excluded from this conversation. My point is rather that Levinas's relationship to Judaism situates his work and his project within a larger Jewish context" (Katz, "'The Presence of the Other Is a Presence That Teaches,'" 101). She thus maintains that "if as Levinas suggests, politics is derivative of ethics, then it is the Jewish tradition from which Levinas's own ethical/philosophical project emerges

a specific practice of Talmudic reading for everyone as especially conducive to moral development.[134] No doubt other Levinasians may disagree with Katz's turn to Jewish practices and instead seek to argue for an alternative set of practices from other traditions they find represented in Levinas's philosophical texts or even from sources external to them. For example, with regard to the former, one might consider "practices and rituals such as those of humanism, fraternity, and solidarity in the context of the modern secular world" which stem "from the French republican context that helped shape Levinas's political sensibility and politics."[135] Either way, however, the lesson drawn from Coakley's approach above is that both options ought to be viewed as the attempted defense and recommendation of specific practices embedded in specific contexts: this is the level at which the debate over "which practices" must take place.

It has been suggested then that Coakley's method for defending her provocative commendation of Christian prayer-practice as a vital means of enhancing moral attentiveness, by being upfront about the significance and inescapability of particular context when it comes to the question of "which practices," in turn challenges others—whether drawing on religious or secular traditions—to be explicit about the commitments informing their own accounts of the "how" of transformation. In other words, to tease out the particular "piety" that informs our pious moral discourses and visions of transformation and, to the extent we find these particulars persuasive, to invest serious

---

that provides us with a more effective pedagogical model that encourages us first to engage with each other face to face" (ibid., 108).

134. This is an education that Katz thinks Levinas's texts implicitly perform and encourage us to adopt, even if they don't explicitly draw attention to this as their method. As she puts it, "Levinas's ethical project points to something more like the Talmudic approach to learning with its focus on a reading of the biblical texts that encourages attunement, questioning and response" (Katz, "'The Presence of the Other Is a Presence That Teaches,'" 107). For Katz's own elaboration and defense of the practice of Talmudic learning as vital for moral cultivation and applicable to everyone, see ibid., 100–108 and Claire Katz, "Educating the Solitary Man: Levinas, Rousseau, and the Return of Jewish Wisdom," *Levinas Studies* 2 (2007): 143–52.

135. Eric Sean Nelson, "Levinas and Early Confucian Ethics: Religion, Rituality, and the Sources of Morality," *Levinas Studies* 4 (2009): 195. In this passage, Nelson compares approaches drawing on secular sources in Levinas's work and those drawing on Jewish sources and aptly presents both as a matter of practices and rituals embedded in specific traditions.

effort in developing defenses of them with which we can engage in dialogue and debate with others.

In relation then to the complaints leveled against continental ethics at the outset of this chapter, the kernel of Coakley's analyses would be to insist that if a philosophical discourse of personal transformation such as Levinas's ethics of infinite responsibility is to avoid amounting to nothing more than empty hyperbolic gestures, then it must take the requisite steps to ensure and sustain the ethical vision it urges. Such discourses, Coakley argues, always provoke "the question of the 'practices' that alone can" effect the desired transformation of self and,[136] furthermore, the question of practices always brings with it the further question of context. As such, for continental ethicists too, there can be no avoiding the necessity to tread the pragmatic path of furnishing a diachronic account of the "how" of transformation and, in conversation with others, of engaging with the difficult issues that come to the fore once one starts to get specific about the question of "which practices."

136. Coakley, *Powers and Submissions*, xx.

3

———

Sacrifice Regained in the Light of *God, Sexuality, and the Self* and "Flesh and Blood": Objections and Replies, or How I Changed My Mind

Eugene F. Rogers Jr.

The title of this volume is *Sarah Coakley and the Future of Systematic Theology*. When I gave an initial version of this essay at the AAR, I called it "Three Friendly Amendments to Coakley's *Sacrifice Regained*."[1] As is often the case with friendly amendments, the paper enjoyed (despite itself) the air of knowing better. There was the Yale-inspired typology to put Coakley into a box; there was the Barth-inspired polemic against

---

1. Sarah Coakley, *Sacrifice Regained: Evolution, Cooperation and God*, five Gifford Lectures delivered at the University of Aberdeen from April 17 to May 3, 2012 and available at http://www.abdn.ac.uk/gifford/about/. Cited in the medieval way by *Lectio* and page number.

natural theology; there was the idiosyncratic or Princeton-specific Aquinas interpretation elevating virtue over "natural law." Coakley was not so sure that *Sacrifice Regained* really needed saving, or that the amendments were really friendly. And now, on longer reflection, I have to admit she was right. Furthermore, I have changed my mind.

This time the essay takes the form of objections posed and replied to. In this I follow the example of Thomas Aquinas when he announces a change of mind by describing an objection as one *quod etiam aliquando mihi visum est*, "which once seemed to be the case even to me."[2] Three objections reflect a reading of *Sacrifice Regained* in isolation and urge their recasting in terms of *God, Sexuality, and the Self*; three replies reflect a reading of *Sacrifice Regained* in light of Coakley's 2004 Hensley Henson lecture series *Flesh and Blood*[3] and reassure the objector that the transformative context is already firmly in place. By "transformative context," I mean a *eucharistic* theory of sacrifice capable of changing scientific water into theological wine, explaining how the Gifford Lectures' natural elements can deliver the real presence of Christ. This rereading is important not only to Barthian and Yale-school interpreters of the latest theology of nature. It confirms the opening to nature that Barth proclaimed when he wrote that there is no one—not a scientist or even a Barthian—who is "living in some forgotten corner of the world, where God is not God or cannot be known as God . . . as if there were a self-contained Gentile world, established, secure, and justified in itself."[4]

The critic might object to three phrases that do a lot of work in Coakley's Gifford Lectures: "Natural theology," "sacrificial theory," and "natural law."

2. *ST* III.70.4c *ca. med.*, newly holding that the grace of circumcision confers the grace of baptism.
3. Sarah Coakley, *Flesh and Blood: The Eucharist, Desire and Fragmentation*, Hensely Henson Lectures delivered at Oxford 2004–2005, typescript provided by the author and quoted with permission.
4. Karl Barth, *Shorter Commentary on Romans* (Philadelphia: John Knox, 1956), 28–29.

Objection 1. The Gifford Lectures seek "the courage to persevere in the task of 'natural theology,'" albeit reconceived.[5]

"Natural theology," as a phrase, has become deeply unpopular, as the Gifford Lectures acknowledge. Barth notoriously called it "*the invention of the anti-Christ*."[6] Catholics associate it with Vatican I. Liberation theology has no use for it. Cosmological arguments sound either medieval or fundamentalist. All that is well known. For that reason, the cost of the phrase is very high. It sounds like a form of what evolutionists call "costly signaling." In Aberdeen it seems hardly worth the cost. At the Center of Theological Inquiry, where the Gifford Lectures were discussed, theologians of various orientations and evolutionary scientists all supposed that despite disclaimers, anything called "natural theology" must import a God-of-the-gaps strategy, making itself hostage to whatever science one allies oneself with—although everyone also saw that that's not what Coakley wants. We saw that "natural theology" has become so unattractive a phrase that it cries out to be reclaimed. We saw, too, that the phrase "natural theology" allows Coakley to stand both *with* the natural world, and *against* an all-too-narrow theological guild. But the evidence suggested that the reclamation wasn't working. It seemed a bridge too far.

Reply to Objection 1. The theological guild is not, in fact, against the sort of theology that Coakley favors, only against the method that they (mis)hear in the phrase—a method Coakley eschews. In *God, Sexuality, and the Self*, Coakley offers a larger method, *théologie totale*. The phrase invites because it implies a theology that *leaves nothing out*, not Trinity, not sexuality, not science. *Théologie totale* invites scientists, too, to see their work as part of a larger whole. It implies openness to science, sacrifice, and feminist critiques of sacrifice, nothing relevant passed over, no artificial barriers, no self-insulation, but the Spirit-led confidence to encounter it all. It includes, as Coakley points out, the courage to push forward to meet the challenge and the refusal to

---

5. *Sacrifice Regained*, Lect. i.1–8 ; *Lect.* vi.1–12.
6. For the citations in the context of others that moderate or undermine Barth's claim, see my *Thomas Aquinas and Karl Barth* (Notre Dame: University of Notre Dame Press, 1995).

withdraw into self-containment. In *content*, *théologie totale* already includes a space for natural theology, by analogy to its treatment of the social sciences, and explicitly provided for in *God, Sexuality, and the Self* (p. 66). The question is then whether natural theology should be allowed to appear as its own *self-insulating, systematic* apologetic enterprise—or whether it too must admit to belonging to something larger, to *théologie totale*; whether it too should submit to the discipline of a larger community, not to suppress its truth, but in order to keep knowledge and mystery together. If God, as Aquinas says, *non est in genere*, is not in a genus or a gender, then theology, too, cannot be confined to a gender or a genus, even a natural one.

The other nice thing about the phrase "*théologie totale*" is that it's distinctively Coakleyan. It ties the sacrifice work to the sexuality work, where of course a deep current already connects them, that of asceticism. In *God, Sexuality, and the Self*, contemplative prayer marks an ascetic moment of self-dispossession. "Sacrifice" expands self-dispossession into self-gift. And yet great discernment—gained perhaps in wordless prayer—is needed to distinguish the false asceticisms imposed by others from the true asceticism of giving up one's false self-images. Contemplation and sacrifice, that is, will always belong together. *Sacrifice Regained* calls upon the theologian to give up the false pride of theological isolation in the Spirit-led conviction that the truth is one.[7]

Despite the deep compatibility of *Sacrifice Regained* with *théologie totale*, the Gifford Lectures read in isolation may leave the false impression that "natural theology" belongs to one type and *théologie totale* to an entirely different type. The disadvantage of the critic's reading (*quod etiam aliquando mihi visum est*) is that it divides Coakley's authorship in two and reads her as inconsistent. To see why this misprision arises, consider the "five types" of Christian theology famously developed by Hans Frei and redescribed by Jeffrey Stout.[8]

---

7. *Sacrifice Regained*, Lect. i.7.
8. Hans Frei, *Types of Christian Theology* (New Haven: Yale University Press, 1992); Jeffrey Stout, "Hans Frei and Anselmian Theology," in *Ten Year Commemoration to the Life of Hans Frei*, ed. Giorgy Olegovich (New York: Semenenko Foundation, 1999), 24–40.

In Stout's version, Christian theology has to relate "biblical language" to nonbiblical languages. Thus five strategies: 1. Esperanto trims from biblical language everything that does not stand to reason, considered without regard to time period, for example Immanuel Kant. 2. Presentese trims from biblical language everything that does not stand to reason as we know it in the present, for example Sallie McFague. 3. Dialogical treats biblical and scientific language as "heterogeneous equals" to correlate by question and answer from either side, for example Paul Tillich. 4. In Anselmian, the motto is "faith seeking understanding," and the goal is for biblical language, in the interest of understanding, to absorb as much of the nonbiblical languages as possible, which it uses ad hoc, nonfoundationally, as a sort of *bricolage* (as Stout described it), a sort of tinkering together of found objects. If the language of nonfoundationalism sounds too 1980s, we can use the language of critical gender theory: the goal is to repeat the deliverances of nonbiblical language; to repeat them subversively; to free them from contexts of oppression; and to use them from an alternative production[9]—as Jesus did when he took the structure of Roman execution and turned it to a peaceful feast, saying "this is my body, given for you." If nonbiblical language describes something true that biblical language cannot absorb, so much the worse for Christianity. The last of Frei's five types Stout calls "Segregationist," where biblical and nonbiblical language remain in separate spheres, as in the vulgar Wittgensteinianism of D. Z. Phillips.

The trouble with "natural theology" is that, read as isolated and unchastened, it sounds like Presentese. *Théologie totale*, on the other hand, is clearly Anslemian. If so, something else from Frei's agenda can help the critic to better understand Coakley's project. That's the idea that the apologetics appropriate to *théologie totale* ought to be read not as systematic but as *ad hoc*.[10] The attempt in *God, Sexuality, and the Self* to overcome the impasse on sexuality in the churches would count as

9. Judith Butler, "Contingent Foundations," in *Feminist Contentions*, ed. Seyla Benhabib et al. (London: Routledge, 1995).
10. The classic essay is William Werpehowski, "Ad hoc Apologetics," *The Journal of Religion* 66 (1986): 282–301.

ad hoc apologetics. A natural theology within *théologie totale* counts as ad hoc, too.[11] If we apply Frei's characterization of philosophy instead to natural science, we get the following statement: "I do not regard [natural science] as having ever achieved that clearly demonstrated set of even formal certainties (and agreements) in 2500 years which would allow it the kind of authoritative status that [natural theology] seems to want to accord it; and yet I believe theology cannot do without [natural science]."[12] That sounds like *théologie totale*. *Théologie totale* can be unapologetic as theology, and modest in its commitments to natural science, which changes far more rapidly than Christian doctrine. If Christianity is committed to love because Jesus preached and practiced it, then *théologie totale* can use Martin Nowak's idea that cooperation is a third principle of evolution as long as that holds up, or switch to Joan Roughgarden's version if that works out better, or wait and see if both fall into retreat.

This is not a modern guerilla strategy. It is an ancient one. It is a principle of biblical exegesis common to Augustine and Aquinas: anything true, which can be adapted (*aptari potest*) to the biblical text (*salva litterae circumstantia*) just *is* a meaning of the text. A meaning, because the text "ought not to be so confined to one meaning (*non cogere*) as to expose the faith to ridicule."[13] This principle of exegesis makes a huge grant of freedom. We ought not, therefore, so confine Christian doctrine that it depends on any one deliverance of evolutionary science, but work *ad hoc* so that scientific commitments can change as science does. As we do not confine God to a genus, so we do not confine the letter of scripture to any one meaning, but allow it

---

11. I thank Anthony Baker for this observation.
12. Letter from Frei to Gary Comstock, November 1985; distributed by Frei to multiple graduate students at the time, including the author.
13. Thomas Aquinas, *De potentia* 4.1–2. The *De potentia* considers precisely the relation of theology to natural science. For an uncontroversial account—because no one cares anymore about Aristotle's views on the creation of the world—consider how Aquinas and Bonaventure handle the potential conflict between Aristotle and scripture in Bruce Marshall, "Absorbing the World: Christianity and the Universe of Truths," in *Theology and Dialogue: Essays in Conversation with George Lindbeck*, ed. Bruce Marshall (Notre Dame: Notre Dame University Press, 1990), 69–102. Now, Coakley may dislike the supersessionist-sounding language of "absorbing," but that need not prevent her from using the traditional, Augustinian-Thomistic solution on science and revelation under a more satisfactory name—such as *théologie totale*.

to author a community. As long as Aristotle, Newton, and Darwin have *some* things right, a *théologie totale* such as that of Aquinas, Edwards, or Coakley was right to use them. *Systematic* apologetics (in isolation from a larger *théologie totale*) is too costly a signal of blowing with the wind rather than with the Spirit. But Coakley's so-called "natural theology" is not a *systematic* or *isolated* apologetics. It is a foray. She has not suddenly forgotten what she wrote about *théologie totale*. When she writes in *Sacrifice Regained* that "I do not either, as a theologian, simply abandon my theological commitments at the door in such an engagement with secular science and philosophy."[14] We see the proof in *Flesh and Blood*. In *God, Sexuality, and the Self*, *théologie totale* accomplishes the same thing with deep dependence on the Spirit, enabling its *ad hoc* use of everyone from Origen to Judith Butler with John of the Cross in between.

Now, I still worry that there is also something distinctive about tone in *Sacrifice Regained*, something of Coakley *contra mundum*. But the triumphalist tone does not drown out the Coakley who, dispossessed by the Spirit,[15] both humbly and sovereignly contemplates the world —even if the Coakley-*contra-mundum* is still a temptation. I prefer the Spirit of Romans 8, who includes all things—even frailty, failure, and death—in the Trinitarian embrace, over the Spirit of the Gospel of John with its dualistic, counter-worldly, light-and-darkness overtones.

All this means that "natural theology" is not wrong. Natural theology is wrong only when isolated and undigested. Under christological discipline—or in Coakley's phrases, under "Christic judgement"[16] or with "Christic orientation"[17] it can be quite alright. Theology must after all exercise her reign as queen of the sciences. That means taking them up in a christological assumption. This is once again the Anselmian paradigm of faith (rather than pure reason) seeking understanding.

---

14. *Sacrifice Regained*, Lect. i.7.
15. Ibid.
16. *Flesh and Blood*, Lect. i.20.
17. Ibid., iv.3.

Objection 2. The Gifford Lectures characterize theories of sacrifice as "the triumph of violence" and blame Girard.[18]

Read in isolation, the Giffords overdetermine "sacrifice" in Girardian terms, and then fight back. But why not step aside, in the judo move, and allow the "all violence" theory to hurtle down, unimpeded, of its own accord? Why not talk about the *practice* of sacrifice rather than fight over theory? We don't need any one theory of sacrifice, although perhaps a thickly developed evolutionary account, if there is one, can help us; we need to be able to leap (like Aquinas) nimbly from one to another, for different interests and purposes. By "practice" I mean something that would continue the self-dispossession of wordless prayer into the self-dispossession of (say) parenting in the distinctively long human childhood described by Melvin Konnor.[19] Here's the point: Human beings do certain vaguely similar things over and over: they are moved to offer their valuables and themselves; and they kill animals and eat them in community. These human practices are vastly overdetermined by multiple overlapping theories. They can be interpreted to mean too many things. They profligately attract interpretation. Among all the theories, Christian theology ought to favor the indigenous ones, precisely as sites of controversy. When I express a suspicion of theory, it's of a general theory of sacrifice that might prematurely shut down or foreclose the deep understanding of the practices of sacrifice indigenous to a community. I don't mind if Christian theology uses theories of sacrifice *small scale* and *ad hoc*, to irritate and elucidate. *Ad hoc*, rather than totalizing accounts (not theories!) of sacrifice would include Aquinas on the incarnation, who simply validates all the theories known to him as useful for different aspects, and such recent authors as Stan Stowers and Kathryn McClymonds.[20] Unless you announce the bounds that keep

---

18. *Sacrifice Regained*, Lect. i.8.

19. Melvin Konnor, *The Evolution of Childhood: Relationships, Emotion, Mind* (Cambridge, MA: Harvard University Press, 2010). Someone at CTI—possibly Celia Deane-Drummond or Agustín Fuentes—suggested childrearing as a sacrificial practice that would fit Coakley's requirements.

20. Stanley Stowers, "The Religion of Plant and Animal Offerings Versus the Religion of Meanings, Essences, and Textual Mysteries," in *Ancient Mediterranean Sacrifice*, ed. Jennifer Knust and

evolutionary theories of sacrifice in check, readers such as myself will worry that the apparent power and generality of an evolutionary theory will wash the interesting content out of theology, or even out of the sociology of religion.

What if sacrifice is not a good candidate for a speculative theory, but for a Wittgensteinian rule? Suppose sacrifice is a skill or practice before it is a concept.[21] We use it to do something. We use it to offer up our suffering for a larger purpose, to join our suffering to the making of meaning, and to help others to do the same. In that way we are less alone—we gain solidarity—we imagine our suffering to be *for* something.

Of course, we even imagine our suffering to be for something when it's not, when suffering needs to be stopped rather than honored with meaning. Is that good or bad? The question, its difficulty and delicacy, does much to tell us what kind of skill it is: the skill of giving meaning rather than taking it away—or indeed of taking meaning away, when it's necessary to unmask injustice. This is why *theories* of sacrifice always fall short: they impose unique strategies for making meaning out of suffering, and we need more strategies than one. Our theories at best summarize our experience of either making meaning out of suffering, or exposing the failure of the attempt for justice' sake. The real skill is the wisdom to tell the difference. A good "theory" of sacrifice, therefore, would hardly be a theory at all, but a quite various and hard-to-summarize set of practices with no essence but a lot of family resemblance that have in common the ability *successfully* to give meaning to the sufferings of others and oneself. Evolutionary biologists like Richard Sosis and students of Vedic and Israelite sacrifice like Naphtali Meshel converge in treating sacrifice as a ritual language with its own lexica and syntax—a language in which metaphysics is made not verbal but palpable.[22] Or if you have a Wittgenstein allergy, so that

Zsuzsanna Várhelyi (Oxford: Oxford University Press, 2011), 35–56; Kathryn McClymonds, *Beyond Sacred Violence: A Comparative Study of Sacrifice* (Baltimore: Johns Hopkins University Press, 2008).

21. Stanley Stowers gives historical rather than Wittgensteinian evidence for this in "Offerings vs. Meanings," cited above.

22. Richard Sosis examines ritual, not specifically sacrifice: Richard Sosis and Jordan Kiper, "Religion Is More Than Belief: What Evolutionary Theories of Religion Tell Us about Religious

talk of "family resemblance" or of practice over meaning makes you break out in hives, you can just follow McClymonds to observe that sacrifice is polythetic rather than all about one thing.

Given that suffering is a bad thing, "sacrifice" is the word we use to describe the bringing of good out of it nevertheless. The reason why *sacri-facio* makes sacred is that it separates good from evil, holy from profane, the good meaning from the bad suffering. In this way even the creation story, which is all about God's separating (light from darkness, water from earth, and so on), is also a story of making holy, making meaning, and therefore of sacrifice: a story of separating meaning out, of skimming it off. (Does creation therefore prefigure atonement, in its emphasis on separation? Does that have anything to do with the role of the Logos in creation and atonement?) Because meaning is a distinctively *human* thing, and sacredness invokes the divine, the human's imaging of the divine takes place here: in our participation in creation's work of separation, *tikkun olam*. This involves sacrifice. But it's unclear whether there is ever meaning without "good" sacrifice (not false sacrifice for its own sake). Note that in connecting meaning and sacrifice in this way I still intend to anchor both to a variety of practices, not something that floats free of concrete attempts to make meaning work.

So "sacrifice" becomes a matter for discernment and the practice of separation gained in deep prayer—another theme of *God, Sexuality, and the Self*—rather than a grand theory that favors some theorists at the expense of others. I suspect we need them all. We need a total and distinctive, or catholic-Coakleyan—not exclusive—theory of sacrifice.

This means that there is less reason to attack (say) Girard, since there is no *one* theory of sacrifice, but multiple practices that overlap. Rather, there is all the more reason to use, absorb, and modify him, so that his later openness to mimesis of the good—which is how we

---

Commitments," in *Challenges to Religion and Morality: Disagreements and Evolution*, ed. M. Bergmann and P. Kain (forthcoming). Naphtali Meshel, *The 'Grammar' of Sacrifice: A Generativist Study of the Priestly Israelite Sacrificial System* (Hebrew University dissertation; book under review). "Metaphysics made palpable" is Robert Parker's phrase in *Miasma: Pollution and Purification in Early Greek Religion* (Oxford: Clarendon, 1996), 19.

apprentice ourselves to the good—controls the interpretation of mimetic violence. Certainly we can be glad, with Coakley, for indications that violence need not go all the way down, in evolution or in God; we can also avoid kenotic theories of the Trinity that make self-emptying prior to the divine fullness; but it is too much to ask for evolutionary science to carry those burdens: they belong to exegesis of the Bible and recovery of the tradition. Only so can we author a community.

Reply to Objection 2. It turns out that a series of recognitions quite like these—down to overdetermination and Wittgensteinian family resemblance already animates the yet-to-be published *Flesh and Blood*. There we read that "the matter [of how to understand sacrifice] has been complicated—or perhaps more truly over-simplified—by a range of beguiling modern theories that have vied in their ambition to simplify the matter of sacrifice into *one* primal meaning, a tactic that we shall stoutly resist."[23] This ambition to reduce led to "over a century of anthropological and psychoanalytic 'overdetermination' of the category."[24] The "classic theories now begin to look—to the jaded eye of the post-modern commentator—distinctively 'modern' and *hubristic* attempts to control multifarious phenomena under *one* constellating idea."[25] Coakley goes on:

> Much better surely to admit, theoretically, with Michael Bourdillon, that "sacrifice" is an umbrella term under which various, "family resemblance," ideas cluster (offering, destruction, division, substitution, commensality, apotropaism, "control of death," moral self-giving) but which are by no means all present in any one cultural or religious context, nor necessarily with the same set of symbolic overtones. Once this has been admitted, as I believe it must be, then the crucial job is to explicate with as much precision as is possible the *particular* sacrificial system one seeks to clarify, and its accompanying "official" theoretic base, but always with the honest acknowledgement that an effusion of additional, and highly *emotive* overtones will most likely be being set off amongst one's audience or ritual collaborators which are hard, frankly, completely to predict or control. That is the "name of the game," in my view, and a

23. *Flesh and Blood, Lect.* ii.2.
24. Ibid., ii.5.
25. Ibid., ii.8.

crucial feature even of "sacrifice's" *current* symbolic power and density, if my analysis is correct.[26]

That, of course, is very far from reducing current sacrifice-theory to Girard alone, and says everything the critic of the Gifford Lectures would wish.

As a corollary to this objection and reply, it's a controversial contention of the Gifford Lectures that Martin Nowak's mathematical "proof" that an altruistic "sacrifice" for others is a real, separate principle of evolution, alongside competition, sexual selection, and the rest. I propose that Coakley take a leaf from *God, Sexuality, and the Self*—which very helpfully invents the word "proto-erotic" for that which, in the work of the Spirit, gives rise to *both* physical desire and desire for God—and invent the word "proto-sacrifice" for that which, in the work of the Spirit, gives rise to *both* evolutionary cooperation *and* the way of the cross. This is of course deeply Thomistic, since Thomas credits the Spirit with both gravitational attraction and the love in the rational lover (*ST* I-II.26.2).

Objection 3. The Gifford Lectures propose to ask the question: Why not use Aquinas to talk about virtue rather than natural law?

The trouble with the natural-law language is threefold. One, it's captive to the Finnis-Grisez-Boyle crowd (sometimes called "the Griffenboyle"[27]), who use it primarily to convince the U.S. Supreme Court to reinforce traditional gender roles.[28] Second, Aquinas himself leaves natural law content-free: All the content comes from the practice of following a wise person, connected (again) to the distinctively human ability to learn by imitation (which chimps, by contrast, do with great loss and inaccuracy). In Aquinas, "natural law"

---

26. *Flesh and Blood*, Lect. 2, 9.
27. Coined in Henry Veatch and Joseph Rautenberg, "Does the Grisez-Finnis-Boyle Moral Philosophy Rest on a Mistake?" *Review of Metaphysics* 44 (1991): 807–30.
28. For the antidote, see Eugene F. Rogers Jr., *Aquinas and the Supreme Court: Race, Gender, and the Failure of Natural Law in Thomas's Biblical Commentaries* (Oxford: Wiley-Blackwell, 2013); here, "How God Moves Creatures: For and Against Natural Law," 83–85.

names a preapprehension of the Good (or *Vorgriff aufs Gute*), a tendency to identify the excellences of a virtuous person with the Good to be pursued. It names the human tendency to say, "That's good! I want to be like that!" The law of our nature is that we imitate those we admire; it is the condition for discipleship; when Jesus says, "follow me," he is, in Thomistic terms, invoking and elevating the law of our nature, the way by which we seek our good.[29] A member of another species might be able to recognize their own excellence (say at birdsong), but not ours. When such naturally developing excellences are *human*, we call them virtues. The third reason, therefore, to prefer talk of virtues, is that it's virtues that give content to morality, that identify and enact what's distinctively human about being in God's image.

In short, Aquinas's appeal to the law of human nature does not so much add anything to virtue theory as *formulate* it (in a remark I owe to Victor Preller). It says that we are in God's image as those who order our deeds to an end, as practitioners of virtue. To do that we do not usually need to "stop and think." Aquinas says virtue is *promptior*, readier or more apparent, in action than in deliberation. In action it moves *suaviter*, smoothly. On his account, as on the accounts of neuroscientists, "stopping to think" represents only special cases. We talk about virtue, in Aquinas, after the fact, to analyze, *post hoc*, an *actus*, something-having-been-done. We talk about virtue, that is, when imitation falls short: "No, do *this*." Talk of virtue, like talk of meaning, represents a second-order practice of dispute or repair.[30]

When the *Summa* says that God "instructs" us with natural law—which certainly sounds like content in English—it sounds like content only because we have ceased to read our Bibles in Latin. In the Vulgate, the primary meaning of *instruo* is to equip an army (*instructus gladio*, "equipped with a sword") or furnish the temple. In "instructing" us, God simply in-structures us with the tendency to pursue (follow thoroughly or imitate) the good person and avoid the evil person, as cognitive science theories of contagion also suggest. Similarly, the

---

29. *Aquinas and the Supreme Court*, 84.
30. Ibid., 78–82.

word *propositio*, which sounds so like a modern philosophical proposition, means in the Vulgate a real proposal, as when God sets before one life and death, or when Israelites set their tables (*le chef vous propose*), so that far and away the commonest use of *propositio* in the Vulgate—with which Aquinas would have been very familiar—occurs in the phrase *panis propositionis*, "the bread of offering." To the author of *Pange Linguae*, if you want to accept a proposition, you first of all take the bread. This is not so much like modern scientific law, and much more like something else that evolution studies, the remarkable human capacity as children from their parents, at table and in church.[31]

All that makes Aquinas's law of nature much too complicated as a category in which to absorb modern evolutionary science. Besides, he devotes only six pages to it. Better to turn to the virtues, to which he devotes 200 *times* as many pages, some twelve hundred.

Virtue is the theory that accords with a human being that develops its distinctiveness in a long childhood, and the long childhood is where parents practice sacrifice. Childhood is also the place where we begin to evolve *culturally*, whatever theory you have about that, and culture is the place where both Christianity becomes distinctive and Darwinian explanations less reductive, where sex (for example) comes unmoored from the need to reproduce and leads to some of the features of Christianity most difficult for evolution to explain, like celibacy. Law, as usually understood, is teleological in a reductive way. Virtue is teleological in an open, self-transcending way.

Virtue also plays well with evolution because it uses contingent disruption to develop excellence. Evolution uses mutations—some of which are adaptive and survive—to develop excellence.[32] Virtue uses obstacles to the good (challenges and misfortunes) to develop moral excellence. Both mutations and moral difficulties are, on different levels, contingent disruptions that may lead to strength. This is in deep harmony with the way that both human evolution and human moral culture work.

---

31. *Aquinas and the Supreme Court*, 89–93.
32. For more, see "How Natural Science Becomes a Form of Prayer," in *Aquinas and the Supreme Court*, 265–88.

Reply to Objection 3. Lecture IV of *Flesh and Blood*, titled "Real Presence, Real Absence," offers a model of reading Aquinas that gives more flesh to the phrase "natural law" while yet admitting that his real contribution is in the virtues. To adopt the eucharistic language of *Flesh and Blood*, Aquinas's account of the so-called "natural law" exposes a "real absence": the absence of any substantive moral content. But Aquinas's retention of the *language* of "natural law," while emptying it of substantive content, can provide a model for interpreting Coakley's own project of retention and new wine in *Sacrifice Regained*. How to take Coakley's retention of "natural law" language seriously? Here too Lecture IV of *Flesh and Blood* paves the way. It describes certain difficult features of Aquinas's eucharistic theory as "resistant markers." "Natural theology" is also such a "resistant marker": a refusal to let go of a marker, to concede a language to one's (perceived) opponents—even while insisting on a "discerning apophaticism."[33] If Coakley's language of natural law also represents a "resistant marker" rather than a full-fledged, systematic account; if it also demands a "discerning apophaticism" of the sort that Aquinas himself requires; then I have no objection. Only in *this* context does it become clear that the remark in Gifford Lecture 6 (7–8)—so distant from the pro-natural law section of Gifford Lecture 3 (11–14)—is in fact to be taken with complete seriousness: "Natural law serves as the basis for our moral *drives*, yet it *does not spell out the details* of moral behavior. Indeed, this is the reason why Aquinas's theory of natural law *requires* a theory of the virtues"[34] (quoted from Craig Boyd). This is true as far as it goes, but it hardly goes far enough. It is not that Aquinas had a six-page theory of natural law, which then "required" a 1200-page theory of the virtues; rather, a 1200-page concrete analysis of the virtues co-opts the language of natural law by appearing to agree with Isidore of Seville in the *sed contra*, but in reality reinterpreting Isidore to entirely different conclusions in the body of every article.[35] As I said before, and

---

33. *Flesh and Blood, Lect.* 4, 8.
34. *Sacrifice Regained, Lect.* vi.7–8, quoting Craig A. Boyd, "Thomistic Natural Law and the Limits of Evolutionary Psychology" in *Evolution and Ethics*, ed. Philip Clayton and Jeffrey Schloss (Grand Rapids: Eerdmans, 2004), 221–37; here, p. 223.

Victor Preller taught long ago, natural law does "not so much add to virtue theory as formulate it,"[36] because by the time Aquinas is through with it, the law of human nature is just to seek human excellence by imitating the just.[37]

Indeed if we may take *théologie totale* as prologue to *Sacrifice Regained*, then even the bravura "new ethico-teleological argument for the existence of God"[38] may pass without anathema, as following Aquinas's (innocent) example. The argument would go like this. Aquinas begins the *Summa Theologiae* by asking what theology is. It is like any Aristotelian science, he answers, in taking its first principles from a new source of insight, or form, that inheres indifferently in minds and things. When this form has impressed itself on the minds of human beings, we have the Scriptures; when this form exists in reality in the world, we have the person of Christ. Therefore, the more Aristotelian the science of theology is, the more scriptural it is; and the more Aristotelian it is, the more christological it is. On Aristotelian, that is, formal grounds, arguments from outside theology can function within theology as "extraneous and probable" arguments (I.1.8), or as we would now say, *ad hoc*. That is the burden of Question 1 of the *Summa Theologiae*.[39] "*Probabilis*" means "testable," neither the modern "probative" nor the statistical "probable." It resembles the vernacular (not statistical) sense of "probably," and—usefully for Coakley—it precisely accommodates her sense of "*contestable*."[40] Thomas did not suddenly backslide from that high vision of theological integrity when he came, in the very next question of the *Summa*, to the Five *Viae* that "demonstrate" nominally "what everyone calls God." If we say he did, we force him to be inconsistent. Rather, he holds a medieval rather than modern notion of demonstration, so that, without equivocation or

35. *Aquinas and the Supreme Court*, 44–50.
36. Ibid., 84.
37. Ibid., 63.
38. *Sacrifice Regained, Lect.* 5, 1.
39. Eugene F. Rogers Jr., *Thomas Aquinas and Karl Barth* (Notre Dame: Notre Dame University Press, 1995), chapter 2.
40. Forms of "contestation," "contestable," and the like feature in the Gifford Lectures as positive terms; e.g., *Lect.* I, 3, 8, 17; *Lect.* II, 2, 3, 5; *Lect.* VI, 1, 3, 6, 8 (esp.), and 15. Compare Th. Deman, "*Probabilis*," *Revue des sciences philosophiques et théologiques* 22 (1933): 260–90.

change of genre, the Son can also "demonstrate" the "via" for us into the Trinity (*Salvator noster Dominus Iesus Christus . . . viam veritatis nobis in seipso demonstravit*, *ST* III, prol.). Rather, Aquinas absorbs theistic arguments into his larger, more integral structure. How do we know this is so? Not only because Christ is himself a "demonstration of the Father."[41] But also because Aquinas sticks to his Aristotelian first principles of quoting *Scripture* as the warrant for the demonstrability of God's existence (Rom. 1:20, "God can be known from the things God has made" in the *sed contra* of *ST* I.2.2) and *Scripture* as the warrant for the argument that God does exist (Exod. 3:14, "I am," in the *sed contra* of *ST* I.2.3). The structure of the argument is, we know God's existence must be demonstrable (in the medieval sense)—somehow!—because Paul says so; and we know God exists because God says "I am"; and therefore familiar theistic arguments have their place in the system as "extraneous and probable" (I.1.8). Thus it is that theology makes its proper and unapologetic claim upon the world. We know this also because Thomas uses three ways as a tool of scriptural *exegesis* when he comes to explicate Rom. 1:20 in his Commentary *In Romanos*.[42]

Like Thomas, like Coakley. We cannot take the Gifford Lectures in isolation without assuming, against the principle of charity, that Coakley has somehow "backslid" from *théologie totale* into some non-Christian theistic genre. (As Durkheim might have said, there is no church of theism.) We ought not read the Gifford Lectures as inconsistent with *God, Sexuality, and the Self.* Natural theology represents an integral part of *théologie totale*, not a denial of it—at least in theory. And the proof in practice is that *Flesh and Blood* provides a eucharistic context and home for the extraneous if probable arguments of Martin Nowak. This does not mean that Christianity falls if Nowak falls. Surely he and Coakley would laugh together at that conceit. It means rather that Christianity must have a place for findings such as his or be desperately the poorer.

---

41. *In Joh.* 5, Lect. 3.
42. *Thomas Aquinas and Karl Barth: Sacred Doctrine and the Natural Knowledge of God*, chapters 4 and 5.

4

———

Getting Lost at Sea? Apophasis, Antisociality, and the (In-) Stability of Academic Theology

Brandy R. Daniels

"Training of any kind . . . is precisely about staying in well-lit territories and knowing exactly which way to go before you set out. Like many others before me, I propose that instead the goal is to lose one's way."

– Judith Halberstam[1]

At the forefront of her long-awaited *God, Sexuality, and the Self: An Essay 'On the Trinity,'* the first volume of her multi-part systematic theology, Anglican theologian Sarah Coakley proposes what she calls a *théologie totale,* a methodology that is built on her thesis that "desire is more

---

1. Judith Halberstam, *The Queer Art of Failure* (Durham, NC: Duke University Press, 2011), 6.

fundamental than 'sex,'" ontologically grounded in God's Trinitarian nature, which is "both the source and goal of human desires, as God intends them."[2] In light of this ontological foundation (and, ostensibly, teleological end) of desire, the task of theology demands "the practices of prayer, contemplation and worship," which, if absent, means that "there are certain sorts of philosophical insights that are unlikely, if not impossible to occur to one."[3] While Coakley grounds her methodology in the practice of contemplation, she also argues for the inclusion of the social sciences and feminism for robust theological reflection, explaining that these "secular" knowledges 1) are vitally important in light of the increasingly "spiritual-but-not-religious" landscape of the contemporary West, and thus must be engaged creatively, and 2) must be grounded in and subordinate to the practice of contemplation, because contemplation reflects the ontology of desire, and concomitantly, it can do what "secular" reflections on power, sex, and gender cannot—it engenders (and demands) a surrender of the self to the Divine, and thus resists the reification of power and mastery.

This chapter will examine the centrality of contemplation in Coakley's methodology, asking whether the practice performs what Coakley suggests. More specifically, this chapter will juxtapose the significance of contemplation to Coakley's *théologie totale* with her efforts to articulate a method that is beyond what she calls "Wigan Pierism," a method that instead engages secular knowledges creatively *and* critically. Whereas Coakley offers a compelling argument regarding the destabilization of identity and "mastery" through the prayerful act of contemplation, it is my contention that her methodology belies and undermines her claims—that, through failing to call into question epistemological and ontological claims regarding not only the identity of God but of the enterprise of academic theology, Coakley inadvertently reifies mastery and identity through other means. Coakley, in short, re-performs mastery through the very

2. Sarah Coakley, *God, Sexuality, and the Self: An Essay 'On the Trinity'* (Cambridge: Cambridge University Press, 2014), 10, 6.
3. Ibid., 16.

practices that are meant to produce un-mastery. This chapter, then, seeks to both build on and challenge Coakley's claims, exploring what it might mean to not find, or even seek, a telos in or through practices, but remaining "lost" in the midst of them.

I. Escaping Wigan Pierism? An Overview of Coakley's *Théologie Totale*

". . . divine desire purgatively reformulates human desire. It follows that all the other problems of power, sex, and gender with which contemporary theory struggles so notably cannot be solved, I dare to say—whether by human political power, violent fiat, or even subversive deviousness or ritualized revolt—without such prior surrender to the divine." – Sarah Coakley[4]

Because desire is ontologically basic and teleologically bound to the Trinity for Coakley, contemplation is not only significant as a theological task, but is inextricably bound to our lives, and thus serves as the starting point for her *théologie totale.* It is through contemplation that our desires are cleansed, reordered, and redirected to the Divine. This reordering to the Divine is one of dispossession that "over time, inculcates mental patterns of 'un-mastery,'" and thus "opens up a radical attention to the 'other.'"[5] Whereas contemplative prayer is central to her method—that "systematic theology without prayer, contemplation, and ascetic practice is void"—Coakley asserts that it "spirals out to acknowledge the messy complexity of the entanglement of the secular and spiritual realms for those who dare to practice it."[6] And so, in the second chapter, "Doing Theology on Wigan Pier? Or Why Feminism and the Social Sciences Matter to Theology," Coakley makes "a case for a continuing, albeit critical, interaction with traditions of political liberalism and feminism."[7]

As the title of her chapter indicates, Coakley supplies the metaphor of Wigan Pier to evocatively illustrate her methodological approach. This metaphor is itself predicated on an earlier theologically minded

4. Coakley, *God, Sexuality, and the Self,* 59.
5. Ibid., 44.
6. Ibid., 47.
7. Ibid., 69.

metaphor—Coakley explains that she is riffing off the poem "Dover Beach," by Matthew Arnold, where he laments the waning "Sea of Faith"[8] during the then-contemporary Victorian Era, when "Christian faith was in decline, overtaken by the modernizing trends of science, industrial revolution, and critical 'rationality.'"[9] Coakley explains that the metaphor of Dover Beach is no longer quite applicable. She surmises that, much to our surprise, the tides of faith did not quite wash away as Arnold had predicted—with the advent of modernity, they undoubtedly "turned," but they moved in an unexpected direction with the subsequent advent of postmodernity and "New Age spirituality."[10] While "institutional Christianity's attraction seems to have washed away . . . various other forms of 'lived religion' have washed back in" in its stead.[11] In light of this tide change—which, for Coakley, is positive, but also dangerous—theologians have been seduced by "Wigan Pier."

In a footnote, Coakley briefly explains her alternate metaphor of "that modest canal jetty at least fifteen miles from any ocean tide."[12] The reference to what is actually a fictional locale was popularized by a George Orwell novel, *The Road to Wigan Pier*, as a descriptor of a town that embodies the dismal conditions plaguing working class England, though it originally stems from a joke wherein a nineteenth-century British comedian, George Formby, mockingly refers to a pier, which in that context referred to a "a device for tipping the contents of coal trucks onto canal boats," as the locale that most of us associate with the term—the seaside walkway that is a source of pleasure and recreation for beach visitors.[13] In short, for Coakley, Wigan Pier functions metaphorically as a falsely luring escape, as a retreat that sounds pleasurable but is, in actuality, dismal. Relatedly, Coakley also implies that theologies reside at this metaphorical docking point when they

8. Matthew Arnold, *Dover Beach and Other Poems* (New York: Dover, 1994). "Dover Beach" was originally published in 1867.
9. Coakley, *God, Sexuality, and the Self*, 71.
10. Ibid., 72.
11. Ibid.
12. Ibid.
13. Ibid., 71n2.

try, and fail, to negotiate the relationship between the sacred and the secular. *Théologie totale*, then, is the methodology she suggests as an alternative, which provides a "methodological pincer movement" that lifts "the decks on the grimy ills of 'Wigan Pier' *without getting stuck there*," and thus leads us to God.[14]

Discussions and diatribes on the relationship between theology and "the secular," broadly construed, are legion, and these conversations and claims have assumed many different forms: from proposals of various typologies regarding the role of the "church" in or to the "world,"[15] to examinations of the role and/or use-value of the Christian tradition in democracy[16] or in the history of empire,[17] to explorations of the relationship between various "secular" disciplines and Christian theology—which, of course, is the "sea-scape" Coakley seeks to chart, exploring how to navigate between systematic theology and the social sciences (as they both relate to feminism). Unlike some other attempts at this navigation, Coakley seeks a sort of middle way—beyond, on the one hand, those positions that eschew the resources and insights of the social sciences as part of their "resistance to 'secular modernity'" and, on the other hand, those that reject "classic Christianity [as] *inherently* 'patriarchal.'"[18]

Coakley offers three examples of the "Wigan Pierism" that she seeks to move beyond, three approaches to the relationship between the sacred and the secular that she eschews and seeks to overcome with her *théologie totale*. The first theological approach Coakley eschews is the "reactive return to a high, authoritarian ecclesiastical Christian

14. Ibid., 36, 85.
15. The literature on this topic is legion, but one useful example would be debates that have arisen between the "church as polis"/"narrative ecclesiology" approach and an "apocalyptic" missiology. The former is represented most popularly, if not ardently, in the works of Stanley Hauerwas and William Cavanaugh. Nathan Kerr offers an apocalyptic response, as well as a useful account of the "church as polis" model in his book on the subject. See Nathan R. Kerr, *Christ, History and Apocalyptic: The Politics of Christian Mission* (Eugene, OR: Cascade, 2008).
16. See, most notably, Jeffrey Stout, *Democracy and Tradition* (Princeton; Princeton University Press, 2004).
17. I.e., Don H Compier, Pui-lan Kwok, and Joerg Rieger, eds., *Empire and the Christian Tradition: New Readings of Classical Theologians* (Minneapolis: Fortress Press, 2007); Bruce Ellis Benson and Peter Heltzel, eds., *Evangelicals and Empire: Christian Alternatives to the Political Status Quo* (Grand Rapids: Brazos, 2008).
18. Coakley, *God, Sexuality, and the Self*, 75.

'orthodoxy,'" which she identifies as being most like the "'Wigan Pier' of the original ironic vaudeville song . . . [having] cut itself off from the messy detritus of the actual 'sea of faith.'"[19] She associates this approach with the Roman Catholicism of John Paul II and Benedict, as well as with various Reformed and Lutheran forms of neoconservatism. Coakley then quickly moves to critique the second Wigan Pier methodology she identifies, an approach that is similar to the first, but different in that its temptations lie in "its own distinctive claims to authority—less institutional, more purely intellectual, in tone."[20] This approach appeals to a certain theological metanarrative, and argues that the "secular" scientific and sociological insights of modernity are "themselves variations on weak theological alternatives" and thus "can be declared intellectually bankrupt."[21]

Whereas these first two Wigan Pier options, while differing in tone and emphasis, share a common resistance to "secular modernity," the third of the unsatisfying approaches in Coakley's typology fails in precisely the opposite way, in that, as opposed to rejecting secular knowledges *tout court*, it instead rejects Christianity, holding that "classic Christianity is *inherently* 'patriarchal,' and that—without necessary ideological correction—it will inevitably tend towards the suppression of the rights and dignity of women and other marginalized people, including ethnic minorities and homosexuals and lesbians."[22]All these approaches fail, then, in that they are unable to articulate some sort of middle way, a way that embraces both the insights of social sciences and the rich history and tradition of the Christian faith. But does this proposed typology actually limit the possibility for the very alternatives that Coakley wants? Whereas contemplation becomes a way of embracing un-mastery, is this desire for a middle ground articulated as such actually a quest for securing Christianity and thus seeking a sort of mastery of the Divine?

Coakley's middle way, I want to argue, is not really a middle way in

19. Ibid., 73.
20. Ibid.
21. Ibid., 74.
22. Ibid., 75.

that it implicitly, if not explicitly, privileges theology over and against "secular" knowledges. This epistemological privileging undermines Coakley's aim; the unreflective assumption and perpetuation of disciplinary categories is its own performance of a kind of mastery. Moreover, through her emphasis on the practice of contemplation, Coakley inadvertently seeks to *master* un-mastery—within her method, there is an implied logic of achievement or success, despite the fact that she disavows the actual attainment of said success. Like Coakley, I do not want to get stuck at Wigan Pier. But what might it mean to avoid the false lure of Wigan Pier while at the same time not rowing fervently toward the shoreline? While Coakley claims to embrace "the 'sea of faith' [which] may be murky, polluted, or marshy," I just wonder if, in the effort to "not get stuck," Coakley too quickly starts searching for dry land, with *théologie totale* as her compass and contemplative prayer as her oars.

The dystopian movie *Children of Men* tells the story of a society in the midst of collapse. The looming threat of extinction, brought on by eighteen plus years of worldwide infertility, has resulted in societal chaos. In the midst of the chaos, we're introduced to a young refugee, Kee, who is pregnant. The story follows Kee, aided by the members of an underground guerilla group, as she travels to seek safe passage with the "Human Project." The movie ends with Kee on a boat, traveling toward *Tomorrow*, the Human Project's vessel. The movie touches on a number of themes (hope, environmentalism, justice, etc.), many of which are discussed in a brief documentary, "The Possibility of Hope," included as a special feature with the DVD of the film. "The Possibility of Hope" consists primarily of reflections by a wide range of prominent academics, with a good portion of the documentary's twenty-seven minutes devoted to musings by the Slovenian philosopher and cultural theorist Slavoj Žižek. "What I like most about the movie," Žižek confesses, "is that the solution is the boat. We must accept how we are rootless," he notes matter-of-factly.[23] It is in embracing this

---

23. Alfonso Cuarón, *The Possibility of Hope*, 2007. While Žižek is featured extensively in the brief documentary, a handful of other celebrated academics are also interviewed, including Naomi Klein and Tzvetan Todorov.

rootlessness, I suggest, that we are enabled to move away from the various iterations of Wigan Pier escapism.

II. Low Theology? Or, a Spongebob Squarepants Approach

"We are all used to having our dreams crushed, our hopes smashed, our illusions shattered, but what comes after hope? . . . What is the alternative, in other words, to cynical resignation on the one hand and naïve optimism on the other?" – Jack Halberstam[24]

A predominant motif in Christian theology is the paradoxical, seemingly nonsensical notion that "Those who find their life will lose it, and those who lose their life for [Christ's] sake will find it."[25] In line with this paradox, I want to suggest that Coakley seeks too hard to succeed at articulating a comprehensive theological approach that avoids the dangers of Wigan Pierism, and in doing so, repeats the very problems she is trying to avoid. I want to suggest, instead, that one must be *willing* to fail, to lose hope in something—in this case, in the discipline of academic theology—in order to have it. In the third section, I will turn to how this embrace of failure aligns with and, again ironically, even strengthens some of Coakley's purported aims; here, I will explore the question, what does failure offer us? Put another way: central to Coakley's critique of the third type of Wigan Pierism, of "liberal feminist theology," is that it has "a striking pessimism about the possibility of any lasting transformation of the institutional churches, and a marked cynicism about prayer as anything other than a delusive 'navel gazing.'"[26] Is "pessimism" necessarily or actually cynicism, or, could it (paradoxically) lead the way to an alternative in the vein that Coakley is seeking? The idea of "queer failure," I propose, suggests the latter.

Like Coakley, cultural theorist Judith Halberstam, in their book *The Queer Art of Failure*, seeks an alternative to the current order of things.[27]

---

24. Halberstam, *The Queer Art of Failure*, 1.
25. Matt. 10:39, NRSV.
26. Coakley, *God, Sexuality, and the Self*, 76.
27. While Halberstam still publishes under the name Judith, they go by, and blog under, the name Jack, and intentionally alternates between male and female pronouns, writing in a blog post that

As the epigraph above notes, Halberstam longs for an alternative to "cynical resignation on the one hand and naïve optimism on the other."[28] However, whereas Coakley's methodological "pincer movement"[29] seeks to valiantly propose a third (fourth?) way through embracing and utilizing *both* the resources of the social sciences and the doctrinal tradition of the Christian faith, Halberstam's embrace of failure, through what they call "low theory," counterintuitively seeks an alternative through embracing our inability to find alternatives, through considering "the utility of getting lost over finding our way."[30]

Halberstam's scholarship in "queer failure" is part of a broader body of increasingly proliferating and diverse scholarship that has come to be called "the antisocial thesis."[31] With its formal articulation found in Leo Bersani's 1995 text *Homos*, where he proposes "questioning the compatibility of homosexuality with civic service," the antisocial turn in queer studies questions the hegemony of normativity and queer desire for inclusion within said norms.[32] For Bersani (and others), this skepticism toward inclusion (belonging/redemption/normativity) is found in the very act of sex and intimacy itself—that "rather than a life force connecting pleasure to life, survival and futurity, sex, and particularly homo-sex and receptive sex, is a death drive that undoes

---

"I think my floating gender pronouns capture well the refusal to resolve my gender ambiguity that has become a kind of identity for me" (Jack Halberstam, "On Pronouns," *Jack Halberstam: Gaga Feminism and Queer Failure*, September 3, 2012, http://www.jackhalberstam.com/on-pronouns/). For ease and clarity of reading, in this essay, I utilize the gender neutral pronoun "they" to refer to Halberstam.

28. Halberstam, *The Queer Art of Failure*, 1.
29. Coakley, *God, Sexuality, and the Self*, 76. Coakley repeatedly refers to *théologie totale* as a "methodological pincer movement" though never defines the term. For those unfamiliar (as I was), a "pincer movement," also referred to as a "double envelopment" is a term traditionally used to describe a military maneuver, where the "enemy" is flanked from combatants from two directions simultaneously, thus being "pinched." For Coakley, then, doctrine and the social sciences serve as the two forces that do the pinching. What they are fighting against is less clear, though it appears that "secularism" and "postmodern New Age spirituality" stand in as key enemy targets.
30. Halberstam, *The Queer Art of Failure*, 2, 15. Cf. n 36.
31. Caserio et al., "The Antisocial Thesis in Queer Theory." Caserio locates the formal inception of the antisocial thesis in Leo Bersani's *Homos* (Cambridge, MA: Harvard University Press, 1996). Caserio explains that Bersani's "questioning [of] the compatibility of homosexuality with civic service," and even its "redefining of relationality," has "inspired a decade of explorations of queer unbelonging" (819).
32. Bersani, *Homos*, 113. Whereas Caserio credits Bersani with the boom in antisocial scholarship, Halberstam has noted that an "anti-communitarian homophilia" has a long genealogy that far predates Bersani. See Halberstam, "The Anti-Social Turn in Queer Studies," 143ff.

the self, releases the self from the drive for mastery and coherence and resolution."[33]

Though various theorists approach this "antisociality" differently (hence the aforementioned caveat regarding queer antisocial scholarship becoming increasingly diverse), even the most presumably cynical proponents find a sort of counterintuitive hope in and through the eschewal of even hope itself. Lee Edelman, for instance, in one of the most provocative accounts of this approach calls for a rejection of "the future" altogether, explaining that

> [q]ueers must respond to the violent force of such constant provocations [of their own lives via/for the "sake of the future"] not only by insisting on our equal rights to the social orders prerogatives . . . but also by saying explicitly what Law and the Pope and the whole of the Symbolic order for which they stand hear anyway in each and every expression or manifestation of queer sexuality: Fuck the social order and the Child in whose name we're collectively terrorized; fuck Annie; fuck the waif from *Les Mis*; fuck the poor, innocent kid on the Net; fuck Laws both with capital l's and with small; fuck the whole network of Symbolic relations and the future that serves as its prop.[34]

Yet, even for Edelman, the rejection of the social order itself is the means through which alternatives are possible—that "[s]uch queerness proposes, in place of the good, something . . . 'better,' though it promises, in more than one sense of the phrase, absolutely nothing."[35]

Whereas Edelman utilizes the language of futurity (and the rejection of it) to articulate an antisocial approach, Halberstam uses the language of failure, and suggests that in and through such failure, we can imagine and engender alternatives. Halberstam leads us into this possibility through a brief narrative of an episode of the popular Nickelodeon cartoon show "Spongebob Squarepants," focusing particularly on a scene involving Spongebob in conversation with his boss, Mr. Krabs. "And just when you think you've found the land of milk and honey," Mr. Krabs tells Spongebob, "they grab ya by the

---

33. Halberstam, "The Anti-Social Turn in Queer Studies," 140.
34. Lee Edelman, *No Future: Queer Theory and the Death Drive* (Durham, NC: Duke University Press, 2004), 29.
35. Ibid., 5.

britches and haul you way up high, and high, and higher, and higher, and HIGHER, until you're hauled up to the surface, flopping and gasping for breath! And then they cook ya, and then they eat ya—or worse." Spongebob, terrified, asks, "What could be worse than that?" to which Mr. Krabs, softly but matter-of-factly, simply notes, "Gift shops."[36] Halberstam uses this silly but significant scene to speak to those of us who don't hope or believe that "a trip to the land of milk and honey inevitably ends at the gift shop."[37] Halberstam proposes their text, then, as a sort of "SpongeBob SquarePants Guide to Life," and suggests this "low theory" as the methodological resource that "loses the idealism of hope in order to gain wisdom and a spongy relation to life, culture, knowledge, and pleasure."[38]

Though she acknowledges the fact that we are at sea and claims to understand and accept said location, Coakley seems quite drawn toward rowing back to shore. Halberstam, on the other hand, asks us to consider "the possibility that alternatives dwell in the murky waters of a counterintuitive, often impossibly dark and negative realm of critique and refusal."[39] How does dwelling in, embracing, our lostness at sea aid in Coakley's aims, even as it pushes against her methodology? Can it be that, in seeking the land of milk and honey—isn't it interesting that this explicitly religious metaphor is what Halberstam turns to—we must embrace being lost at sea if we want to avoid the gift shop? Instead of rowing toward land, seeking higher ground where we don't risk drowning, can we counterintuitively seek the aims that Coakley articulates through embracing a low, Spongebob Squarepants, theology? This is the question to which I now turn.

---

36. This transcribed dialogue from Spongebob Squarepants comes directly from Halberstam, *The Queer Art of Failure*, 1.

37. Ibid.

38. Ibid., 1, 2. Halberstam employs and adapts the term "low theory" from cultural theorist Stuart Hall who proposes a Gramscian concept of theory as a "detour en route to something else." See, for instance, Stuart Hall, "Cultural Studies and Its Theoretical Legacies," in *Cultural Studies*, ed. Lawrence Grossberg, Cary Nelson, and Paula A. Treichler (New York: Routledge, 1992), 277.

39. Halberstam, *The Queer Art of Failure*, 2.

III. Towards a Theology of Getting Lost at Sea, Or, I Don't Want to Pray!

"She pole-dances to gospel hymns. Came out to her family in the middle of Thanksgiving grace. I knew she was trouble two years before our first date. But my heart was a Labrador Retriever, with its head hung out the window of a car, tongue flapping in the wind on a highway going 95 whenever she walked by.

So I mastered the art of crochet, and I crocheted her a winter scarf, and one night at the bar I gave it to her with a note that said something like, I hope this keeps your neck warm. If it doesn't, give me a call.

The key to finding love, is fucking up the pattern on purpose, is skipping a stitch, is leaving a tiny, tiny hole to let the cold in and hoping she mends it with your lips."

– Andrea Gibson, "Pole Dances to Gospel Hymns"[40]

After articulating the need for a way beyond Wigan Pierism, Coakley outlines the methodological hallmarks of *théologie totale*, articulating how this approach navigates beyond the problematically polarized forms of such escapism. The first of these hallmarks, the pinnacle of the methodology, as I have already noted, is contemplation. Contemplation *does* a great deal for Coakley: it, among other things, enables one to attend to the other;[41] "engenders courage to *give voice*, but in a changed, prophetic key";[42] "involves a progressive—and sometimes painful—incorporation into the life of God," an incorporation that gradually purifies desire and metabolizes anger "into the energy of love";[43] and in doing so, it also transforms gender, as it "involves a rendering labile of gender to the workings of divine desire, a loosening of the restrictions of worldly presumptions about gender as selfhood expands into God, and is thereby released for the same great work of love."[44] This section, while recognizing the significance of what contemplation can accomplish, seeks to question

---

40. Andrea Gibson, "Pole Dancer," *Pole Dancing to Gospel Hymns* (Nashville: Write Bloody Publishing, 2008), 7.
41. Coakley, *God, Sexuality, and the Self*, 84.
42. Ibid., 85.
43. Ibid., 87.
44. Ibid.

the scope of Coakley's emphasis on contemplation—suggesting that the scope is simultaneously skewed: that, on the one hand, it too narrowly defines contemplation, and, on the other hand, too broadly (and somewhat ironically) presumes an effectiveness of contemplation, even as it situates that effectiveness as a kind of un-mastery. The resources of queer failure, I propose, "de-skew" this scope by recognizing and embracing how skewed the whole project really is. Queer failure can "(de-) skew" a *théologie totale* in three key ways: destabilizing "practices," confounding categorization, and eschewing order.

§1: Destabilizing "Practices"

In laying the groundwork for her *théologie totale*, Coakley explores various critiques that are leveled against systematic theology, and thus methodically is able to address how her approach is beyond these critiques. One of the main reasons systematic theology is distrusted, Coakley explains, is the philosophical critique of "onto-theology," which "claims that systematic theology idolatrously turns God into an object of human knowledge."[45]

Théologie totale does not fall prey to this critique, Coakley argues, because contemplation is a *practice* that constitutes an "appropriately apophatic sensibility."[46] Coakley explains that

> the very act of contemplation—repeated, lived, embodied, suffered—is an act of grace, and over time, inculcates mental patterns of "un-mastery," welcomes the dark realm of the unconscious, opens up a radical attention to the "other," and instigates an acute awareness of the messy entanglement of sexual desires and desire for God. The vertiginous free-fall of contemplation, then, is not only the means by which a disciplined form of unknowing makes way for a new and deeper knowledge-beyond-knowledge; it is also—as I have already argued—the necessary accompanying practice of a theology committed to ascetic transformation.[47]

---

45. Ibid., 43.
46. Ibid., 46.
47. Ibid., 44.

Cannot, though, even an emphasis on the practice of contemplation reinforce a sense of mastery? On the one hand, Coakley recognizes that systematic theology can oppressively reinforce hegemony. She explains that

> [t]he social theorists who have decried "hegemony" are rightly calling attention to ways in which powerful discourses, especially ones that aspire to a total picture, can occlude or marginalize the voices of those who are already oppressed, or are being pushed into a state of subjection. "System" here tends to connote "systemic" oppression—deep-seated political violence or abuse; "hegemonic" discourses—consciously or unconsciously—seek to justify such oppression. Does systematic theology do this too? The short answer, again, is that it certainly can . . .[48]

While it is laudable of Coakley to recognize and name this risk, she fails to acknowledge that it can manifest even *in* practices. Turning to contemplation does not *necessarily* engender un-mastery—*pace* Foucault's claims about the productiveness and diffuseness of power, "contemplation" can function both practically and discursively as power dressed in new garb—it can represent and function as not (only?) an assent of un-mastery but as a technique of power that smartly and subtly has shifted its locus from faithful assent to certain theological claims or from superior logic to its new locale in practices of piety.[49]

In light of his theorizations on power, Foucault offers his own methodology—though, precisely because of his own reflections on the complexity of power, he notes that these methodological "rules" he proposes are "not intended as methodological imperatives; at most they are cautionary prescriptions."[50] While all of these cautions

---

48. Ibid., 48. What words Coakley chooses to place in scare quotes strikes me as especially interesting. For instance, throughout the text, she scare-quote's the word "hegemony," "sex," "gender," and "sexuality," but does not, at any point, do so to "secular," let alone "God," "tradition," or "church." Coakley here again reifies and (re-) performs a logic of mastery through particular discursive/grammatical choices and assumptions.

49. For a concise introduction to his theorizing of power, see Part Four: "The Deployment of Sexuality," in Michel Foucault, *The History of Sexuality, Vol. 1: An Introduction*, trans. Robert Hurley (New York: Vintage, 1990), 75–132, most notably chapter 2 on "Method" (92–102). In his lecture series, which has now been transcribed and published as *"Society Must Be Defended": Lectures at the Collège de France, 1975-1976* (New York: Picador, 2003), Foucault also provides a useful summary of his genealogical method and analysis on the history of power as it has morphed to take different forms. See especially lectures one, two, three, and eleven (1-64, 239-64).

potentially hold some relevance to my argument here, it is the third that I want to briefly turn to here, the "rule of double conditioning."[51] Foucault explains:

> No "local center," no "pattern of transformation" could function if, through a series of sequences, it did not eventually enter into an over-all strategy. And inversely, no strategy could achieve comprehensive effects if did not gain support from precise and tenuous relations serving, not as its point of application or final outcome, but as its prop and anchor point . . . one must conceive of the double conditioning of a strategy by the specificity of possible tactics, and of tactics by the strategic envelope that makes them work.[52]

It is this "rule" that Coakley seems to fail to acknowledge, which places her at risk of reproducing the very power relations she seems to dismantle. Rather, Coakley places enormous faith in the "pattern of transformation" that contemplation engenders, and in doing so, fails to attend to how this practice itself can function to bolster certain hegemonies of power—in this instance, the hegemony of academic theology.

Perhaps one of the most salient examples of how this emphasis on contemplation reinforces the hegemony of academic theology is found in Coakley's critique of contemporary gender theory. Working towards full gender equality and justice, Coakley argues,

> is—to say the least—an exercise of historical, religious and political sophistication, requiring distinctive spiritual strengths of self-knowledge and humility. It is not, then, a task best accomplished by a divestment from religious practices and traditions, as is still assumed in dominant "secular" circles: on the contrary, it may be that contemplative religious practices of "effacement" are precisely the enabling incubus for such reconsideration.[53]

Leaving aside, at least for the moment, Coakley's claim that contemporary "secular" gender theory demands "a divestment from

---

50. Foucault, *The History of Sexuality, Vol. 1*, 98.
51. Ibid., 100. See 98–102 for his other "rules," as well as for analysis on the ways they intersect.
52. Ibid., 99.
53. Coakley, *God, Sexuality, and the Self*, 81.

religious practices and traditions" (I do not think this critique is correct, for the record), Coakley's proposition puts enormous faith in the supposed effectiveness of religious practices, and in the traditions on which they're grounded. Coakley claims to resist a theological approach that "has cut itself off from the messy detritus of the actual 'sea of faith,' [whose] exponents can enjoy a certain delusion about the ecclesiastical realities around them."[54] How is it not delusional to suggest that the more religious among us are more self-knowledgeable or humble, that the more spiritual in our midst are more attuned to the rights of marginalized and oppressed peoples?

While such a question is perhaps unfairly uncharitable in its framing, as there are assuredly individuals whose spiritual practices have engendered these kind of attributes, it is nevertheless foolhardy to propose such a tight correlation. While I certainly have had experiences where I have "seen God" in and through other people in my life—experiences and relationships that have caused me to embrace my faith, serving as life-rafts during times I've almost drowned—there have, regrettably, been more instances in my life where I have witnessed those who express and experience a closeness to the Divine acting in ways that are incredibly oppressive and harmful.[55] Given that I was a precocious child in a fundamentalist church, and then a queer teenager in that same church, this is not all that surprising. My anecdotal experiences are not unique, of course—not only have my own experiences brought me into encounter and relationship with a number of people with similar narratives, but sociological research has suggested that many in the modern West experience Christians as particularly homophobic, judgmental, and hypocritical.[56]

---

54. Ibid., 73.
55. I have been exceptionally lucky to have a number of people who have been "life-rafts" for me and for my faith in the midst of moments where drowning seemed inevitable. While it is impossible to list or even recall all of them, a handful stand out—Kathryn and Jeff Manildi, Elizabeth Clift, Kaitlyn Dugan, Amelia Hube, and Kayla Brandt. It is to these extraordinary people that I dedicate this chapter. Thank you for not just being a life-raft, but for teaching me how to swim.
56. In *Unchristian: What a New Generation Really Thinks About Christianity—and Why It Matters* (Grand Rapids: Baker, 2012), lead researchers David Kinnaman and Gabe Lyons present and explicate the results of their extensive research (conducted by the Barna Group) on young adults who do not identify as religious, a rapidly growing demographic in contemporary America (they note that "outsiders"—the term they use to describe the nonaffiliated—represent about one-quarter

Whether one interprets these data as an image problem (as the authors of one of the studies cited above do) or as a substantive critique, it nevertheless is a bright pink elephant in the room that suggests that religious practices necessarily correlate with justice and equality. The elephant becomes all the brighter still when one considers the complex history of the relationship between faith practices and justice aims—yes, religious beliefs and practices have been used to combat slavery, apartheid, domestic servility, and many other societal injustices, but so have they also been used to *justify* such injustices. As Isaac Asimov quipped, "Properly read, the Bible is the most potent force for atheism every conceived."[57] Some might, perhaps, extend his claim from the Bible itself to the people that believe and uphold its words.

This is not to say, however, that religious practices should be seen as inherently problematic—the critique that Coakley suggests that liberal feminist theology wrongly makes. Here, then, is where queer failure provides a useful rejoinder—it does not eschew practices, but nor does it seek a clear aim in and/or through them; rather, queer failure embraces the messiness of them—not searching for an end through practices, but simply abiding in them, being content in being lost in the midst of them. What queer failure, and Spongebob Squarepants, recognizes is that in searching for the land of milk and honey too fervently, we end up at the "gift shop." What might it mean to embrace practices amidst being lost at sea, or, to utilize another apt metaphor, while wandering in the wilderness?[58] In searching for the land of milk and honey, are we perhaps not trusting God to provide as we wander;

---

of Boomers and one-third of young adults/millennials [18]). Through their data analysis of over 45,000 participants, Kinnaman and Lyons found that, whereas merely ten to fifteen years ago, 85 percent of outsiders viewed Christianity's role in society favorably, currently 38 percent of young outsiders—2 out of every 5—have a "bad impression of present-day Christianity" (24). Young adult outsiders, they found, view Christianity as overwhelmingly hypocritical (85 percent), homophobic/"antihomosexual" (96 percent), and judgmental (87 percent).

57. Isaac Asimov, letter, February 22, 1966, in Stanley Asimov, ed., *Yours, Isaac Asimov: A Lifetime of Letters* (New York: Doubleday, 1996), 315.

58. I am indebted to my colleague Russell Johnson for this rich, and apt, biblical metaphor of wilderness wandering. Moreover, he, along with Elizabeth Antus, Anthony Paul Smith, Joshua Brockway, and Bo Eberle graciously read earlier versions of this essay and offered thoughtful and incisive feedback, for which I am very thankful.

are we complaining about yet another day of eating manna? As opposed to seeking to be found in God, could we perhaps consider being *lost* and thus continually discover that God is there in our lostness, even in surprising, unexpected, "secular" places? Could embracing such uncertainty and failure be precisely what it means to be "cruciform," to follow a "failed" Messiah who "had no place to rest his head"?[59]

Coakley briefly attempts to address "the *non-Christian* religious response," a position that might imply that her "appeal to Christian contemplation is an insidious new 'hegemonic' move, replacing doctrinal supersessionism with a more covert supersessionism of practice."[60] While she correctly acknowledges the critique of her appeal to practice, her analysis of what fuels this critique is misplaced. Coakley posits that this object is "fuelled . . . by the presumption that religious 'practice' is precisely what engenders and mandates a sectarian *withdrawal* from public commitments and shared projects"[61] Ironically, Coakley performs the inverse of what she critiques about the non-Christian religious response. The critique, at least the one that I am leveling here, is not fueled by concerns that religious practices equal or demand withdrawal; rather, the contention is with the claim that *only* religious practices can invoke certain insights or enable certain virtues. For instance, Coakley notes that to "contemplate is to invite uncomfortable change, not to bludgeon the other with one's certainties. To ask its exponents then to *relinquish* their practice in order to join a common discussion is to vitiate precisely the subtle distinctiveness of its contribution."[62]

Coakley offers no examples of instances where Christians are asked to relinquish practices for the sake of dialogue or change. It is, in fact, quite the opposite, as Coakley is the one who argues that

> if one is resolutely *not* engaged in the practices of prayer, contemplation and worship, there are certain sorts of philosophical insights that are

59. Luke 9:58.
60. Coakley, *God, Sexuality, and the Self*, 86.
61. Ibid.
62. Ibid.

unlikely, if not impossible to occur to one. So it now becomes clear why theology, thus understood, must be a form of intellectual investigation in which a *secular*, universalist rationality may find itself significantly challenged—whether criticized, expanded, transformed, or even at points rejected.[63]

An account of failure, then, recognizes the way that contemplation *can* function as a source of insight and knowledge, but also importantly recognizes the way that it can also become its own sort of hegemony as it serves as both the ends and means of a certain philosophical and religious telos—a certain end that does not so much resist as it does reinforce a sense of mastery. More significantly, beyond recognition, it locates hope and possibility precisely in . . . well, in failure. Not only does it affirm the reality that we "will wander, improvise, fall short, and move in circles," but boldly asserts that not in spite of said wandering but precisely "*in* losing we will find another way of making meaning."[64] Relatedly, this stabilizing of practices and of the possibilities they not only engender but presuppose not only re-performs mastery through a clearly proscribed path, it also makes assumptions about what constitutes the steps on that path.

§2: Confounding Categorization

In correspondence with his colleague Armin Mohler, the German philosopher and political theorist Carl Schmitt reflects upon an interesting—and, I would argue, profound—insight that was made by the Jewish philosopher Jacob Taubes. "Taubes is right," he muses. "Today everything is theology, with the exception of what the theologians talk about . . ."[65] Taubes's insight is reminiscent of David's psalm to God: "Out of the mouths of babes and infants you have founded a bulwark because of your foes, to silence the enemy and

---

63. Ibid., 16.
64. Halberstam, *The Queer Art of Failure*, 25, emphasis mine.
65. Carl Schmitt, letter, August 14, 1958, in Jacob Taubes, *To Carl Schmitt: Letters and Reflections* (New York: Columbia University Press, 2013), 26.

avenger."[66] What might it mean to take Schmitt's observation seriously within and for the field of theological studies?

A *théologie totale,* on the one hand, might be upheld as a methodology that seeks to do just this—the fifth hallmark of this methodological approach is "the overcoming of false divides."[67] Coakley notes a number of said false divides that her methodology confounds: belief and practice, academic and pastoral theology, liberal feminism and postmodern gender theory, etcetera. Interestingly, a divide that fails to make Coakley's list is the assumed divide between sacred and secular knowledges. Rather, Coakley frequently affirms this divide, and elevates religious and spiritual knowledges and forms of knowing over and against the "secular." Her abasement of said "secular" fields and knowledges is pervasive, even if it is at times subtle, and couched within a desire to resist mastery. She critiques, for instance, "the seemingly immoveable stuckness of what secular gender theory gloomily calls 'the gender binary'";[68] argues that theology is "a form of intellectual investigation in which a *secular,* universalist rationality might find itself significantly challenged";[69] and notes that the resources of the social sciences are useful when they are "stripped of secularizing pretensions."[70]

---

66. Psalm 8:2. Jesus also references this psalm as he cleanses the temple; see Matt. 21:12-17. I'm grateful to J. Kameron Carter for this reference and insight.

67. Coakley, *God, Sexuality, and the Self,* 90.

68. Ibid., 61. It remains unclear to me what Coakley's critique is here, as she fails to offer any particular or substantive examples of exactly how "secular gender theory" remains stuck in a "gloomy" gender binary. First, "secular gender theory" is not a singular entity, as Coakley assumes—rather, there are a multiplicity of gender theories, which overlap and diverge in myriad ways in their articulations of gender, analyses of the theoretical and practical concerns, and methodological approaches to change. Moreover, my reading of much of "secular gender theory" suggests quite the opposite of what Coakley purports—though, again, differing in their analyses, many influential, canonical figures in gender theory, from Irigaray and Kristeva to Wittig and Butler, cite contemporary constructions of a gender "binary" as a key locus of the oppression of women, as a paradigm to be critiqued.

69. Ibid., 16.

70. Ibid., 82. Coakley's critique strikes me as painfully one-sided. While she does acknowledge the usefulness of the "secular" social sciences and feminism, she subordinates the value of said knowledges—while secular knowledges *add* and *refine* theological insights for Coakley, they are never employed or valued on their own terms, and never function within those terms as a source of critique of theology proper. The inverse, however, is one of Coakley's key points—what the secular knowledges lack, in her paradigm, is precisely what theological reflection can offer. I will return to this point later in the chapter when I juxtapose Coakley and Halberstam's differing interpretations of the significance of the ethnographic and critical work of Saba Mahmood.

Coakley charges that there is a "moral and epistemic stripping that is endemic to the act of contemplation."[71] Yet, in assuming clear lines between the sacred and the secular, Coakley is performing a different kind of mastery—a purity that is found in the very category of contemplation and within the academic theology that claims to stem from its practices. Coakley exclaims that theology must be about "not merely the *metaphysical* task of adumbrating a vision of God, the world and humanity, but simultaneously, the *epistemological* task of cleansing, re-ordering, and re-directing the apparatuses of one's own thinking, desiring, and seeing."[72] This is thus not an epistemological stripping, but a reassertion of epistemological certainty simply functioning on a different plane.

Queer failure, conversely, embodies the epistemological un-handing that Coakley seeks, precisely through not seeking to achieve it, recognizing that it is not about what one achieves, but what one escapes. "Perhaps most obviously, failure allows us to escape the punishing norms that discipline behavior and manage human development with the goal of delivering us from unruly childhoods to orderly and predictable adulthoods," Halberstam writes. "Failure preserves some of the wondrous anarchy of childhood and *disturbs the supposedly clean boundaries between adults and children, winners and losers.*"[73] Failure does not simply free us from the mastery that comes with the assurance of practices, it frees us from the epistemological mastery that is concomitant with clear disciplinary and categorical assumption.

Halberstam, relying again on Foucault, explores how disciplinarity and categorical clarity reproduce norms and reify power. Foucault, of course, speaks at length regarding the imperialistic impulses undergirding knowledge production and classification. Through providing an "archaeology of knowledge," Foucault excavates the relationship between knowledge and power throughout history.[74]

---

71. Ibid., 49.
72. Ibid., 20.
73. Halberstam, *The Queer Art of Failure*, 4, emphasis mine.
74. See Michel Foucault, *The Archaeology of Knowledge & the Discourse on Language* (New York: Tavistock,

Foucault writes at length about the classificatory gestures of knowledge formation and production, pointing to its culturally constructed character as well as its function as a mode of control.[75] "Once knowledge can be analysed in terms of region, domain, implantation, displacement, transposition," he explains, "one is able to capture the process by which knowledge functions as a form of power and disseminates the effects of power."[76] Knowledge as a classifying system of control, what Foucault defines as discourse, operates as a social code that punishes deviancy, ultimately creating conforming subjects.[77] In making these claims, Foucault critiques a Kantian epistemological framework, explaining that modern thought has problematically merged objective knowledge with experience, seeking "to articulate the possible objectivity of knowledge."[78] While Coakley too seeks something beyond the hubris of knowing, through making the classificatory and disciplinary assumptions that she does, she unwittingly reproduces an epistemological imperialism.

Conversely, Halberstam embraces failing even in this, in upholding or assuming such categories and disciplinary lines; that while doing so risks illegibility, it is by traveling down such unclear paths and embracing illegibility that we discover and generate "new forms of knowing."[79] Failing means being "undisciplined," because disciplines "qualify and disqualify, legitimate and delegitimate, reward and

---

1972). The relationship between power and knowledge is a central theme in Foucault's work. See also, *Power/Knowledge: Selected Interviews and Other Writings* (New York: Vintage, 1982).

75. Discussions of classification are dispersed through Foucault's texts. On the one hand, classifications serve as keys for understanding the construction of subjectivity in the development of what he calls the human sciences, new schemas for classifying information elucidating underlying conceptual shifts. Classifications also operate as the tools that produce those shifts, functioning as instruments of power. Foucault's historical analyses—of mental health: *Madness and Civilization: A History of Insanity in an Age of Reason* (New York: Random House, 1965); prisons: *Discipline & Punish: The Birth of the Prison* (New York: Vintage, 1995); and sexuality: *The History of Sexuality, Volume 1: An Introduction* (New York: Vintage, 1990)—all examine how classifications operate in these ways. *Archaeology of Knowledge*, as well as *The Order of Things: An Archaeology of the Human Sciences* (New York: Routledge, 2002), offers deeper examination of the role of classifications in Foucault's methodology.

76. Coakley, *God, Sexuality, and the Self*, 46.

77. Foucault's discussion of discourse can be found primarily in *Archaeology of Knowledge.* See also his essay "Subject and Power," in Michel Foucault, *Power*, ed. James D. Fabion, trans. Robert Hurley. Essential Works of Foucault, 1954-1984: volume 3 (New York: New Press, 1994), 326–48.

78. Foucault, *Power/Knowledge*, 69.

79. Halberstam, *The Queer Art of Failure*, 7.

punish."[80] Coakley assumes very clear lines of what is legitimate and what is not through privileging theological discourse, even if/though that discourse presumes and demands a recognition or assent of unmastery via contemplation.

A key example of Coakley's performance of mastery in regard to disciplinarity and categorization occurs when Coakley discusses the "secular riddle of gender," which she argues can only be solved when "its connection to the doctrine of a Trinitarian God" is understood and embraced.[81] This claim, and the argument that follows, makes a number of epistemological assumptions that are concerning, the most obvious one being that there *is* a sort of ontological twoness of gender, even if it is fallen and subject to a "transfiguring interruption" (58). Mapping the threeness of the Trinity onto the twoness of gender assumes and reproduces—ontologizes—gender. Coakley supports this, suggesting that the Trinity and our participation in the triune life of God "does not obliterate the twoness of gender" but rather transforms and redeems it (59). While Coakley's suggestion that this moves us beyond being "endlessly and ever subject to the debilitating falseness of fallen gender, fallen twoness," might fit within an Irigarayan paradigm, the contributions of poststructuralist feminist theory and the growing field of trans* scholarship raise significant concerns about such a presumption of twoness.[82]

Relatedly, what is perhaps even more problematic is that Coakley's assumption of twoness and of its redemption suggests that the "problem" of gender is something that *can* and *should* be *solved*. Coakley suggests that turning our attention to desire and to the Trinity enables us to move beyond "the seemingly immoveable stuckness of what secular gender theory gloomily calls 'the gender binary.'"[83] Not only

---

80. Ibid., 10.

81. Coakley, *God, Sexuality, and the Self*, 54.

82. See, for instance, Pheng Cheah and Elizabeth Grosz, "Of Being-two: Introduction," *Diacritics* 28, no. 1 (1998): 3–18; Elizabeth A. Grosz et al., "The Future of Sexual Difference: An Interview with Judith Butler and Drucilla Cornell," *Diacritics* 28, no. 1 (1998): 19–42. These essays together function as a useful introductory foray into debates/critiques on "twoness" and sexual difference, and are accompanied by other similarly themed essays and reviews in the specially edited edition of *Diacritics* on "Irigaray and the Political Future of Sexual Difference."

83. Coakley, *God, Sexuality, and the Self*, 61.

does Coakley again falsely read a nihilism *into* "secular gender theory" and fail to take the nuance of said theory's understanding of subjectivization seriously (as poststructuralism's acknowledgment, and critique, of the gender binary strikes me as anything *but* "gloomy"), but she sees the move beyond this as achievable.

Halberstam, on the other hand, most clearly does not see a transformation and solving of the gender binary as achievable. Nor does she, however, see this un-achievability as gloomy—quite the contrary! What the failure that Halberstam calls for recognizes is how any real grab at solving and/or at classifying, is precisely a reproduction of norms that forecloses other knowledges and thus leads to oppression—that, again, it is in *the failure itself* that we can "locate all the in-between spaces that save us from being snared by the hooks of hegemony and speared by the seductions of the gift shop."[84] In the third chapter of *The Queer Art of Failure*, Halberstam uses the image of the butch lesbian as one example of the effectiveness of failure—and of the dangers of seeking success. Turning to the popular Showtime series *The L Word*, Halberstam explains that the show's attempt to represent the lesbian as successful demands repudiating the image of the butch lesbian. Halberstam explains that

> in *The L Word* we see that in order to make "lesbians" appealing to men and straight women, the specific features which have stereotypically connoted lesbian in the past—masculine appearance and interests and jobs—must be blotted out to provide a free channel for commodification. Indeed commodification as a process depends completely upon a hetero-normative set of visual and erotic expectations. While even feminine gay men can function within this framework (because they still model a desire for hetero-masculinity) the butch lesbian cannot; she threatens the male viewer with the horrifying spectacle of the "uncastrated" woman and challenges the straight female viewer because she refuses to participate in the conventional masquerade of hetero-femininity as weak, unskilled, and unthreatening.[85]

The effort to succeed, we see through this example, fails in that it

---

84. Halberstam, *The Queer Art of Failure*, 2.
85. Ibid., 95–96.

excludes and normativizes; the butch lesbian, then, precisely in *failing*, succeeds, refusing to contort to fit into the boxes she is repeatedly shoved into. What might it mean, then, to fail at resisting "secularizing pretensions," or, even, to fail at contemplation itself? Where a theory of queer failure departs most sharply from Coakley's methodology is precisely at this point, through eschewing order. Yet, I will argue that the rejection of order is what a liberative theological method demands—or, rather, what it enables, through attending to and embracing failure.

§3: Eschewing Order

Coakley's *théologie totale* delineates between mastery and order—eschewing the former while retaining the latter. Coakley proposes that hierarchy-as-order is not only consistent with but perhaps even necessary for feminist aims. She explains:

> Where hierarchy simply means order, then, it is not clear that feminism should oppose it. Anyone who has worked in circumstances of institutional chaos knows that some such order, organizationally, is preferable for everyone; it is sexed subordination that feminism opposes. And participation in God, in contrast . . . may precisely be the means of undermining such subordination.[86]

Is this appeal to order that Coakley affirms consistent with her efforts to avoid mastery? Is it consistent with a telos of liberation? Moreover, does order reflect Coakley's claims regarding the ontology of desire?

A key insight of queer theory, stemming back to Nietzsche's *Genealogy of Morals*, is that "history is written by the winners."[87] The "order of things," as Foucault puts it, is a reflection of and perpetuation of power, and through the creation of norms and the construction of order, we are disciplined to conform, and this conformity is far more often oppressive than it is liberative.[88] As Judith Butler puts it,

---

86. Coakley, *God, Sexuality, and the Self*, 273.
87. Whereas this quote, though often attributed to Nietzsche (as well as to Winston Churchill) actually comes from an essay written by George Orwell in *Tribune* (February 4, 1944). Halberstam, citing Walter Benjamin, conveys the same sentiment: "empathy with the victor invariably benefits the rulers" (120–21).

the "ordering" of gender establishes "the ontological field in which bodies may be given legitimate expression," which is oppressive, as it is not reflective of the reality of people's lives.[89] What queer theory recognizes is that order is not reflective of the nuances and complexities of reality, that it is always socially constructed, thus always limiting, and often oppressive.

The insights of queer theory are especially salient when one takes into account the ways that order has functioned as a theological justification for (oppressive) power, an insight that has rich roots (as well as avenues for resistance) in liberation theologies.[90] Theological conceptions of providence, sovereignty, and natural law, among others, have been used to justify and perpetuate subordination and oppression.[91] What might it mean, then, to embrace queer failure, which is all about failing at assenting to the order of things—recognizing that not only do we ultimately not have control or order, but that—through the grace of God—it is paradoxically when we "fuck up the pattern" that we find liberation? Coakley implicitly connects order with "participation in God."[92] But what kind of possibilities might emerge if participation in God demands and/or engenders a *failure*—demanding and producing a disorder of the current fallen, oppressive order of things?

Halberstam turns to James Scott's text *Seeing Like a State: How Certain Schemes to Improve the Human Condition Have Failed*, as an example of the failures of order, and thus of the success of the failure of disorder. In short, Halberstam references Scott's metaphor of "the Germanic ordered forest" as order manifests in and through regulation and bureaucracy.[93] Halberstam explains that Scott's analysis reveals that

88. See Michel Foucault, *The Order of Things: An Archaeology of the Human Sciences*, 1st edition (New York: Vintage, 1994); Foucault, *Society Must Be Defended.*
89. Judith Butler, *Gender Trouble: Feminism and the Subversion of Identity*, 1st edition (New York: Routledge, 2006), xxiii.
90. This assumption is fundamental to liberation theology. For instance, throughout *A Theology of Liberation: History, Politics, and Salvation*, Gustavo Gutiérrez writes that "[t]he denunciation of injustice implies the rejection of the use of Christianity to legitimize the established order," and he continues to use language throughout his work about overturning the "existing social order."
91. I am indebted here to Willie Jennings's Divinity School course "Slavery and Obedience."
92. Coakley, *God, Sexuality, and the Self*, 273.
93. Halberstam, *The Queer Art of Failure*, 9.

thinking "with the logic of the superiority of orderliness ... we erase and indeed sacrifice other, more local practices of knowledge ... ," knowledges that may be less "efficient" but that are ultimately more sustainable.[94] Embracing failure, then, means recognizing and embracing "the thicket of subjugated knowledge that sprouts like weeds among the disciplinary forms of knowledge, threatening always to overwhelm the cultivation and pruning of the intellect with mad plant life."[95]

This begs the question of the presumed order/stability of academic/ systematic theology. Coakley argues that systematics as a discipline

> does not convey the hubristic idea of a totalizing discourse that excludes debate, opposition, or riposte; but on the other hand, it does not falter at the necessary challenge of presenting the gospel afresh in all of its ramifications—systematically unfolding the connections of the parts of the vision that is set before us.[96]

Is not part of the gospel afresh the way it always confounds the systems we build, because it always exceeds them? Is not then an attempt to fit the system together, like pieces in a puzzle, an attempt at control, at mastery?

Interestingly, both Coakley and Halberstam reference the work of Saba Mahmood, a cultural anthropologist who has done profound ethnographic work on the Islamic Women's movements calling for a reexamination of the relationship between religious practices, secular politics, and agency. Coakley aligns her own work with that of Mahmood's, noting that both of their projects point out the idolatry of "even liberal feminist theology," and highlight "the distinctive power of submission to the divine."[97] Interestingly, Halberstam also praises Mahmood, but her analysis operates on a different plane. Referencing her ethnographic work, Halberstam notes that Mahmood's work is compelling not because of its emphasis on "submission" over and against liberal feminism, but rather, because it demonstrates that

94. Ibid.
95. Ibid.
96. Coakley, *God, Sexuality, and the Self*, 42.
97. Ibid., 99, 98.

"[c]onversation rather than mastery indeed seems to offer one very concrete way of being in relation to another form of being and knowing without seeking to measure that life modality by the standards external to it."[98] For Halberstam, Mahmood's work is profound precisely because it does *not* seek to fit (religious) practices squarely within a system—that allowing conversation that exceeds (normative) systems and presumptions enables Mahmood's creative insights. Halberstam's interpretation elucidates how Coakley's analysis of Mahmood's work ironically ends up performing precisely what Mahmood is resisting: in reading Mahmood's scholarship as an eschewal of liberal feminism and as a treatise on submission, Coakley obscures the agency of the Muslim women's voices that Mahmood is highlighting, thus re-performing the cultural colonization that Mahmood critiques, simply for different ends.[99] What might it look like when one applies the insights garnered through queer accounts of failure to Coakley's methodology? In the conclusion, I offer a few brief suggestions.

IV. Dying for Nothing? A Théologie Bricolage?

"There is nothing in bricolage worth dying for." – John Howard Yoder[100]

"Such queerness proposes, in place of the good, something I want to call 'better,' though it promises, in more than one sense of the phrase, absolutely nothing." – Lee Edelman[101]

---

98. Halberstam, *The Queer Art of Failure*, 12.
99. Cf. n 69. Mahmood makes the aim of her work clear when she writes, "My intention here is not to question the profound transformation that the liberal discourse of freedom and individual autonomy has enabled in women's lives around the world, but rather to draw attention to the ways in which liberal presuppositions have become naturalized in the scholarship on gender. Saba Mahmood, *Politics of Piety: The Islamic Revival and the Feminist Subject* (Princeton: Princeton University Press, 2012), 13. Moreover, Mahmood also articulates her *own* discomfort *as* a "liberal feminist" of the mosque movement, but explains that it is the discomfort that is part of what is generative about her analysis. She explains: ". . . I was forced to question the repugnance that often swelled up inside me against the practices of the mosque movement, especially those that seemed to circumscribe women's subordinate status within Egyptian society. . . . In many ways, this book is an exploration of . . . the 'visceral modes of appraisal' that produce such a reaction among many fellow liberal-left minded intellectuals and feminists, as much as it is an exploration of the sensibilities that animate such movements" (37–38).
100. John Howard Yoder, *For the Nations: Essays Evangelical and Public* (Grand Rapids: Eerdmans, 1997), 76.
101. Edelman, *No Future*, 5.

"We will wander, improvise, fall short, and move in circles. We will lose our way, our cars, our agenda, and possibly our minds, but in losing we will find another way of making meaning in which, to return to the battered VW van of Little Miss Sunshine, no one gets left behind." – Jack Halberstam[102]

In the same paragraph that she aligns Mahmood's project with her own, Coakley also cites Luke Bretherton's *Christianity and Contemporary Politics: The Conditions and Possibilities of Faithful Witness* as a text that adeptly introduces the debates between religion and secularism in the political sphere and suggests "modes of Christian political activism even within a religiously plural and 'secular' society."[103] In *Christianity and Contemporary Politics*, Bretherton, building on Yoder's critique of bricolage (see epigraph above) notes that in contrast to bricolage, "a theological account of politics does not seek to only transgress the prevailing hegemony but acts in expectation of its transfiguration."[104] Bretherton goes on to explain Michel de Certeau's account of bricolage in more detail, and proposes that it "has an intrinsically agonistic and violent understanding between those forced to deploy tactics and the holders of strategic power" and that this assumed antagonism establishes "a Manichean false dichotomy between church and world."[105]

I have (hopefully) argued in the sections above that it is only by way of bricolage, through a nuanced recognition of what Bretherton describes as the antagonism of power, that one can break free of such a dualism, and that it is only *through* transgressing the prevailing hegemony that one is able to witness to and participate in its transfiguration—that, this side of the eschaton, what is required is a constant vigilance directed at the normalizing and disciplining reaches of power, that one must not get too close to a shoreline, as it is likely only a form of Wigan Pier escapism. Halberstam explores how collage functions as one artistic example of queer failure. "Collage precisely references the spaces in between," she notes, "and refuses to respect

102. Halberstam, *The Queer Art of Failure*, 25.
103. Coakley, *God, Sexuality, and the Self*, 98.
104. Luke Bretherton, *Christianity and Contemporary Politics: The Conditions and Possibilities of Faithful Witness* (Chichester, UK and Malden, MA: Wiley-Blackwell, 2010), 191.
105. Ibid., 191, 192.

the boundaries that usually delineate self from other, art object from museum, and the copy from the original. In this respect, as well as in many others, collage (from the French *coller* to paste or glue) seems feminist or queer."[106] Bricolage and collage are, of course, near-synonyms—sharing similar meanings and the same etymology—and function as such here. A théologie bricolage, then, has the same aims as a théologie totale—incorporation into the triune life by way of desire. It differs, however, in that it believes that the path towards the Divine, like desire itself, is far more circuitous and complicated and paradoxical—but in that, it is quite fun, as traversing the sea allows one to experience a whole range of adventures and encounters that we would not have seen otherwise.

German theologian Dietrich Bonhoeffer's *Creation and Fall* offers an explicitly theological account of what I am calling a théologie bricolage. Whereas I, building on Coakley, have used the metaphor of the sea, Bonhoeffer speaks more abstractly, suggesting a theology that is done from "the middle." Bonhoeffer recognized that to firmly articulate our origins, or our telos, is not only dangerously imperialist but is hopeless. As he puts it:

> To take a gigantic leap back into the world of the lost beginning, to seek to know for ourselves what humankind was like in its original state and to identify our own ideal of humanity with what God actually created is hopeless. It fails to recognize that it is only from Christ that we can know about the original nature of humankind. The attempt to do that without recognizing this, as hopeless as it is understandable, has again and again delivered up the church to arbitrary speculation at this dangerous point. Only in the middle, as those who live from Christ, do we know about the beginning.[107]

For Bonhoeffer, it is through Christ that we are freed to not simply tolerate but to embrace this "twilight" existence, this lost-at-sea-ness. Failure is inevitable, and it is only through embracing it that we can find our way. Or, again, in Bonhoeffer's words:

---

106. Halberstam, *The Queer Art of Failure*, 136.
107. Dietrich Bonhoeffer, *Creation and Fall (Dietrich Bonhoeffer Works, volume 3)*, John W. De Gruchy, ed. (Minneapolis: Fortress Press, 2004), 62.

Those who, in acting responsibly, seek to avoid becoming guilty divorce themselves from the ultimate reality of human existence; but in doing so, they also divorce themselves from the redeeming mystery of the sinless bearing of guilt by Jesus Christ, and have no part in the divine justification that attends this event.[108]

In embracing being lost at sea, we may be able to, as Halberstam puts it, see possibilities beyond the "gift shop." That only in risking dying for "nothing," in failing, can we flourish.

---

108. Dietrich Bonhoeffer, *Ethics*, ed. Clifford J. Green (Fortress Press, 2005), 276.

5

The Body and the Body of the Church: Coakley, Yoder, and the Imitation of Christ

Myles Werntz

Throughout her career, Sarah Coakley's work has been marked by two intertwined concerns: the place of contemplative prayer and the role of gender in Christian theology. As Coakley's work has become increasingly attentive to the ways in which prayer and gender are intertwined, it has become more textured, and more provocative in both its direction and implications for the future of theological work. Coakley proposes to integrate Trinitarian systematic reflection with practices of contemplative prayer; such a *théologie totale* attends to not only the intellectual reflection upon God but the affective engagement with God as well.[1]

---

1. Sarah Coakley, *God, Sexuality, and the Self: An Essay 'On the Trinity'* (Cambridge: Cambridge University Press, 2013), 43–51.

In this essay, I will examine Coakley's use of the Philippian "*Christus* hymn*,*" which appears in her early work as a model for the integrative praxis that stands at the heart of her more recent work.[2] In her reading of the hymn, Coakley argues that the contemplation of Christ's submission provides the basis for undoing gender norms, insofar as contemplation of a God who is beyond gender transforms our often-damaging assumptions about gender. As provocative as Coakley's proposal is, I will argue that her argument remains insufficiently attentive to the communal context necessary for enacting this important work.

To propose one way to repair this, I will turn to John Howard Yoder's paradigmatic use of the *Christus* hymn in his own work, arguing that Yoder's reading of the passage offers a vision of the social context that Coakley sees as intrinsic for her project's success. Yoder's proposal is not without its own problems, most glaringly in that his reading of Philippians as socially paradigmatic has the potential to sublate the individual narratives to which Coakley's work draws attention. Recently, Yoder's own sexual misconduct has prompted questions about this aspect of his theology, among other aspects. By focusing on the communal nature of witness, Yoder's ecclesiology runs the risk of being unable to do justice to individual narratives that do not cohere with the corporate witness, including gendered narratives.

Coakley and the Submission of Christ

In the first volume of Coakley's long-awaited systematic theology, she proposes that a *théologie totale*—a joining together of ascetic and

---

2. For the purposes of this essay, Philippians 2:5-11 will be referred to simply as the "*Christus* hymn," while acknowledging there is much scholarly debate about the nature of the passage as a hymn. Cf. Gordon D. Fee, "The New Testament and Kenosis Christology," and Thomas R. Thompson, "Nineteenth-Century Kenotic Christology: The Waxing, Waning, and Weighing of a Quest for a Coherent Orthodoxy," in *Exploring Kenotic Christology: The Self-Emptying of God*, ed. C. Stephen Evans (Oxford: Oxford University Press, 2006), for the historical options. Many contemporary appropriations of kenosis have centered on kenosis as descriptive of the act of creation and not primarily applicative to the work and person of Christ. While attempting to draw kenosis into a fully Trinitarian context, these appropriations raise their own questions regarding the emptying of God's divine attributes, questions that will not be dealt with here. Cf. *The Work of Love: Creation as Kenosis*, ed. John Polkinghorne (London: SPCK, 2001).

contemplative practices with intellectual reflection—provides a better way forward for theology. By this, she means theological reflection must remain grounded in bodily reflection if it is to "do justice to every level, and type of religious apprehension."[3] Specifically, this means giving priority to contemplative prayer in theological reflection. But in many ways, this unfolding of her integrative approach is nothing new for Coakley, as this is at the heart of her early work, such as *Powers and Submissions.*

In *Powers*, Philippians 2:5-11 functions paradigmatically for her work, the backdrop for how gender might be rethought. The submission of Christ, she notes, has often been eyed with suspicion by those who would see the submission of Christ as antithetical to the Christian feminist's quest for self-identity and freedom from domination and hierarchy.[4] For Coakley, however, retrieval of Christ's submission is integral to undoing gender domination.

There have been two basic readings of the hymn, Coakley argues: either the hymn is speaking of Christ's kenotic divestment of divine attributes in the act of incarnation, or the hymn is describing a moral paradigm that Christians are to imitate.[5] Coakley threads between these options, reading the passage as describing the ways in which Christ *handled* power; in doing so, she avoids the conclusion, on the one hand, that the hymn is uncritically calling for submission to abusive power, and on the other hand, avoids interpretations of the passage that require Christ to be shorn of certain divine attributes in the incarnation.[6]

Coakley's concern here is twofold. If she follows the first interpretation—that Christ relinquished ontological attributes—God is unable to enter creaturely life intact such that what Christ offers is not the transformation of creaturely life, but only solidarity within

---

3. Coakley, *God, Sexuality, and the Self*, 48.

4. Sarah Coakley, *Powers and Submissions: Spirituality, Philosophy, and Gender* (Oxford: Blackwell, 2002), 3. As Diane Hampson, *Theology and Feminism* (Oxford: Blackwell, 1990), 155 notes, "For women, the theme of self-emptying and self-abnegation is far from helpful as a paradigm."

5. Ibid., 7. These are simply the modern positions, which are asking very different questions than the patristic period, Coakley notes.

6. Ibid., 11.

injustice and abuse. As Coakley writes, God is "sheared down to human size, [made] intrinsically powerless, incapable of sustaining the creation in being."[7] If she follows the second interpretation—that Christ's submission is a moral paradigm—then Christ's dual nature is downplayed, such that human participation in the triune life is diminished.

Coakley resolves this conundrum by recourse to Cyril of Alexandria's solution, which presupposes no loss or emptying of the divine person as is characteristic of many modern explications of *kenosis*.[8] Because Christ—as fully human and fully God—joins with us, our accompanying "submission" to God through Christ becomes an entrance into divine strength.

> The hymn of Philippians was, from the start, an invitation to enter into Christ's extended life in the church, not just to speculate dispassionately on his nature. The "spiritual" extension of Christic kenosis, then . . . involves an ascetical commitment of some subtlety, a regular and willed practice of ceding and responding to the divine.[9]

For Coakley, both men and women in Scripture embody this fundamental attribute of human creatureliness—dependency before God—with the apex of this dependency and submission occurring in the person of Christ on the cross.[10] The admonition of Philippians 2:5-11 is thus not an admonition that encourages female subordination; Christian traditions that have unreflectively imbibed a patriarchal version of this submission are to blame here.[11] Coakley's reconsideration of submission to God is rooted in an analogy-of-Christ: that the narration of Christ's weakness and dependency is *paradigmatic*

---

7. Ibid., 24.
8. Cyril of Alexandria, *Third Letter to Nestorius*, translated in T. H. Bindley and F. W. Green, eds., *The Ecumenical Documents of the Faith* (London: Methuen, 1950), 213ff., in Coakley, *Powers*, 13ff.
9. Ibid., 34.
10. Ibid., 60–61.
11. Ibid., 38. Coakley distinguishes between the negative ways in which kenosis has been articulated to codify suffering and submission in specifically gendered ways, and a kenosis that is the manner in which humanity comes to embody "prophetic resistance, courage in the face of oppression, and the destruction of false idolatry." In *God, Sexuality, and the Self*, Coakley continues this criticism of traditional modes of contemplation that undermine the possibility that the Holy Spirit might revise our gender stereotypes, 126–31.

for human existence.[12] Prayerful inhabitation of this reality, then, provides apophatic access to a way that the contemplative might "construct a vision of the Christic self that transcends the gender stereotypes we are seeking to up-end."[13] Describing her experience in leading Boston convicts in hesychastic prayer—a foretaste to her more recent *théologie totale* approach—she comments:

> Gentleness, poise, peace and solidarity: these were indeed manifest ways of "bucking the system," if only for a short and blessed interval in the prison day. . . . I was suddenly reminded of Elijah's posture of despair on Mt. Carmel (1 Kings 18:42) and of the later Christian hesychasts' imitation of this posture in the practice of the Jesus prayer—their theory being that the posture expressed physically the "bringing of the mind down into the heart."[14]

"Contemplation" as "a divine infusion of prayer into a passive recipient"[15] unveils a number of undercurrents of the spiritual life that threaten authoritarian abuses.[16] This is because the Trinitarian God—the object and source of contemplation—refuses these common gender assumptions.

> If we think of the Trinity not as a set of perfect mutual relations into which the (known) gender binary somehow has been interposed in a cleansed, but rather as an irreducible threeness that always refuses a mere mutuality of two . . . we do not allocate the binary of "masculinity" and "femininity" to different "persons," or even to their relation, but instead step into a circle of divine desire . . . which is necessarily beyond our comprehension and categorization, but is drawing us by degrees into the "likeness" of the "Son."[17]

In sum, the vision of the *Christus* hymn invites us into the contemplation of God. In this contemplation we encounter the

---

12. Coakley, *Powers*, 30.
13. Ibid., 33. See also "Living into the Mystery of the Holy Trinity: Trinity, Prayer and Sexuality," in *Anglican Theological Review* 80 (1998): 223.
14. "Meditation as Subversive Activity," in *The Christian Century*, June 29, 2004, 18–21.
15. Coakley, *Powers*, 41.
16. Ibid., 54. Coakley argues that simply dismissing contemplative prayer dismisses the "messy entanglement of authoritative claims to divine power" and "creative gender play" that are often left covered in meditative techniques such as advocated by John Chapman.
17. Sarah A. Coakley, "The Trinity and Gender Reconsidered," in *God's Life in Trinity*, ed. Miroslav Volf (Minneapolis: Fortress Press, 2006), 140.

eschatological self, which we are then invited to enact in the present age in sociopolitical ways. For Coakley, while we are transformed in contemplation to be able to thus enact the eschatological "self," there are still present constructions of gender that must be reckoned with.

The Locus for Reconstructing Gender

Coakley envisions the resources for gender reconstruction as being accessed by means of the contemplative act, through prayer in which we receive the work of God. But these practices are, by definition, individual forays into the apophatic realm. This is not to say, however, that the empowering results of such apophatic encounters are primarily the property of the individual. The "self" that is affected by contemplation is not a Cartesian mind, but a unity that is psychosomatic and sociosomatic.[18] The effects of contemplation, as indicated in Palamite theology, are not primarily for the benefit of some disembodied mind or soul, but the whole person in community.

> Whilst debates about identity and the nature of the self must of course continue to be conducted with the utmost philosophical rigour, it is none the less as well to be aware of the political and ideological undertow of our discussions in this area . . . as the anthropologist Mary Douglas is wont to remind us: "the public idea of the self is part of a cultural commitment. . . . *Both self and community have to be examined together.*"[19]

Thus the effects of contemplation are to be conceived of, not in terms of one's own personal piety, but by necessity, as an invitation to personal and corporate critique and renewal. The self, a matter of usage rather than static ontological definition, is malleable and open to reconstrual—hopefully away from abuse.

But in what kinds of communities does Coakley conceive of this re-creation occurring? Here, Coakley has in the past been less explicit.[20] In

---

18. Ibid., 85.
19. Ibid., 86, italics mine.
20. On the whole, Coakley shies away from programmatic implications of her suggestions, except to note that they must be "incarnational" (68), that "our prayer is enfleshed" (ibid.). As one reviewer has noted, however, Coakley leaves much to be desired in actual concrete suggestions. See Ellen T. Armour's review in *Journal of the American Academy of Religion* 73 (2005): 239–42.

God, Sexuality, and the Self, significant attention is given to charismatic communities, which she sees as embodying the gender-transforming implications of prayer, which is an advance over her previous work;[21] however, even in this fieldwork, her observations focus more on the doctrinal implications of the life of prayer as experienced in these groups. For example, she describes the transformative life of "tongues" and personal transformation within the liturgical life, but does not give attention to whether these personal experiences have yielded a transformed corporate life of the congregation.[22]

If as Coakley notes, the self is a matter of social negotiation, a matter of use in a particular context, the flexibility and specificity of the *locus* in which these transformations take place must be accounted for, lest "self" remain an abstracted concept. This is precisely what Coakley wants to resist: if our re-gendered existence is a marker of its Trinitarian origin,[23] it follows that gender transformation will play out in the communal life of the church as well. For Coakley, this is important insofar as the reconstruction of gender relies upon a community to both incarnate and evaluate these mystical transformations.[24]

In her recent book, she echoes earlier concerns that institutional voices will work against these insights, leading to "implicitly, for a woman, the ceding to potentially repressive and patriarchal structures in church and society."[25] To be sure, Coakley rightly worries about the manner in which power has been inscribed upon female bodies in abusive ways across church history, leading to her choice to "make space" in the opening provided by apophatic prayer. But the lack of concrete discussion on communal dynamics ultimately proves to be a problematic lacuna for Coakley's project. Having experienced the "empowering darkness" in its unity, and not wanting to once again segment life into binary opposites, she does not speak to the practical

---

21. Coakley, *God, Sexuality, and the Self*, 163–86.
22. Ibid., 170–74.
23. Coakley, "Mystery," 231.
24. Coakley, *Powers*, 58.
25. Ibid., 57.

dimensions of these enactments. As William Cavanaugh has argued, apart from a specific location to narrate identity, identities remain open to recolonization by the very powers that Coakley seeks to avoid.[26]

Given the liturgical orientation of Coakley's project, it is also surprising that the issue of space is not developed alongside her project, a project that would appear is implicated by the use of Philippians 2:5-11 as a hymn, if not by Paul's use of the passage to negotiate differences within Philippian congregational life. To address this, I now turn to John Howard Yoder's use of this passage, to explore whether Yoder's approach may aid us.

John Howard Yoder and the Imitation of Christ

As with Coakley, the *Christus* hymn of Philippians 2:5-11 appears prominently in a number of John Howard Yoder's works, including his seminal *The Politics of Jesus*, and his posthumously published *Preface to Theology*.[27] That Scripture appears prominently, for a biblical and Mennonite theologian such as Yoder, is no surprise, but the persistence with which this passage appears and appears paradigmatically within Yoder's corpus should draw our attention.[28]

At the onset of *The Politics of Jesus*, Yoder claims

> that Jesus is, according to the biblical witness, a model of radical political action ... this "stating it" is all the present study tries to do; to let the Jesus

26. William Cavanaugh, *Torture and Eucharist: Theology, Politics, and the Body of Christ* (Malden, MA: Wiley-Blackwell, 1998), 70ff. Recent work by Coakley has been largely suggestive here. In "Why Gift? Gift, Gender and Trinitarian Relations in Milbank and Tanner," *Scottish Journal of Theology* 61 (2008): 224–35, Coakley offers that, because issues of gender are intimately tied to issues of economy, it may very well be that "the poor" are the location for this renarration. Her naming "the poor" is suggestive, but not developed. Cf. "Is There a Future for Gender and Theology? On Gender, Contemplation, and the Systematic Task," *Svensk Teologisk Kvartalskrift* 85 (2009): 52–61, for other recent reflections on this nexus.

27. John Howard Yoder, *The Politics of Jesus: Vicit Agnus Noster* (Grand Rapids: Eerdmans, 1972); *Preface to Theology: Christology and Theological Method* (Grand Rapids: Brazos, 2002).

28. The passage also appears centrally in Yoder's final, posthumously published essay, "On Christian Unity: The Way from Below," *Pro Ecclesia* 9, no. 2 (2000): 165–83, where Yoder, discussing the epistemic humility required of ecumenical talk notes that "[t]he kenosis or humiliation which God chooses as the path to Lordship is not merely a mentality of self-abnegation or servanthood. ... Jesus' choice of the cross is the pinnacle and prototype of that divine self-emptying, and it has been followed by the Romeros and Kings and Gandhis who have retrieved and re-incarnated that suffering servant vision for our century" (182).

story so speak that the person concerned with social ethics, accustomed as he is to a set of standard ways to assume Jesus not to be relevant to social issues, or at least not relevant immediately, can hear.[29]

In other words, Yoder's baseline hermeneutic is that what we see in the life of Jesus is and should be a model of social and political action, a view consistent with Yoder's "biblical realism."[30] It is to this end that Yoder sets out, establishing Jesus as one intimately concerned with social issues and ethics, and correspondingly, the need for those who would follow Jesus to be the same.[31]

Yoder's excavation of Jesus' original *Sitz im Leben* reveals a continuity between the individual's life and their social setting, that "Jesus doesn't know anything about radical personalism," but rather that "the personhood which he proclaims as a healing, forgiving claim to all is integrated into the social novelty of the healing community."[32] Whatever we say concerning the meaning of Jesus, it will thus refuse a separation between the personal and social; Jesus' paradigmatic action is viewed in distinctly corporate terms, as the community bears visible witness to the one it follows.[33] This concern for the visible witness of the community consequently shapes Yoder's subsequent discussion of "participation" in Christ. As Yoder claims, Jesus is "the bearer of a new possibility of human, social, and therefore political relationships."[34] It follows then, that when we read images of "imitation" in the New Testament, we should not read these as mystical encounters, but as metaphors for discipleship.[35]

It is with this understanding of imitation in hand that Yoder arrives

---

29. Yoder, *Politics*, 12.
30. Ibid., 14. This immediate reading and practice by the people of God is set in opposition to the "crypto-systematics" by scholars of Scripture (14), which Yoder sees as creating a distance between theology and ethics.
31. Jesus is "in his divinely mandated . . . prophethood, priesthood, the bearer of a new possibility of human, social, and therefore political relationships" (62–63). This theme of Jesus as the inauguration of a new humanity will become more significant as we approach the issue of "imitation" of Jesus.
32. Ibid., 113.
33. Speaking of the kingdom of God that Jesus inaugurates, Yoder notes that "it is a visible socio-political, economic restructuring among the people of God, achieved by his intervention in the person of Jesus as the one Anointed and endued with the Spirit" (39).
34. Ibid., 63.
35. Ibid., 118.

at his first treatment of Philippians 2:5-11. The self-denial and humiliation of Jesus, Yoder notes, does not refer to a loss of metaphysical attributes, but to Jesus' paradigmatic bearing of the form of a servant.[36] The submission referred to entails obedience, but not originally questions of metaphysics.

> The thought of "seizing equality with God" may be in contrast to the example of Lucifer or of Adam. In the very earliest stages of Christological thinking the concept of "grasping equality with God" might not have presupposed the preexistence of the Son . . . it may originally have referred to his renunciation of Zealot kingship.[37]

In the context of Philippians, Yoder notes that the exhortation to imitate Jesus takes on a third level of meaning: "self-denial which fosters the unity of the church."[38] In light of how Yoder views Jesus—as a model for radical, corporate political action—it is not surprising that the imitation of Jesus is seen in terms of what this means for the church's subsequent activity.[39] Accordingly, for Yoder, the implications of Philippians 2:5-11 for the Christian community of "imitating Christ" includes accepting innocent suffering, martyrdom, and the acceptance of servanthood in place of dominion,[40] concluding that "servanthood" replaces dominion, forgiveness absorbs hostility. As communities of imitation, Christians are called to "be like Jesus."[41]

This interpretation of Philippians 2 continues in later writings, as in his 1984 *Priestly Kingdom*:

> The imagery behind the hymn would seem to be that of a Prometheus/Adam/primeval king, who as representative of the human race grasped at equality with God, thereby representing the picture the poet projected of the human predicament.[42]

Occurring within the context of how the New Testament texts conceive

36. Ibid., 125.
37. Ibid., 125n24.
38. Ibid., 125.
39. Ibid., 126.
40. Ibid., 126–28.
41. Ibid., 134.
42. John Howard Yoder, *The Priestly Kingdom: Social Ethics as Gospel* (Notre Dame: University of Notre Dame Press, 1984), 52.

of Jesus' relation to God, Philippians 2:5-11 is again discussed, not as evidence of "proto-Gnostic cosmology," but rather an affirmation of the Logos' identification with humanity:

> No longer does the concept of Logos solve a problem of religion, reconciling the eternal with the temporal; it carries a proclamation of identification, incarnation, drawing all who believe into the power of becoming God's children [emphasis mine].[43]

Again, in his lecture notes, edited and published as *Preface to Theology*, Yoder recounts what is now recognizable as his standard treatment of the passage, concluding with the affirmation that

> [i]n this view the self-emptying, the kenosis, or the humiliation consists not in divesting oneself of absolute attributes of divinity in order to become a man, but rather, after the model of what Adam should have done . . . refusing to disobey.[44]

In sum, the significance of the hymn is that Jesus provides a present moral paradigm that the community exercises in their corporate life. By viewing Philippians 2 as immediately descriptive of the community's vocation rather than how an individual enters into the triune life, Yoder immediately redresses a shortcoming in Coakley's approach. But this is not to say that Yoder's approach does not come without a deep lacuna of its own.

The community that is constructed by the following of Jesus' paradigm is thus one that carries forth its mission in faithful, countercultural response. Or to use Yoder's language, the gospel is seen as ethics.[45] It is with this communal focus that we see both the strength and weakness of Yoder's project. While recovering the vitality and centrality of the Christian community as witness to and

---

43. Ibid., 51.
44. John Howard Yoder, *Preface to Theology: Christology and Theological Method* (Grand Rapids: Brazos, 2002), 84. See also 86: "If we came to this text with a full concept of the prior exalted status which he forsook, then we would tend toward this idea of emptying out . . . if however, we were to take the other line of interpretation, we would see Jesus as tempted, in the line of Adam, to add to 'being the divine image' a further God-likeness that he would have grasped. Yet he didn't grasp it. . . . *The point of the quotation is to make a different connection between the Christian and Christ* . . . that because he was humiliated we should accept humiliation."
45. The subtitle of *Priestly Kingdom*.

transformative agent in the world, Yoder's suspicion of speculative metaphysics and an invisible church lead him to emphasize the communal ordering of the church, without adequate attention to the individual narrative, which might, as Coakley suggests, subvert or revise the assumptions embedded within a community. In order to refocus the church's life and categories in communally visible and practiced entities, Yoder trades Coakley's apophatic and contemplative theological categories for visible ones, seeing the contest as an either/or.[46] This move need not be conceived, as Oliver O'Donovan has charged, as "neoliberal," of sociality purchased at the expense of belief.[47] However, it would appear that in his desire to maintain the visibility of the church, as Travis Kroeker has suggested, Yoder has neglected certain nonmaterial dimensions of the Christian life that cannot be fully accounted for by social practices, and thus places in question how one can make sense of Christian teaching (Trinity, eschatology, etc.) that cannot be accounted for in the terms of practices of the Christian life.[48]

When it comes to the issue raised most presciently by Coakley—the issue of gender—Yoder's emphasis upon a *community's* visible formation takes a more troubling turn. Attention has recently turned toward Yoder's relationships with women, some of which were abusive; Yoder was disciplined toward the end of his life for sexual harassment, an aspect of his life neglected by a number of Yoder's commentators.[49] In a widely disseminated work on Yoder's behavior,

46. The most radical example of this can be seen in his late "Sacraments as Social Practice," *Theology Today* 48 (1991): 33–44, where Yoder discusses the traditional Catholic sacraments in terms of community discipline. The great irony with this explanation is that it defies Yoder's own understanding of Scripture: by collapsing the sacraments, which are and are not the thing they signify, into a single dimension, Yoder dismisses his own earlier explication of Anabaptist hermeneutics of Scripture, in which Scriptures are themselves of dually layered, having both an inner and outer sense.

47. Oliver O'Donovan, *Desire of the Nations: Rediscovering the Roots of Political Theology* (Cambridge: Cambridge University Press, 1996), 221–24.

48. P. Travis Kroeker, "The War of the Lamb: Postmodernity and John Howard Yoder's Eschatological Genealogy of Morals," *The Mennonite Quarterly Review* 74 (2000): 305.

49. For periodical accounts of the disciplinary proceedings concerning Yoder's sexual conduct, see Tom Price, "Theologian Cited in Sex Inquiry," *Elkhart Truth*, June 29, 1992; Tom Price, "Theologian's Future Faces a 'Litmus Test': Yoder's Response to Allegations Could Determine Standing in the Field," *Elkhart Truth*, July 13, 1992; "A Known Secret: Church Slow to Explore Rumors Against Leader," *Elkhart Truth*, July 14, 1992; Tom Price, "Yoder's Actions Framed in

Ruth Elizabeth Krall concludes that Yoder's theology is written as a justification for his behavior, a claim that remains to be investigated fully.[50] But Krall, while acknowledging the institutional failures that did not hold Yoder to account, she locates his moral failure not in these institutional dynamics, but in "fantasies of violence," which, Krall confesses, is purely speculative.[51]

Krall's analysis on institutional dynamics is more convincing than her speculation on Yoder's inner life; as such, I think her exploration of Yoder's moral failures with respect to his writings is not a faulty approach, but wrongly attuned.[52] In other words, Yoder's moral failures—if linked to his theology—are indicative not simply of Yoder's views on sex primarily, but his views on sexuality in relation to the church's corporate witness; as we have seen, Yoder's theology rests upon the corporate witness of Christians, and as Krall notes, it was this church that failed to hold Yoder accountable for a number of years for his actions. Though Yoder himself was disciplined by his Mennonite community, what remains troubling about the episodes is that little attention was given to the victims of these abuses themselves; little attempt was made to reconcile the abused to the church, as much of the Mennonite Church's focus was centered on Yoder's actions.[53]

It is not the case that Yoder's emphasis on the corporate nature of Christian witness will *necessarily* lead to the institutional failures Krall describes; maintaining an emphasis on communal witness and formation does not, *as such*, lead to silencing of individuals whose stories do not fit with the overarching narrative of the community. But, as Cynthia Hess has pointed out, sublimation of aberrant voices is a danger within communities whose witness attends to corporate forms of witness, but not to the individual voices whose lives have been silenced by a corporate model.[54] What is needed, I suggest, is not a

Writings," *Elkhart Truth*, July 15, 1992; Tom Price, "Teachings Tested: Forgiveness, Reconciliation in Discipline," *Elkhart Truth*, July 16, 1992.
50. Ruth Elizabeth Krall, *The Elephants in God's Living Room*, vol. 3: *The Mennonite Church and John Howard Yoder* (Enduring Space Publications, 2013), 199–200, accessed at www.ruthkrall.com.
51. Ibid., 206.
52. Ibid., 195ff.
53. Ibid., 236.

rejection of Yoder's ecclesiology *as such*, but precisely the attentiveness to individual narratives—particularly gendered narratives—though this may complicate Yoder's corporate emphasis. Ultimately, attention to individual narratives and gender experiences create, I contend, a stronger communal witness, by creating the possibility for the church to be patient in its differentiation and able to attend to the blind spots created by a singularly communal focus.

Between Coakley and Yoder

It would appear thus far, that while sharing a desire to conceive Christianity as providing the resources to combat a range of dehumanizing and violent forces, Yoder's and Coakley's projects suffer from equal and opposite deficits. Though both take the cues for their project from the paradigm of the *Christus* hymn, there emerges an apparently unbridgeable divide in their approaches.

Yoder, emphasizing the practical dimensions of corporate Christic imitation in Philippians 2:5-11, opens the possibility that the corporate narrative will succeed at the expense of individual ones. In the case of Yoder, the corporate narrative was seemingly prized at the expense not only of attending to Yoder's misconduct, but also at the expense of the women who were abused. Coakley, on the other hand, by focusing on the contemplative aspects of Philippians 2:5-11, emphasizes the ways in which gender assumptions can be overturned. She, however, has yet to fully attend to the corporate context that would allow these individual narratives to take root.

Where there *is* traction between the two approaches, however, is in the specifically embodied approach that both Yoder and Coakley affirm. For Coakley, the contemplation of Christ invites the pray-er into the triune life, leading to a bodily narration of gender identity.[55] Likewise, Yoder emphasizes that the manner in which the imitation of Christ is to be pursued is through the corporate, practiced life of

---

54. Cynthia Hess, *Sites of Violence, Sites of Grace: Christian Nonviolence and the Traumatized Self* (Lanham, MD: Lexington, 2009), 105–11.

55. Coakley, *Powers*, 163–67. For Coakley, this narration is ultimately an eschatological one, following Gregory of Nyssa, but one that appears within bodies in time.

discipleship.[56] I suggest that, despite their qualms about the other's approach, it is this point of contact in the bodily existence of Christian life that draws the two together, and the point at which these two very different voices may be of aid to one another.

Yoder consistently emphasizes that when we are talking about the church, we are talking not about ecclesiastical structures but about the gathered body of believers.[57] Coakley's proposal, emphasizing the mystagogical aspects of discipleship, finds itself in need of precisely this aspect. By reading the *Christus* hymn as a practical exercise, Yoder posits the corporate church as the locus for God's activity. In Coakley's project, the triune God's subversion of our assumptions about gender has corporate implications, since it means that God's effect upon one life cannot be sealed off from the lives of others.

Likewise, Yoder's project benefits from Coakley's insights concerning the reformation of this body in and through the acts of prayer. Because empowerment of the believer for Coakley occurs through the renewing life of the triune God (and in specific opposition to patterns of gender discrimination that become entrenched in ecclesiastical structures), Christians are not left to work with only the materials available in immanent communities, nor to speak only of the corporate witness. Insofar as both individual Christians and churches exist by the work of God, there is no reason not to attend to the gendered narratives of men and women. Together, they provide a vision of God's empowerment, remaking the community of faith *in their humanity*, empowering the church to live as a witness to what is not yet seen elsewhere. In this sense, though divided in other ways, Coakley's work is not competitive with Yoder's vision of churches as

---

56. Cf. *The Fullness of Christ: Paul's Revolutionary Vision of Universal Ministry* (Elgin, IL: Brethren Press, 1987), 71–74.

57. Cf. "The Hermeneutics of Peoplehood," in *The Priestly Kingdom* (Notre Dame: University of Notre Dame Press, 1984). Within Yoder's writings on ecumenicity, he consistently views "institutional" structures as impediments to the command of unity, similar to the manner in which war stands as a form of idolatry in which one nation is preferred over another. Cf. "A Historic Free Church View," in *Christian Unity in North America: A Symposium*, ed. J. Robert Nelson (St. Louis: Bethany, 1958), 87–97; *The Ecumenical Movement and the Faithful Church* (Scottdale, PA: Mennonite Publishing House, 1958), 4–6; and "The Nature of the Unity We Seek," *Religion in Life* 26 (1957): 225, for various versions of the argument against "institutional" preferences within ecumenical dialogues.

communities of practice, but helps bring it to fullness. Coakley's vision, of a church fully transfigured by the triune life, additionally helps illuminate the dark corners of Yoder's work, by ensuring that individual narratives are not reducible to how they fit within the corporate witness; if the church exists by God's work, then the corporate witness must always be attentive to how God is recasting and remaking the individual lives of its members for its corporate witness to not silence those whose voices need to be heard the most.

6

The Winnowing and Hallowing of Doctrine: Extending the Program of the Father of Modern Theology?

Nicola Hoggard Creegan

As a theologian who has interacted with feminism and science, I have picked up Sarah Coakley's work from time to time with enormous interest, sensing that here is way of progressing in theology which gives some sort of priority to directions that are otherwise seen in some quarters as distractions from the pure discourse of systematics. The whole enterprise of systematic theology in its claim to provide the metanarrative *par excellence* can be quite contrary to the spirit of postmodern feminism. Coakley, however, in marrying experience of a certain kind, "field work" and doctrine, overcomes these phallocentric tendencies.[1]

This brings her into comparison, of course, with that other great systematizer for whom experience was also key: Schleiermacher. I realize that a comparison with Schleiermacher is not always flattering, and that his failure to develop in a trinitarian direction marks Coakley as distinctly different from him. I will argue, however, that there are many points of convergence as well, and I explain why I think this comparison is not only apt but complimentary, and why it is that Coakley has extended the Schleiermacherian program. Further, I will argue that the two theologians reveal a deeper pattern—explicated through the work of Iain McGilchrist—that can be extended in a number of different ways. Moreover, for Coakley, as for Schleiermacher, her method allows natural and easy means of interacting with the arts and sciences. Providing an anchoring in experience that makes her theology authentic, her method also answers to some extent the very cogent critiques of Christian theology coming from numerous directions. In the end I claim that Coakley's method—which in some form was also Schleiermacher's—gives both a winnowing and hallowing of doctrine.

Schleiermacher

Some years ago a Schleiermacher scholar gave a paper at the AAR Annual Meeting that was titled "Schleiermacher: Theologian of Vatican XX." Now Vatican XX would indeed be many millennia in the future and in this paper's light-hearted scenario the pope was a Baptist woman. The point of the paper was serious—that Schleiermacher's theology would eventually return to prominence in a time in the future that might be otherwise unrecognizable in the present.

Schleiermacher was the first great systematizer of the contemporary age, but his work was also a theology of and for the church, and was deeply rooted in piety. Like Coakley he started with the essence of being a human oriented toward God. Schleiermacher

---

1. This approach is detailed in her first volume of Systematic Theology. See Sarah Coakley, "Prelude: God, Sexuality, and the Self: The Arguments of This Book," in *God, Sexuality, and the Self: An Essay 'On the Trinity'* (Cambridge: Cambridge University Press, 2014).

described this as piety, defined as "neither a Knowing nor a Doing, but a modification of Feeling, or of immediate self-consciousness."[2] He argued that our day-to-day consciousness involves a brokenness, a dialectic, between feeling and perception, between "abiding within" and moving out, between a sense of relative freedom and relative dependence on the world around us. Against this brokenness is a consciousness of unity, of being at one with the world that is itself dependent, not owing its existence to itself but dependent on something beyond it. Toward this "Other" Schleiermacher famously argued we have no sense of freedom, but instead only a consciousness or feeling of "absolute dependence."[3] Making links between all people and Christians, he argued that the universal mode of dependence became for the Christian the "sense of sin and of grace."[4] In Schleiermacher's *On Religion*, the first great work of apologetics in the contemporary world, he makes the point that when poets and artists are seeking beauty and the infinite they are longing for God.[5] Artists and people of faith are therefore fellow travelers.

Now something of this desire for God that people experience unawares is common to both Schleiermacher's and Coakley's work. In both cases they recognize that basic human responses need to be winnowed and hallowed, by prayer in Coakley's case, and by exposure to the Word in the church, that corporate world of "mutual interaction and co-operation," in Schleiermacher's understanding.[6] For absolute dependence, desire, and sexual desire can all be problematic, leading to hedonism and idolatry as easily as to piety and the experience of participating in the triune God. In chastened circumstances, however, they are the beginning of theology. Schleiermacher and Coakley, standing before and after Barth respectively, are in contrast to the dominant strand of twentieth-century Barthianism that considered the

---

2. Friedrich Schleiermacher, *The Christian Faith* (Edinburgh: T. & T. Clark, 1999), §3.
3. Ibid., §5.
4. Ibid., §63.
5. Friedrich Schleiermacher, *On Religion: Speeches to Its Cultured Despisers* (Cambridge: Cambridge University Press, 1988), 32.
6. *Christian Faith*, §115.

natural too fallen and too corrupted to be an entryway to the foundation of theology.

Schleiermacher argued that when others glimpsed God through art or infinity they participated, albeit less intensely, and sometimes misdirectedly, in this grammar of faith. He says in *On Religion*:

> [T]hat first mysterious moment that occurs in every sensory perception, before intuition and feeling have separated, where sense and its objects have, as it were, flowed into one another and become one, before both turn back to their original position—I know how indescribable it is and how quickly it passes away.... But I wish that you were able to hold on to it and also to recognize it again in the higher and divine religious activity of the mind.[7]

He goes on to say, "It is as fleeting and transparent as the first scent with which the dew gently caresses the waking flowers, as modest and delicate as a maiden's kiss, as holy and fruitful as a nuptial embrace; indeed, not like these, but it is itself all of these."[8] Thus he, like Coakley, parallels the intensity of sexual desire with desire for God, sees them in fact as entangled and enmeshed.

Schleiermacher's theology had dialogue partners: the confessions of the church and the scriptures, the corporate body of the church, and the cultured despisers of religion. For some, Schleiermacher has been seen as hopelessly anthropocentric and experience based. He is read as though his dogmatics refers only to internal religious states of being. On this matter there is much confusion. Schleiermacher's method is certainly phenomenological, and certainly includes centrally the phenomenon of human consciousness, but these observations are crucially made in the context of the church and the church's preceding proclamations. Nothing human exists for Schleiermacher without utterance—everything is signed.[9] Schleiermacher acknowledges subjectivity, that the person is made to be in relationship with God, that is, related to but ultimately transcending of all other relationships in and of the natural and social worlds. But he does not end there;

7. *On Religion*, 31–32.
8. Ibid., 32.
9. *Christian Faith*, §6.

rather he moves into a dense dialogue between the phenomenon of piety and the confession of the church and the proclamation of the Word. Nevertheless the sense of absolute dependence is the religious form of consciousness that opens us up to know the spiritual dimension. It is the means of knowing anything at all, and especially any "other" in a human way, moving from the prereflective to the reflective, always mindful that the knowing in relationship precedes knowing in a more objective, more separated way.

Coakley has similarly begun with the person and their affective states and perceptions. She has done a great deal of work on bodily "spiritual perception" in the early fathers, especially Gregory of Nyssa and Origen.[10] Origen, in particular, she argues, talks about the parallel development of physical and spiritual senses. So that in the mature person "one can speak of an 'inner' life of sense that is ultimately safely *disjoined* from the snares of physical and material sensuality."[11] In her systematic work Coakley is trying to answer the question: "why perfect relationship in God was understood as triadic in the first place."[12] One of her distinctive marks is her insistence upon wordless prayer as the beginning of all theology. But she links prayer with desire, especially sexual desire, and a threefold trinitarian movement, arguing in fact that this connection between desire and Spirit, and ultimately participation in God is the "soft underbelly" of trinitarian development that has been ignored because it was so fraught and controversial.[13] Using Romans 8 and Paul's description of prayer in the Spirit with groans too deep for words she says:

> what is being described in Paul is *one* experience of an activity of prayer that is nonetheless ineluctably, though obscurely, triadic. It is *one* experience of God, but God as simultaneously (i) doing the praying in me, (ii) receiving that prayer, and (iii) in that exchange, consented to in me, inviting me into the Christic life of redeemed sonship.[14]

---

10. Sarah Coakley, ed., *Re-thinking Gregory of Nyssa* (Malden, MA and Oxford: Wiley-Blackwell, 2003).
11. Sarah Coakley, "Beyond Belief: Liturgy and the Cognitive Apprehension of God," in *The Vocation of Theology Today: A Festschrift for David Ford*, ed. Tom Greggs, Rachel Muers, and Simeon Zahl (Eugene, OR: Cascade, 2013), 141 (emphasis original).
12. Sarah Coakley, "The Trinity, Prayer and Sexuality: A Neglected Nexus in the Fathers and Beyond," accessed April 14, 2013, http://www.atonementfriars.org/centro_lectures/1999 Coakley.doc.
13. Ibid.

The move from wordless prayer to the Trinity is a jump, but an interesting one, and one that Schleiermacher conspicuously did not make. Coakley takes the desire of the human being, at an inchoate level, and sees it as the sign of the Spirit already possessing and indwelling the human who is oriented to God through this Spirit.

That this type of prayer is often deeply linked to an ecstasy related to sexual intimacy—also a leap—allows her to name sexual intimacy itself as a clue to the Spirit, and hence to the triune life of God. This is justified by reference to Origen, who also links sexual desire and desire for God, though he is worried enough about this connection to recommend it only to celibates and "manly women."[15] Coakley wants to generalize much further than Origen, even while insisting that the desire be always chastened. Schleiermacher, in contrast, has only the controlling power of the Word, which does not in the end do the work that prayer effects for Coakley.

Nevertheless we can draw parallels between this passage and the one from Schleiermacher's *On Religion* above, though he does not take the extra step of pointing to the trinitarian force of the experience, nor does he go back to the early fathers and suggest that this type of experience was once perhaps developed as an alternative route to the Trinity.

Points of Connection and Difference

At this point then I would like to suggest three points of connection between Coakley and Schleiermacher, but also to note that there are a further three points where Coakley differs from or has extended the program of the Father of Modern Theology.

First, both Schleiermacher and Coakley, in beginning with the universal flowerings of human consciousness, are theologians of continuity. They are not prepared to pluck doctrine fully formed from the shelves or the pages of history, or indeed only from scripture. Both see a whole range of continuities that are important. Consciousness

14. Ibid.
15. Ibid.

itself in Schleiermacher's case, or desire in Coakley's work, can be hallowed and chastened, or it can simply be generic. One might be a pointer to the other in the right context, and one is always open to being transformed into the other. Neither theologian, then, is given to the harsh category differences that typify much of modernity: dividing the world into the saved and unsaved, the secular and the holy, the bodily and the sacramental, or nature and grace, for instance—or even animal and human. There are differences between people but there is much that all share in common as well. Continuity as well as discontinuity typifies the boundary between the world and the pious. In the end this makes dialogue with other religions and with science much less problematic.

Secondly, both see in the passions and consciousness of human life vestiges of the life of God. In Schleiermacher the argument is more incipient, but present in his recognition of god consciousness in the creative life of the artist and poet. In Coakley there is an explicit sense of the trinitarian vestiges in the life of prayer and indeed in any sexual yearning. In Coakley's case this vestigial theology is further progressed by her insistence that God also is yearning and desiring us. So much for the aseity of God.

Thirdly, this method for both theologians allows an easy interaction with both science and the arts. In Coakley's case, for instance, her starting point in desire and sexual desire is pointing to something that is shared by all animals; higher primates and mammals also have complex cultural patterns surrounding the management of sexual desire. As far as we know these animals do not pray, although if they did their prayers would be wordless, but they participate in the same intense sexual activity. Thus Coakley is pointing here to aspects of the creation that are shared by large numbers of higher animals and it becomes then much easier to accommodate these animals into the theological enterprise than it might otherwise be. She is not deriving her trinitarian theology from some abstract view of *imago Dei*, for instance. Thus the continuities and discontinuities that science recognizes in the evolutionary process are more easily paralleled in her writing as well. It is shocking of course to have this feeling we have all wished to relegate to the edges of faith discourse find a place so central in theology; on the other hand without it the human race and all other species as well would cease. Sexual desire is at the core of most narrative tension, most mimetic rivalry, most violence and sin, most beauty, and all evolutionary movement.

Schleiermacher too, in beginning with immediate self-consciousness is nevertheless starting with a facet that exists in shadow form in other animals, as even he recognized. He says, for instance:

> [I]f we go back to the first obscure period of the life of man, we find there, all over, the animal life almost solely predominating, and the spiritual life as yet entirely in the background . . . and so we must regard the state of his consciousness as closely akin to that of the lower animals.[16]

Although the animal state is to us "strange and unknown," there is a "general agreement that, on the one hand, the lower animals have no knowledge, properly so called, nor any full self-consciousness which combines the different moments into a stable unity." Feeling and perception "are not really distinct from each other." In this he draws links between the consciousness of animals and that of small children.[17]

These continuities are particularly important at this time when religion is being "explained" away by evolutionary cognitive science. Religion is often depicted as the transfer or co-option of cognitive traits like essentialism, anthropomorphism, or hyperactive agency detective device (HADD). In these fields religion is explained without any need for the claims of religion to be true. A theology that acknowledges the embodiedness of religious belief has a much easier time reconciling itself with this science than does the Barthianism of the twentieth century.[18]

---

16. *Christian Faith*, §4.
17. Ibid., §5.
18. See for instance, Pascal Boyer, "Religious Thought and Behaviour as By-Products of Brain Function," *Trends in Cognitive Sciences* 7 (2003): 119–24. Boyer does not absolutely claim to explain religion away, but he does offer what is to his satisfaction a plausible explanation of how ubiquitous human cognitive traits get applied to the religious sphere, thus undermining if not invalidating truth claims.

On the other side there are differences, or sometimes extensions in understanding when we move from Schleiermacher to Coakley. First, only Coakley extends the basic theological move to the Trinity. Coakley, of course, moves quickly from sexual desire to the Spirit, and hence to the Trinity, before which and in light of which Schleiermacher always hesitated. In Schleiermacher, however, there is much talk of the common Spirit arising from the community linked to Christ. This, when combined with proclamation of the Word, is the Holy Spirit.[19] The Holy Spirit in Schleiermacher, though, remains bound to the community, and is never seen as the external disrupter of the status quo, coming among God's people. The New Testament depictions, says Schleiermacher, "represent the Holy Spirit to us as always and only in believers."[20] Rather there is always the sense that this Spirit emerges from the long line of the historic community so long as the Word is proclaimed. If anything, the Word itself bears the weight of the Spirit. Although the Spirit is mentioned, as is prayer, the emphasis is upon how our prayers might or might not accord with those of the will of God, not on the role of the Spirit and of prayer in the believer themselves, as some sort of mystical union between the two.

In retrospect we can see Schleiermacher grasping after the Spirit, but not quite getting there. He gets to within a hair's breadth of something very close to Coakley's position. If he had of course, his doctrine of the Trinity, which for Schleiermacher is an afterthought, would have been quite different. He did not live in times that were right for an engagement with the Spirit. But this makes his statement about the Trinity interesting. He says:

> We have less reason to regard this doctrine as finally settled since it did not receive any fresh treatment when the Evangelical (Protestant) Church was set up; and so there must still be in store for it a transformation which will go back to its very beginnings.[21]

It is almost as though he knew there was something missing, and

---

19. *Christian Faith*, §121.
20. Ibid.
21. Ibid., §172.

it is easy to interpret this "something" as exactly what Coakley is describing, the acknowledgment of the Spirit in apophatic prayer, the hints of the spirit in all desire and especially in the strong desire for union experienced in sexuality. Not that the Spirit has been missing in the trinitarianism of twentieth-century theology, but that was the neglected person of the Trinity, rather than the one who might chasten our desires and thus give us a clue to God. This is what Schleiermacher's project was crying out to have done.

Secondly, Coakley extends Schleiermacher in insisting that a practice sits at the heart and the entryway to dogmatics. That practice is silent prayer. Schleiermacher also, in his reflections on prayer, deemphasizes the purely cognitive and speaks of an orientation to the future and to the kingdom of God that is fused with god consciousness.[22] Although for some things there might be gratitude and for others resignation, all other concerns are to be in a sense wordlessly given over to God in awareness of god consciousness. Here we find a great deal of similarity to Coakley's theology of prayer, but Schleiermacher does not make the links to the exercise of theology and then to the Trinity.

Thirdly, Coakley, unlike Schleiermacher, also extends the metaphors of desire to an insight into the passion of God *for us*, reflecting and mirroring our desire, and no doubt the source of our passion for others and for God.[23] Thus Coakley offers us a dynamic, interrelational metaphor for human-divine relationships that is consistent with and synergistic with our growing understanding of matter and life, social life and spiritual reality.

Thus I hope to have shown that Schleiermacher and Coakley bear more than faint family resemblance, but that Coakley has extended enormously the method and coherence of the former theologian of experience. Why do we have theologians beginning in very different but parallel places? What does it mean? I think we can understand this

22. Ibid., §146.
23. Coakley, "The Trinity, Prayer and Sexuality."

better if we divert briefly to examine the work of Iain McGilchrist and his recent book, *The Master and His Emissary.*

McGilchrist as Hermeneutic

I turn to McGilchrist because he enables us to link the approaches of Coakley and Schleiermacher, and indeed others, and because he also gives us in his book, *The Master and His Emissary*, an interesting window into the functioning of the brain and the light it might shed on the different types of conscious processing humans can do.[24] After all, Schleiermacher starts with what he calls an abiding-in-self, and Coakley with desire linked to prayer. Is this just wishful thinking? Can a humane science shed any light on why it might be fruitful to start theology in this way? Unlike most recent neurological literature McGilchrist is anything but reductionist. He is both a psychiatrist and philosopher, and brings his long clinical practice, and his knowledge of philosophy and art as well as neurology to bear on the problem of our consciousness. In drawing together and integrating numerous other studies his work is nothing if not idiosyncratic, but his underlying point, that within the single brain we are capable always of two ways of seeing and dealing with the world, is a point worth pondering. His book makes for interesting reading on how it is that we interact with the world, the state of our consciousness, and the place of emotions and sexuality in the wider scheme of things. Unlike most works on mind and body in recent history this book not only attempts to chart some of the centers of brain function, but it does so in light of the broad sweep of the history of philosophy and of art.

Homo sapiens, as most people are aware, functions with a divided brain. The brain is not just divided into two, but joined as well by the *corpus collosum*. In fact we possess a trinitarian brain, as is appropriate to the divine ape, though this arrangement, like most other surprises, is not found in humans alone, but in other mammals and corvids. McGilchrist is at great lengths to explain that there is no neat division

---

24. Iain McGilchrist, *The Master and His Emissary: The Divided Brain and the Making of the Western World* (New Haven: Yale University Press, 2012).

of the hemispheres, and that most human activities require an exquisite involvement of both brain hemispheres. In humans, however, one hemisphere is importantly dominant and there can be a rough attribution of the primary functions of the hemispheres. He argues that unless the brain has no impact at all on how we experience the world, the divided nature of the brain must mean something.

There is beneath the brain's geometry an astounding division of functions in different parts of the brain, all of them interacting and for the most part also very plastic, so that loss of function in one part of the brain can with effort and help be compensated for in other parts of the brain. All of this McGilchrist recognizes, but he is willing nevertheless to make interesting arguments about what happens when the dominant hemisphere becomes too dominating.

Arguing from an extensive literature and from his own clinical observation, he claims that the left hemisphere in most right-handed people is the dominant half of the brain. The left specializes in processing abstract information in isolation. It prefers what it knows already, and has a mechanical view of reality. It is parasitic on the right brain but is unaware of this. The left brain deconstructs, or reduces into parts and prefers to deal with nonliving objects. The left brain allows sharp focus. It "sees" in terms of machines.[25]

The right brain in contrast deals not in details but in the gestalt of a situation, but also with individuals in particular. It is open to metaphor, sees things as a whole and in context. It deals with the emotional content of situations and lives. The right deals with novelty and with life, with faces and with empathy.[26] It is easy to see how our contemporary world minimizes right-brain input and emphasizes instead the left brain's skills.

McGilchrist's thesis, not surprisingly, is that we have become a left-brained civilization, preferring to deal with information at a distance and in isolation from context, and by using mechanical models. The objectification and isolation of knowledge is not just a matter of the

25. McGilchrist, *The Master and His Emissary*, 55–56.
26. Ibid., 51–64.

hemispheres but is facilitated in humans also by the frontal cortex, which has enormously magnified in humans and allows us the distance from reality that has made our knowing so powerful, but also at times illusory.

Representing a human figure with overtones of both tragedy and "fallenness," he argues that where the hemispheres should be cooperating in their interactions with the world they are in fact competing. The result is that the "what" of a situation becomes more dominant than the "how."[27] The nonliving and mechanical become more evident than the living and irreducible. We become ill-adept at seeing things in context and as a whole.

While the left brain specializes in what it has constructed itself, the right brain is aware of the world out there, even if its very focus and awareness is a part of what brings this world into being for us.

> Ultimately I believe that many of the disputes about the nature of the human world can be illuminated by an understanding that there are two fundamentally different "versions" delivered to us by the two hemispheres, both of which can have a ring of authenticity about them, and both of which are hugely valuable; but that they stand in opposition to one another, and need to be kept apart from one another.[28]

One can easily see that religion will never get going at all if the left brain dominates to the exclusion of the right, if the left's way of seeing eclipses the right's. Schleiermacher's sense of absolute dependence, I would assert, requires a properly contributing right brain because it is only there that we get a sense of gestalt that makes possible an intuition of the unity of all that is there and its dependence on an Other. And Coakley's attention to prayer is also a way of forcing the silence of the left brain long enough for the right to function.

It is the same with relationships. Given only a left brain the person becomes autistic, acknowledging no other minds as real. Where in the past, religion and the arts might have brought us back again and again to the natural world and to emotion, this is no longer the case.

27. Ibid., 93.
28. Ibid., 5.

That we live instead in "[a]n increasingly mechanistic, fragmented, decontextualised world, marked by unwarranted optimism mixed with paranoia and a feeling of emptiness, has come about, reflecting, I believe, the unopposed action of a dysfunctional left hemisphere."[29]

McGilchrist goes on to say that attention is of enormous importance. Attention is not just another "function" alongside other cognitive functions. Its ontological status is of something prior to functions and even to things. The kind of attention we bring to bear on the world changes the nature of the world we attend to, the very nature of the world in which those "functions" would be carried out, and in which those "things" would exist. Attention changes what kind of a thing comes into being for us: in that way it changes the world. In language very similar to that of the Spirit, McGilchrist insists that attention is not a thing, but a relationship. It is a "howness," something between, an aspect of consciousness itself, not an object of consciousness. "It brings into being a world and, with it, depending on its nature, a set of values."[30]

Interestingly McGilchrist sees morality as a matter of emotion. "Moral values are not something that we work out rationally on the principle of utility, or any other principle, for that matter, but are irreducible aspects of the phenomenal world, like colour." Morality is intimately connected to empathy and a deep intuitive connection with others. Morality and music may be related, he suggests, perhaps predating both language and religion.[31] In music of course, there is a way of sharing emotion, at a level that goes under the radar of ordinary language and communication.

"Where the thing itself is 'present' to the right hemisphere," explains McGilchrist, "it is only 're-presented' by the left hemisphere, now become an idea of a thing. Where the right hemisphere is conscious of the "Other," whatever it may be, the left hemisphere

---

29. Ibid., 6.
30. Ibid., 29.
31. There is now much controversy over whether or not music in some sense predated or accompanied the evolution of language in humans. See, for instance, Steven Mithen, *The Singing Neanderthals: The Origins of Music, Language, Mind, and Body* (Cambridge, MA: Harvard University Press, 2007).

is conscious only of itself.[32] The right brain has access to wonder, produces wonder and awe, and this then progresses to the more analytical processing of the left brain.

Schleiermacher and Coakley

A number of conclusions can be reached by using McGilchrist as a heuristic to explain both Coakley and Schleiermacher. First, McGilchrist explains how it is that the focus and quality of our attention will determine the kind of picture we see. This is not so surprising in a postmodern world; perhaps more surprising is his insistence that our brains/minds can see in two different ways, but one way of seeing is more easily eclipsed than the other. This dominant rationality is evident not only in the rationality of some scientism and fundamentalism, but also in some circular and highly abstract forms of postmodernism. There is an obvious synchrony here with Schleiermacher's and Coakley's method of doing theology. They both insist that an attitude of submission to all that is there is the beginning of piety. In other words, theology cannot be done as an objective exercise alone. It cannot be done without a particular kind of attention being paid.

Secondly, the whole divided, but unified picture McGilchrist gives us is very similar to Schleiermacher's reflections on consciousness arising from the antithesis of the passive/reflective and Knowing/Doing states. Although Schleiermacher characterizes those latter states as extending beyond the self, the extension to which he refers is a focused controlling attention in contrast to the passive/receptive attention that typifies the right hemisphere in McGilchrist's schema. Certainly the passivity and longing facilitated by the right brain fits with Schleiermacher's understanding of this feeling leading to our sense of absolute dependence and acknowledgment of God. For the right brain is conscious of and alert to "other" and "Other." It is not surprising, then, that too much left-brained activity can drive out faith altogether.

---

32. McGilchrist, *The Master and His Emissary*, 174–75.

Similarly this fits with Coakley's beginnings in the receptive task of submission and wordless prayer, which is the beginning of her recognition of God as acting within.

Thirdly, I pursue this interlude here to show that there is independent substance to Schleiermacher's prophetic thought and to his reflections on consciousness, its divided and antithetical nature, and his insistence that it is a part of the consciousness that gives us clues to God. We now know that this reflectivity is vulnerable and quite easily overwhelmed, especially in the type of material culture we inhabit.

But I pursue this line also to show that in fact the right-brain function is quite broad; it is receptive to new impressions and to life, to emotion and sexuality and to the particular in context as well as the whole. Any of the colorful right-brain functions might be described as having a similar function. Mediated by McGilchrist we can see that there are obvious parallels between starting with absolute dependence and starting with desire chastened by the hallowing power of the Spirit in prayer. Schleiermacher may never have said it like that, but absolute dependence and prayer both cut short the totalizing tendencies in all systematic theological knowledge of God. Systematic theological thought is too frequently involved in abstract loops, more interested in analysis of what has already been given than in new experience. Schleiermacher's absolute dependence entails that all doctrine be rephrased as springing forth from the individual's consciousness and piety that is indeed the sense of being not in charge, but dependent upon that on which the whole of one's milieu is also dependent. Abstract knowledge that is only abstract knowledge has no place in his systematic. In Coakley's emphasis on prayer, there is similarly an insistence that all knowledge of God must spring out of the mind and heart oriented toward God, and indeed led by God. Coakley says, for instance:

> Rather, what is blanked out in the regular, patient attempt to attend to God in prayer is *any* sense of human grasp; and what comes to replace such an ambition, over time, is the elusive, but nonetheless ineluctable,

sense of *being grasped*, of the Spirit's simultaneous erasure of human idolatry and subtle re-constitution of human selfhood in God.[33]

Thus I am enthusiastic about Coakley's enterprise because it seems to be Schleiermacher taken to the next level. And even in Schleiermacher, I would hasten to add, I see a systematic theology that is relatively free of the problems Coakley has identified in systematic theology: hegemony, phallocentrism, and especially that of reifying theological language.[34]

Desire and Empathy

Coakley's emphasis upon desire is instructive and interesting, then, but raises questions about how sexual desire works as an analogy of or pointer to the desire or longing for God. Certainly this emphasis upon sexual desire places the ubiquity of sexual passion in the evolutionary process and in the animal world (where it is ironically more controlled than in humans) in a new light. I am interested, however, in an even more basic capacity that precedes and undergirds sexuality: that is, empathy.

In a recent book Simon Baron-Cohen has argued that empathy is what makes us moral.[35] Some people because of circumstances or unhappy combinations of genes have very little or zero empathy for others. This can make them dangerous. Others, however, have so much empathy that living becomes extremely painful. Baron-Cohen is attempting to defuse the concept of evil, ridding it of its religious overtones. Evil can be explained, he says, in terms of a lack of empathy. Baron-Cohen recommends training and education in empathy as the only means by which violence and aggression can be limited in human society. There has been much discussion of this idea and there are many ways in which it is far from being the full explanation of evil done by ordinary people in vicious circumstances. Nevertheless

---

33. Coakley, "Prelude."
34. Sarah Coakley, "Is There a Future for Gender and Theology?: On Gender, Contemplation, and the Systematic Task," *Criterion* 47, no. 1 (2009): 2–12, 4–5.
35. S. Baron-Cohen, *Zero Degrees of Empathy: A New Theory of Human Cruelty* (London: Allen Lane/ Penguin, 2011).

empathy and the capacity for empathy are an important part of what makes us human, and the first imprint of empathy is well documented in other mammals. I wonder whether empathy cannot also be seen as a pointer to God—in direct contrast, of course, to those who would argue that empathy in lower animals obviates the need for God. Empathy gives us clues that we are made to be in relationship with one another and empathy is potentially extendable to the whole of life, but especially to those animals that themselves exhibit empathy. Empathy is that which lies behind and is the precondition of sacrificial love and sexual ecstasy. Empathy can give us a clue to God because it draws us out of ourselves and into the other. Empathy is the clue to the interrelatedness of all things.

A long ethical conversation has gone on in history concerning the need for emotion in doing good. J. S. Mill, Bentham, and arguably Kant, would argue that ethics should be worked out rationally before it is felt. Reasons matter more than emotions in doing good, and in fact, they would argue, we can be led miserably astray if we stick to emotions. This is the kind of thinking that has been associated with the elevation of reason over emotion, and of men over women and nature. But the long virtue theory tradition would argue otherwise. Humans have long recognized that virtue and emotion can be trained. We can also at times make decisions that will take us into the orbit of the other whether we feel kinship or not. The highest moral codes would enjoin us to do good and give to others whether we feel like it or not, but always, I would argue, with the expectation that feeling would follow in time. So we might open up a conversation with another by an act of will, but expect that this would lead us into a closer bond with that person in time. What funds human kindness is a deep-seated biological empathy together with the will to do good. Kindness that comes from empathy is in the end trusted better than that which is reasoned out; this may be why we trust our dogs more than our well-trained psychotherapist at times.

Empathy also changes the territory of sacrifice. For sacrifice without empathy or love is all that the critics take it for—a blind and distasteful transaction that binds and oppresses the object of sacrifice as much as the doer. But sacrifice as an accompaniment of love or empathy is perhaps the most powerful moral and religious practice possible. I would argue, therefore, that perhaps it is empathy, shared by all mammals at least, which is the kernel of moral life, and the clue to God and to the primacy of interrelationship. Empathy can also awaken a sense of being in the world, a compassion for all that breathes and has spirit. A natural extension of this empathy is longing, longing for the whole or complete or most fulfilled connection. There are glimpses of heaven, I would argue, not only in a chastened sexual desire, but in the shared conversation that is open and wondering and reaching for God, where the questions and the answering emerge from deep empathy, and in humans a shared focus of attention.

The possibility of such conversation takes us back to Schleiermacher and to his *Christmas Eve*.[36] In this short novel which comes out of another longing, a longing for home, that which he saw as so much epitomizing the human state, Schleiermacher gives us a picture of friends gathering before a holy feast, in a state of wonder, with questions and responses emerging out of a deep yearning and deep empathy for one another. Out of this conversation comes a sense of being in the other, and of being finally within the God who encompasses all.

The Winnowing of Doctrine

With Schleiermacher the sense of absolute dependence under the influence of Christ worked to winnow doctrine, excluding speculation in areas that were most distant from this sense; he did work very much within the circle accessible to the sense of absolute dependence and refused to speculate outside it. So prelapsarian Adam and Eve, and for him the Trinity, were in some senses off limits.[37] For Schleiermacher the sense of absolute dependence gave humans a solidarity that

---

36. Friedrich Schleiermacher, *Christmas Eve Celebration: A Dialogue*, ed. T. Tice (Eugene, OR: Wipf & Stock, 2010).
37. *Christian Faith*, §61.

contradicted any Reformed doctrine of election, or merged election to the general election of all in Christ.[38]

This makes Schleiermacher's doctrine at times appear to be not much concerned with scripture. In Schleiermacher, however, doctrine and knowledge and God were all a unified and holistic whole. The story was always there, but it was linked inevitably to others' stories, and linked also to the human's emotions and consciousness. Not for Schleiermacher was the human out of sync with the natural world and the body and/or the transcendent. We were made for God and we were made to know God, but these senses and natural proclivities were born out of lower or lesser capacities. His vision was always of the human standing between the lower divided world and that of God. He would surely have embraced the theory of evolution as a magnificent affirmation of all that. In evolution too there is the insistence that even belief in God is built upon lower propensities and cognitive functions present in all mammals and some other genera as well. Thus for Schleiermacher we know as we are absorbed into the text using all our human and religious capacities. We might be guided to the truth by Scripture, but it is such a unified whole that its truths are now the truths of the community of blessedness, and they are proclaimed in the natural spirituality of the faithful one in the world.

Coakley has another type of differentiation, between doctrine that seeks to grasp God and that which emerges from the sense of "being grasped, of the Spirit's simultaneous erasure of human idolatry and subtle re-constitution of human selfhood in God."[39] For Coakley also there is a unified holistic vision in which so-called lower practices and passions become the means by which truth is known and mediated; not just by finding propositional knowledge in Scripture but by relating the how and now and the immediacy of faith to that which is proclaimed and revealed in Scripture. I wait with interest to see how this plays out in the coming volumes of her systematic.

---

38. *Christian Faith*, §163.
39. Coakley, *Prelude*.

The Conversation with Science

The other way in which Coakley is theologizing in the spirit of Schleiermacher is in her engagement with science as part of a much more holistic systematic. It was Schleiermacher—also the scientist and artist and poet—who asked two hundred years ago: "shall the tangle of history so unravel that Christianity becomes identified with barbarism, and science with unbelief?"[40] Outside of rarefied centers of great theological scholarship, this is the case today.

We must interact with nature for two reasons. For in nature there is *logos*, and life breathed by the Spirit, and as one philosopher has said, nature is "turned radically and ecstatically toward a distance unto which all the resonance of that life is directed, and from which that life is itself derived."[41] How can we theologize without it? In nature we find our own history, which is also the history of God. Eco-theology in recent times has indeed shown us that we have been reading the text not only in a patriarchal fashion but in one that ignores the habitat, the earth, and its fruits. The scriptures are studded with reference to these other players if we are attentive. Moreover, the mysticism of the past was often done in the context of nature, inspired by its liveliness and care. We have been reading nature through the dead lenses of modernity and have long believed, as Mary Midgley has pointed out, that we are the only beings with life and consciousness.[42] Theology must repent of this perspective. But I suspect also that the same chastening prayer that might give us discernment of God will also give us eyes to see nature in relationship to God. Where Schleiermacher emphasized our human solidarity we might now extend this solidarity deep into the animal world, so influencing our theological reflection. In beginning with sexual desire Sarah Coakley leads us in this direction.

The other reason that an interaction with nature is part of the

---

40. Friedrich Schleiermacher, *On the Glaubenslehre: Two Letters to Dr Lücke*, trans. J. O. Duke and F. Fiorenza (Chico, CA: Scholars, 1981), 61.
41. B. V. Foltz, "Nature's Other Side: The Demise of Nature and the Phenomenology of Givenness," in *Rethinking Nature*, ed. B. V. Foltz and R. Frodeman (Bloomington: University of Indiana Press, 2006), 330–42, 334.
42. Mary Midgley, *Beast and Man* (Oxford: Routledge, 2002), xxix.

theological task is that nature through science presents the greatest challenge to coherent Christian faith. In returning to the missional face of systematic theology, to its interface with the unbeliever in the skeptical naïve atheist who stumbles across the Word, their problem of alienation is not only that the language of faith has been so disjoined from their everyday experience, but also that they know that science tells another story. They might not know much at all about science, but the high priests of science have done a good job of communicating the redundancy of any faith position. Dawkins inspired ad on the London buses: There's probably no God. Stop worrying and enjoy your life.. In other words: without God there is no need of sacrifice; there is no conflict between the good life and enjoying yourself. A sacrificial life is one demanded by the pretense of God and religion, they are saying, but is not required for any other reason.

Thus systematic theology must interact with science if it is to maintain its missional objective, and even if it is to speak to the doubting heart at the center of church, faith, and theology. If the future of systematic theology must be done much much more closely in dialogue with science, it does not mean that it should become more science-like or that some sort of concordant partnership take place. Scientists on the whole are not engaged in theological progress and imagination; the merging of disciplines would only increase the need for the critiques outlined by Coakley. Rather, a true difficult dialogue of the kind that van Huyssteen calls transversality is needed, holding the tensions and integrity of different disciplines while juxtaposing them and placing them in serious conversation.[43]

Science disturbs the theological systems of systematic theology in three ways. First, in its very completeness and the breadth of its scope science appears to trump all talk of other realms and other realities. Where is there to hide a God or a transformed soul, or the dead? Secondly, the problem of evil in a post–Adam and Eve world is huge. Animals suffering, predation, selfish genes extinction, all require

---

43. J. Wentzel van Huyssteen, *Alone in the World: Human Uniqueness in Science and Theology* (Grand Rapids: Eerdmans, 2006), 18.

explanation. Systematic theology once had a kernel that could be defined as paradise, fall, and redemption. This kernel has been undermined. Moreover, Christian faith once had a simple response to evil: the fall of Adam. Now all manner of complicated responses are necessary. The atheists' response that there is no God has simplicity on its side. Thirdly, the long long period of supposedly purposeless prehuman history deconstructs the purpose with which we invest the last five thousand years of human history. All of this threatens systematic theology to the core. Responding, however, requires not only scientific understanding but deep discernment.

Summary: The Winnowing and Hallowing of Doctrine

I have argued then, that Sarah Coakley's work has many of the overtones of Schleiermacher. She can in many ways be seen as Schleiermacher taken to the next stage. Both Coakley and Schleiermacher, I have argued, can be defended from the critiques of systematic theology and both, but especially Coakley, are able to place theological discourse in a place that is hallowed while also being within the realms of reason and rhetoric. Sarah Coakley does this directly, by advocating that the theologian be an ascetic, one who practices prayer and therefore open to the chastening power of the Spirit.

Coakley, while going further than Schleiermacher into the realms of both spirit and Trinity, nevertheless also like him is involved in a winnowing and searing of doctrine. Purely abstract reasoning for its own sake, or metatheories that claim to have distance and objectivity (even if scripturally based) are eschewed for the insights that are born out of the vulnerability of prayer and spiritual struggle and tested in the field.

7
———

Why Kenoticism Rests on a Mistake: Reflections on the Christologies of Sarah Coakley and Gregory of Nyssa

Dennis W. Jowers

I. Introduction

In her essay "Does 'Kenosis' Rest on a Mistake?"[1] Sarah Coakley conjectures that "two-minds"[2] and kenoticist[3] Christologies abound

1. *Exploring Kenotic Christology: The Self-Emptying of God*, ed. C. Stephen Evans (Oxford: Oxford University Press, 2006), 246–64.
2. A two-minds Christology is an account of Christ's ontological constitution according to which Christ's humanity and his divinity co-instantiate a single individual nature that possesses two consciousnesses, one divine and the other human. Contemporary advocates of two-minds Christologies include Thomas V. Morris (*The Logic of God Incarnate* [Ithaca, NY: Cornell University Press, 1986], esp. chapters 1–4); Richard Swinburne (*The Christian God* [Oxford: Oxford University Press, 1994], 192–215); and Douglas K. Blount ("The Incarnation of a Timeless God," in *God and Time: Essays on the Divine Nature*, ed. Gregory E. Gannsle and David M. Woodruff [Oxford: Oxford University Press, 2002], 236–48).

in today's theological climate for three primary reasons. First, she asserts, classical Chalcedonian Christology appears to many powerless to account for the moral and psychological development of Jesus that the synoptic gospels attest.[4] Kenoticists seek to remedy this flaw in the old Christology, Coakley observes, by minimizing Christ's deity and thus immersing him more fully in the vicissitudes of history.[5] Second, contemporary Christologists tend to neglect the vitally important subject of the *communicatio idiomatum*;[6] and third, moderns tend at least subliminally to regard human and divine greatness as quantities that vary in inverse proportions.[7] This supposition, she holds, combined with otherwise admirable humanitarian instincts, leads Christologists to derogate from the integrity of Christ's divine nature in order to concede maximal autonomy to Jesus, the human being.[8]

Coakley, a skeptic of two-minds and kenoticist Christologies, addresses these concerns with a twofold response. First, she proposes to retrieve substantial elements of Gregory of Nyssa's thought for contemporary Christology: especially Gregory's views on the relation between Christ's divinity and his humanity.[9] Attention to this aspect of Gregory's Christology, she believes, will: (a) show how, within the framework of classical Christology, one can do justice to the human

---

3. Kenoticist Christologies are accounts of the Incarnation according to which Christ, in becoming incarnate, emptied himself of certain divine properties and/or functions. Prominent contemporary kenoticists include Stephen Davis ("The Metaphysics of Kenosis," in *The Metaphysics of the Incarnation*, ed. Anna Marmodoro and Jonathan Hill (Oxford: Oxford University Press, 2011), 114–33); Ronald J. Feenstra ("A Kenotic Christological Method for Understanding the Divine Attributes," in *Exploring Kenotic Christology*, 139–64); and C. Stephen Evans ("The Self-Emptying of Love: Some Thoughts on Kenotic Christology," in *The Incarnation: An Interdisciplinary Symposium on the Incarnation of the Son of God*, ed. Stephen T. Davis, Daniel Kendall, and Gerald O'Collins [Oxford: Oxford University Press, 2002], 246–47). One can integrate elements of kenoticism and the two-minds theory into a single account of the Incarnation. Cf. e.g. Brian Hebblethwaite's "The Propriety of the Incarnation as a Way of Interpreting Christ," in his *The Incarnation: Collected Essays in Christology* (Cambridge: Cambridge University Press, 1987), 53–76, esp. 68.
4. Ibid. 263.
5. Ibid., 246.
6. Ibid., 247–48, 260–61.
7. Ibid., 262, 264.
8. Ibid., 264.
9. Ibid., 248, 257, 263–64. Cf. also Coakley's "'Mingling' in Gregory of Nyssa's Christology: A Reconsideration," in *Who Is Jesus Christ for Us Today? Pathways to Contemporary Christology*, ed. Andreas Schuele and Günter Thomas (Louisville: Westminster John Knox, 2009), 72–84, at 72–73 and 80.

frailty, struggles, and growth of Jesus highlighted by the synoptic gospels;[10] and (b) help goad contemporary theologians and philosophers out of their indifference to the *communicatio idiomatum*.[11]

Second, in order to address concerns about the putative incompatibility of Christ's deity with his humanity, Coakley exposes a patently fallacious premise that frequently underlies such worries: viz. the notion that God and human beings resemble each other sufficiently to compete for power and dignity. God transcends the created universe so vastly, Coakley observes, that creaturely flourishing cannot conceivably encroach on the divine prerogatives.[12]

The cure Coakley proposes for what she considers the regrettable attachment of theologians and philosophers to kenoticist and "two minds" Christologies, then, is: (a) the selective appropriation of Gregory of Nyssa's understanding of the relation between Christ's human and divine natures; and (b) a healthy appreciation for the ontological distance that distinguishes God from creatures. To remedy (b), I have no objection. Remedy (a), however, the proposal that contemporary theologians take up certain elements of Gregory of Nyssa's Christology, gives reason for pause. In the following, therefore, I hope to outline my concerns about the wisdom of reviving Gregory's Christology.

After so doing, then, I shall briefly take up the question of how one might satisfy Coakley's legitimate concerns without invoking problematic aspects of Gregory's thought. I shall argue, specifically, that, in order to remedy the shortcomings Coakley perceives in contemporary Christology, one must achieve two objectives. First, one must vindicate the patristic and medieval conceptions of nature and person that orthodox Chalcedonian Christology presupposes. Second, one must uncouple the notion of a hypostatic union from that of the communication of the highest degree of created grace conceivable to Christ's humanity from the first moment of its existence. For it is the assumption that the former entails the latter that motivates

10. Ibid., 248, 257, 263.
11. Ibid., 248, 264.
12. Ibid., 261–62, 264.

most ascriptions to Jesus' humanity of superhuman qualities like omniscience and immunity from illness: precisely the kind of ascriptions that lead two-minds and kenoticist Christologists to reject classical Christology as implausible.

I agree, then, with Coakley's negative assessment of kenoticist and two-minds Christologies. I disagree, however, with her views as to the origins of these aberrations from conciliar orthodoxy, and I regard the principal remedy she proposes for them as problematic. In the following, therefore, I shall argue that the aspects of Gregory's Christology that Coakley proposes to revive entail highly undesirable consequences and that one can address her legitimate concerns by less problematic means. Before criticizing Coakley's proposal, however, I should like to emphasize my agreement with the broad outlook on questions of Christology and the relationship between God and the world that Coakley defends. I wholeheartedly endorse the following theses, for example, each of which Coakley enunciates herself and each of which I take to be fundamental to her approach to Christology:

1. Incarnation is not metamorphosis. The two notions are distinct and, in principle at least, need not intersect at any point.[13]

2. The eternal Son is capable of assuming a human nature into hypostatic unity with his person without forgoing the possession of a single divine attribute: indeed, without forgoing the full use of the divine attributes.[14]

3. The hypostatic union in no way compromises the integrity of Christ's human nature.[15]

4. The nature of God and that of human beings differ so radically that exalted conceptions of the former cannot conceivably detract from the dignity of the latter.[16]

The reflections that follow, accordingly, by no means constitute assaults on Coakley's overall christological project. They constitute,

13. Ibid., 261.
14. Ibid., 248.
15. Ibid., 262, 264.
16. Ibid., 262.

rather, tentative suggestions as to the course she should pursue in advancing her christological agenda.

II. Gregory of Nyssa on the Hypostatic Union

1. *Introduction.* Three primary difficulties, it seems, limit the usefulness of Gregory of Nyssa's Christology for the purpose of reconciling conciliar orthodoxy with the synoptic gospels' testimony to human frailties, struggles, and growth in the human life of Jesus. First, Gregory sometimes speaks as if he advocates a *homo assumptus* Christology: a Christology, that is to say, in which Jesus the man and the eternal Logos constitute distinct ontological subjects. Second, Gregory also suggests at times that Christ's divine nature may transform Christ's human nature so radically that this nature comes to lack all distinctively human characteristics and to exhibit instead the characteristics of the divine. Third, at least as Coakley understands Gregory, he maintains that the Logos progressively unites Christ's human nature to his divine person by communicating the properties of the divine nature to the human in the degree in which the human can absorb them. In the following, I shall elaborate on the nature and implications of each of these concerns and so justify my designation of them as difficulties.

2. *Proto-Nestorianism?* Numerous statements in Gregory's corpus suggest that he attributes a human hypostasis distinct from that of the divine Logos to the man Jesus. He refers, for instance, to Christ's human nature as "the man who was united to him"[17] and "the man according to Christ."[18] After speaking of how Christ "bore our sicknesses and carried our plagues" (Isa. 53:4), he avers that Christ's divinity did not suffer, but rather "the man conjoined to the divinity by the union."[19] Referring to Christ's prayer in Gethsemane, "Not my will, but yours be done" (Mark 14:36; Matt. 26:39; Luke 22:42), Gregory asks, "Is the

---

17. *Antirrheticus adversus Apolinarium* 53 in *Gregorii Nysseni Opera* [henceforth cited as *GNO*], ed. Werner Jaeger et al., 10 vols. (Leiden: Brill, 1921–), 3/1:222. I shall cite the full title of each of Gregory's works when I first refer to it. Thereafter, I shall employ the standard abbreviations for these given in the *Lexicon Gregorianum*, ed. Friedrich Manns, 7 vols. (Leiden: Brill, 1998–).
18. *In illud, Tunc et ipse filius (GNO* 3/2:14).
19. *Antirrh* 21 (*GNO* 3/1:160).

one who prays man or God? If one holds that it is God who prays, God appears as weak as human beings. How, then, is it that God, who has no need of good from without, prays for assistance from above? How is it that he condemns his own will?"[20] Gregory scoffs, that is to say, at the notion that the eternal Logos, whose will is identical with his Father's,[21] utters the prayer, "Not my will, but yours be done."

Gregory, likewise, harshly censures Apollinarius for asserting that God was born of a woman, ate food, experienced fatigue, and died at Golgotha.[22] He censures Apollinarius, that is to say, for employing precisely the sort of language that the Councils of Ephesus and II Constantinople endorse as orthodox in view of the unity of Christ's person.[23] Many regard the Christology of Gregory and the other Cappadocians, moreover, as foundational for that of Nestorius.[24]

These considerations, admittedly, hardly suffice to convict Gregory of Nestorianism *avant la lettre*. For Gregory vigorously disputes the charge of Apollinarius and Eunomius that he proclaims two Sons, a divine and a human, in Christ,[25] and he usually refers to that which Christ assumes in the Incarnation as human nature: not a man. His discussions of Phil. 2:6–7, furthermore, typically make it plain that he conceives of the one who exists in the form of God and the one who assumes the form of a servant as the same subject;[26] and unlike Nestorius, he does not shrink from calling Mary the Mother of God.[27]

Gregory, then, as I shall demonstrate more fully below, is no

---

20. Ibid., 32 (*GNO* 3/1:180).
21. Gregory specifically denies that the Father and Son differ in will (*Ad Graecos* [*GNO* 3/1:25]). Indeed, he admits no distinction whatsoever between them except that between a cause and that which it causes (*Ad Ablabium, quod non sint tres dii* [*GNO* 3/1:56]).
22. *Antirrh* 25–6 (*GNO* 3/1:167–68, 171–72).
23. Cf. esp. the twelfth of Cyril's anathemas (DH 263) and the second, third, and tenth canons of II Constantinople (DH 422–23, 432).
24. Cf. e.g. the assessments of Aloys Grillmeier, *Christ in Christian Tradition 1: From the Apostolic Age to Chalcedon (451)*, trans. John Bowden, 2nd ed. (London: Mowbray, 1975), 368; and John A. McGuckin, *St. Cyril of Alexandria: The Christological Controversy: Its History, Theology, and Texts*, Supplements to *Vigiliae Christianae* 23 (Leiden: Brill, 1994), 130n19.
25. Cf. *Antirrh* 35, 53 (*GNO* 3/1:185, 221) and *Contra Eunomium* 3.3 (*GNO* 2:128–33).
26. Cf. e.g. *Antirrh* 20 (*GNO* 3/1:159); *Eun* 3.2 (*GNO* 2:70); *Refutatio confessionis Eunomii* (*GNO* 2:319); and *De beatitudinibus* 1.4 (*GNO* 7/2:84). For more on Gregory's interpretation of these verses, cf. Lucas F. Mateo-Seco, "Kénosis, exaltación de Cristo y apocatástasis en la exegesis a Flp 2, 5–11 de Gregorio de Nisa," *Scripta Theologica* 3 (1971), 301–42, esp. 305–18.
27. Cf. Gregory's *De virginitate* 13 and 19 (*GNO* 8/1:306, 322) and *Ep.* 3.24 (SC 363:142). Gregory's at least verbal acceptance of Mary's divine maternity, incidentally, does not preclude his making

Nestorian. He writes as if he were, however, because he lacks the sophisticated understanding of the nature/hypostasis distinction necessary to make sense of the ontology of the Incarnation. One cannot reasonably fault Gregory for this deficiency, because the understanding in question emerges only after centuries of theological reflection subsequent to Gregory's death. It seems instructive, nonetheless, to sketch the concepts required to articulate Gregory's Christology in such a way that it does not savor of Nestorianism.

In order to avoid unintentionally Nestorianizing statements like those into which Gregory falls, it seems that one must distinguish sharply between a hypostasis and a nature when discussing Christ's ontological constitution.[28] Christ's human nature, as the most acute patristic defenders of Christological orthodoxy conceive of it, is not the human species as such, but the nature of this species as it exists in the one man Jesus: an individual nature, in other words, rather than a generic one.[29] Christ's person, in the view of these thinkers, is a hypostasis in the sense that it constitutes a concrete whole that is not part of anything more comprehensive than itself.[30] Natures, in this view, do not exist in isolation from hypostases, i.e., individual, concrete things.[31] "Treeness," the nature of a tree, for example, exists only in individual trees; and natures constitute the means by which hypostases are what they are. They are not hypostases, sc. the individual, concrete things, themselves.

An intelligent person, who employs the terms "nature" and "hypostasis" in these senses and is not a Nestorian, accordingly, will

statements like the following: "He who was formed in the belly of the virgin, according to the word of the prophet, is the slave, not the Lord" (*Ad Simplicium, de fide* [GNO 3/1:63]).

28. His signal contribution to the establishment of this distinction on the plane of Trinitarian theology notwithstanding, Gregory almost never applies his nature/hypostasis distinction to the ontology of Christ.

29. Cf. e.g. Leontius of Byzantium, *Epilyseis* 1 (PG 86:1917); Leontius of Jerusalem, *Contra Nestorianos* 1.20 (PG 86:1485); and John of Damascus, *Expositio fidei* 55 in *Die Schriften des Johannes von Damaskos*, ed. Bonifatius Kotter, 5 vols., PTS 12 (Berlin and New York: De Gruyter, 1969–88), 2:131.

30. Cf. e.g. Leontius of Jerusalem, *Contra Nestorianos* 2.1, 5 (PG 86/1:1529, 1544); John of Caesarea, *Apologia concilii Chalcedonensis* 4.6 (CCG 1:55); and Maximus the Confessor, *Opusculum* 23 (PG 91:264).

31. Cf. e.g. Leontius of Byzantium, *Contra Nestorianos et Eutychianos* 1 (PG 86/1:1280); Leontius of Jerusalem, *Contra Nestorianos* 2.13 (PG 86/1:1560–61); and John of Damascus, *Expositio fidei* 53 in Kotter 2:128.

never refer to Christ's human nature as a man, because a man is a hypostasis, not a nature. Likewise, such a person will never deny, at least in an unqualified manner, that he who suffered on the cross is God or that he who was a carpenter in Nazareth is the Father's eternal Word. For the pronoun "he," *per definitionem*, refers to a person, not a nature. Whether the name by which one refers to Christ's person derives from his divine nature (e.g., "God") or from his human nature (e.g., "a carpenter in Nazareth"), therefore, one must assert that this person performed all acts done through Christ's divine or his human nature. Only thus can one ensure that she does not implicitly deny the hypostatic union of Christ's natures.

Gregory's inability to articulate the nature/person distinction in a way that is adequate to the task of formulating an orthodox Christology, then, renders it difficult for him to reflect on these subjects without occasionally compromising the unity of Christ's person and thereby anticipating Nestorius.

3. *Proto-monophysite?* In addition to the Nestorianizing aberrations we have considered, Gregory also often appears to espouse a mitigated Eutychianism. Specifically, although he recognizes that Christ's flesh remains visible and undergoes all of the hardships of human life before Jesus' resurrection, he often speaks as if, after Christ's ascension, his divine nature transforms his human nature so radically as to render it indistinguishable from the divine. Gregory claims, for instance, that the Son, after his ascension, "having suffused with the infinity of divine power that humble first-fruit of our nature, made this [the first-fruit] also to be that which he himself was . . . making all things, as many as are considered by pious thought to be in God, to be also in that which was assumed by the Word."[32] In the post-ascension Christ, he asserts:

> All things that formerly appeared "according to the flesh" [2 Cor. 5:16] are transformed into the divine and undefiled nature. Neither weight, nor form, nor color, nor solidity, nor softness, nor spatial limitation, nor anything else of the things that formerly appeared endures. Through

32. *Eun* 3 (*GNO* 2:132).

mixture with the divine, the humility of the fleshly nature takes on the divine characteristics.[33]

Indeed, Gregory appears at least once baldly to declare that Christ's human nature no longer exists after his ascension. "Christ," he writes,

> was always, both before the *oikonomia* [the Incarnation] and after it. The man [i.e., Christ's human nature], however, existed neither before this nor after these things, but only in the time of the *oikonomia*. For neither before the virgin did the man exist, nor after the ascension into the heavens did the flesh retain its own characteristics. "For though we knew Christ according to the flesh," it says, "now we know him thus no longer" [2 Cor. 5:16].[34]

These quotations, which one could easily multiply, might appear to establish conclusively that Gregory endorses post-ascension monophysitism. A wider reading of Gregory's works, however, indicates that Gregory does not intend to eradicate all distinctions between Christ's deity and his humanity even after the ascension. For Gregory regards human salvation as contingent on the union of human beings with Christ's body: not merely his mystical body, the church, but his individual, human body.[35] "Since only that God-bearing body received this grace," he writes, "our body cannot become immortal otherwise than by participating in incorruption through fellowship with that immortal body."[36]

The church militant realizes this fellowship most intensely in the

---

33. *Antirrh* 42 (*GNO* 3/1:201).

34. Ibid. 53 (*GNO* 3/1:222–23).

35. Gregory rarely, if ever, unambiguously distinguishes between Christ's physical and his mystical body. This omission presumably reflects scriptural usage and Gregory's distinctive ideas about universals: the same ideas that lead him to deem the term "men," as opposed to "man," catachrestical (*Abl* [*GNO* 3/1:40–41]; *Graec* [*GNO* 3/1:26–28]). Also worthy of notice, however, is the polemical exigency of interpreting in a non-subordinationist fashion 1 Cor. 15:28: "When all things have been subjected to him, then the Son himself will be subjected to the one who subjected all things to him, that God may be all in all." In his brief tractate devoted to the problem, Gregory accomplishes this by equating the Son's final subjection to his Father with the ultimate submission of the church, his body, to God (*Tunc et ipse* [*GNO* 3/2:20–23]). For further discussion of Gregory's interpretation of 1 Cor. 15:28, cf. Elena Cavalcanti, "Interpretazioni di 1 Cor. 15, 24, 28 in Gregorio di Nissa," in *Origene e l'Alessandrismo Cappadoce (III–IV secolo)*, ed. Mario Girardi and Marcello Marin, Quaderni di "Vetera Christianorum" (Bari: Edipuglia, 2002), 139–70.

36. *Oratio catechetica* 37 (*GNO* 3/4:94). For the risen Christ's ongoing consubstantiality with the human beings who comprise his mystical body, cf. also *De perfectione* (*GNO* 8/1:197) and *In Canticum Canticorum* 13 (*GNO* 6:381–82).

Eucharist, and Gregory does not consider the utter transformation of Christ's humanity after the ascension as a hindrance to this. In Gregory's view, rather, this transformation is a prerequisite *sine qua non* of the divinization of the human race. After identifying the Holy Spirit with the glory, which the Father gave the Son (John 17:22), and he in turn gave to his disciples, which the Son also possessed with the Father before the creation of the world (John 17:5), Gregory explains:

> It was also necessary for the flesh [i.e., Christ's flesh], by mixing with the Word, to become that which the Word is. This happens when that [the flesh] receives that which the Word had before the world. This was the Holy Spirit; for nothing else was before time except the Father and the Son and the Holy Spirit. Therefore . . . the text says, "The glory that you have given to me, I have given to them" [John 17:22] so that through this [i.e., the glory, the Holy Spirit] they might be united to me and through me to you.[37]

For the world to be united through Christ to the Father, Gregory believes then, Christ's flesh must become that which the Word is, viz. divine. The post-ascension transformation of Christ's human nature that Gregory envisions thus plays a crucial role in his soteriology.[38]

That Gregory affirms the continued existence of Christ's human nature after the ascension, however, scarcely suffices to obviate the difficulty posed by the apparent indistinguishability of the two natures as Gregory conceives of them. His emphasis on the continuing role of Christ's post-ascension flesh in the salvation of humankind, in fact, seems to render this difficulty more acute.

In Gregory's defense, admittedly, one might argue that his distinction between the divine essence, on the one hand, and the divine attributes and energies, on the other, enables him consistently to assert that the risen Christ's natures are ontologically distinct even if they are qualitatively identical.

---

37. *Tunc et ipse* (GNO 3/2:22).

38. Aloys Grillmeier is correct, naturally, in observing that Gregory strips the risen Christ's humanity of its distinctive attributes and replaces them with divine properties at least partially in order to counter the Apollinarian charge that he acknowledges two Sons in Christ (*Christ in Christian Tradition* 1, 375–76). The radical divinization of Christ's post-ascension humanity, however, also functions in Gregory's theology as the initial stage in the divinization of all humanity. Cf. e.g. *Ref Eun* (GNO 2:368) and *Or cat* 25 (GNO 3/4:63).

Gregory distinguishes, that is to say, between God's nature, which is utterly incomprehensible by creatures, and his attributes and energies, through which creatures can know something of God. "The divine nature as it is," Gregory explains,

> remains unexpressed by any of the names that are conceived for it. . . . For when we learn that [God] is a benefactor, and a judge, and good and just, and however many such things there may be, we are taught distinctions of energies. Yet we are not at all capable of knowing the nature of the one who works by consideration of the energies. For when one assigns a definition to each of these names and a definition to the nature of that to which the names refer, one will not assign the same definition to both. Because the definitions are different, however, the natures of these things are different as well.[39]

Gregory seems to posit, then, not merely a logical, but an ontological distinction between the divine essence and those attributes and/or energies to which the divine names refer.[40] It might seem possible to reconcile Gregory's affirmation of the enduring distinctness of Christ's divine and human natures with his attribution of the same properties to each, therefore, by arguing that, given Gregory's essence/attribute distinction, he could consistently assert both that Christ's risen humanity remains distinct from his divinity and that this humanity exemplifies all of the divine properties.[41] Certain of Gregory's

---

39. *Ad Eustathium, de sancta trinitate* 8 (*GNO* 3/1:13).

40. Cf. e.g. *Eun* 1 (*GNO* 1:86); *Abl* (*GNO* 3/1:42–43) and *Beat* 6.3 (*GNO* 7/2:140–41). I am not unaware of texts in which Gregory might appear to identify one or more divine attributes with the divine essence: e.g. *Eun* 1 (*GNO* 1:95); *In Ecclesiasten homiliae* 7 (*GNO* 5:406–7); and *Vita Moysis* 1.7 (SC 1:50). Gregory never argues for this position, however, and one can plausibly interpret the few statements in which he seems to identity essence and attribute in God as hyperbole. Gregory argues extensively, by contrast, for the necessity of distinguishing between the divine essence and God's attributes/energies, contending, among other arguments, that one who identified the two would implicitly compromise God's simplicity and transcendence. Cf. e.g. *Eun* 2 (*GNO* 1:315) and 3 (*GNO* 2:308). It seems safe to conclude, therefore, that Gregory does posit an ontological, and not merely an epistemic, distinction between the divine attributes/energies and God's essence. For more thorough discussions of these issues, cf. Basil Krivocheine, "Simplicity of the Divine Nature and the Distinctions in God, according to St. Gregory of Nyssa," *SVThQ* 21 (1977): 76–104 and Andrew Radde-Gallwitz, *Basil of Caesarea, Gregory of Nyssa, and the Transformation of Divine Simplicity*, Oxford Early Christian Studies (Oxford: Oxford University Press, 2009), 175–224.

41. George Dion Dragas, for example, vindicates the coherence of Gregory's Christology with precisely such an argument. Cf. his "The Anti-Apollinarist Christology of St. Gregory of Nyssa: A First Analysis," *GOThR* 42 (1997): 299–314 at 309–10.

utterances about the role of properties in distinguishing diverse natures, however, tend to blunt the force of this defense.

Gregory explicitly states, for example, that distinct entities can instantiate different natures only if the characteristics of the two entities differ in some respect. "Each subject," he writes,

> possesses certain tokens through which the distinctive character of the subject's nature is recognized. . . . A tree and an animal are not known by the same marks. Nor, among animals, do the distinguishing signs of the human being have anything in common with those of irrational animals. Nor, again, do the same indicators manifest life and death. In every case, rather . . . , the differentiation of subjects is unconfused and exclusive. Nor are any things confounded by some sharing of the tokens by which things are recognized.[42]

Gregory holds, then, that beings of a given nature necessarily differ from those of other natures in that they possess certain identifying tokens that characterize beings of their nature alone. This implies, he recognizes, that if two entities possess precisely the same attributes, they must possess the same nature as well, for, if they differed in nature, this difference would manifest itself by the presence of diverse characteristics. Given two subjects, he writes, "If they were to declare them [the subjects' attributes] to be the same, there would no longer be diversity of nature between them. By the sameness of the distinguishing characteristics they would be combined."[43]

The risen Christ's human nature, as Gregory envisions it however, seems to exhibit no characteristics that distinguish it from Christ's divinity. "Whatever is weak and subject to death in our nature," Gregory writes, "by being mingled with the divinity, has become that which the divinity is. . . .For whatever one might see in the Son is divinity."[44] By asserting that God communicates the divine attributes to Christ's humanity, therefore, Gregory implies that this humanity has metamorphosed into the divine.[45]

---

42. *Eun* 1 (*GNO* 1:174–75).
43. Ibid. (*GNO* 1:176).
44. *Ad Theophilum adversus Apolinaristas* (*GNO* 3/1:126).
45. Gregory arguably expects the entire human race to undergo a similarly radical transformation in the eschaton. For, first, he holds that the ideal divine image of Gen. 1:26–27a resembles the divine

Admittedly, as Coakley[46] and Brian Daley[47] observe, Gregory's comparison of the Son's human nature to a drop of vinegar mixed with the ocean does not imply that, in his view, the intermingling of Christ's two natures entails the obliteration of Christ's humanity.[48] Admittedly, moreover, the Pauline analogy of a seed growing into a plant (1 Cor. 15:35–50) undercuts many arguments from the radical disparity between Christ's post-ascension and his pre-ascension humanity to an essential distinction between the two.[49] These considerations, nevertheless, seem insufficient to eliminate the difficulty posed by those statements of Gregory that seem implicitly to identify Christ's post-ascension humanity with his deity.

4. *A progressively enacted hypostatic union?* Coakley raises the specter of yet another difficulty for Gregory's Christology when she appears to conjecture that, in Gregory's view, the eternal Logos becomes the subject of Christ's human nature only gradually over the course of his earthly sojourn. According to Gregory, she asserts, the change effected in Christ's humanity by the hypostatic union does not occur instantly. Rather, she explains,

nature in an extraordinary degree. He characterizes it, for instance, as not merely immortal and incorruptible, but also as ἀπαθής (*Or cat* 6 [*GNO* 3/4:25]), asexual (*De hominis opificio* 16.7 [*GNO* 4/2:200]), and incorporeal (*De mortuis* [*GNO* 9:62–63]). Twice, moreover, he poses the question of how the ideal divine image differs from God and identifies only two respects in which the ideal image falls short of deity: viz. createdness (*Op hom* 16.12 [*GNO* 4/2:204]) and mutability (ibid.; *Or cat* 21 [*GNO* 3/4:51]). Second, Gregory holds that at the general resurrection, God will restore all human beings to this ideal divine image. Cf. e.g. *Op hom* 17.2 (*GNO* 4/2:210); *In Eccl* 1 (*GNO* 5:296); and *De anima et resurrectione* (PG 46:148). For more on the nature of the ideal divine image as Gregory conceives of it, cf. esp. Jérome Gaïth's *La conception de la liberté chez Grégoire de Nysse*, Études de philosophie médiévale 43 (Paris: J. Vrin, 1953), 40–66. One should note, incidentally, that in Gregory's view, God does not create Adam and Eve in the ideal divine image referred to in Gen. 1:26–27a. God supplies them with corporeal, sexual characteristics that are incompatible with the ideal image, rather, in order to ensure the continuance of the human race after the fall. On this, cf. *Op hom* 17.4–5 (*GNO* 4/2:211–12) and J. Warren Smith's "The Body of Paradise and the Body of the Resurrection: Gender and the Angelic Life in Gregory of Nyssa's *De hominis opificio*," *HTR* 92 (2006): 207–28.

46. "'Mingling' in Gregory of Nyssa's Christology," in *Who Is Jesus Christ for Us Today?* 77, 82–83.
47. "Divine Transcendence and Human Transformation: Gregory of Nyssa's Anti-Apollinarian Christology," in *Re-Thinking Gregory of Nyssa*, ed. Sarah Coakley (Oxford: Blackwell, 2003), 67–76 at 71–72.
48. Anastasius of Sinai (*Hodegos* [PG 89:240]), nonetheless, finds it necessary to argue against the monophysites that Gregory does not intend by his analogy to confound Christ's natures. Anastasius implausibly argues that Gregory means merely to illustrate how vastly the divine nature transcends humanity (*Hodegos* 13 [PG 89:240]).
49. This analogy figures prominently in the argument for the bodily resurrection of human beings that Gregory places on Macrina's lips in *An et res* (PG 46:152–60).

it is throughout the lifetime of Jesus' ministry, life, and death—and supremely and decisively in the resurrection—that this purification and transformation occurs; not that there is *sin* to be removed in Jesus himself, but merely a plumbing of every weakness and *pathos* that is characteristic of the genuinely human. . . . The "personhood" of Christ is thus not, as in Cyril, already pre-identified (*qua* Logos) such that . . . the assumption of human characteristics looks like a mere takeover bid that instantly trumps weakness—or else rhetorically declares the Logos the subject of it without further explanation. . . . What Gregory proposes is a real, but gradual, transfusion of divinity into the human until, as he memorably puts it, the humanity is "absorbed by the omnipotent divinity like a drop of vinegar mingled in the boundless sea."[50]

This characterization of Gregory's views on the hypostatic union seems problematic for two reasons. First, it is not certain that Gregory would recognize his Christology in Coakley's portrait of it. After mentioning Luke 2:52, "Jesus grew in wisdom, stature, and grace," for instance, Gregory writes:

> Let no one, because of this, wrongly interpreting the Gospel, believe that by a certain progress and gradual succession our nature in Christ was transformed into something more divine. For "he grew in wisdom, stature, and grace" is recorded in Scripture to show that the Lord was truly in our lump [i.e., human nature][51] in order that there may be no place for the view that, instead of a true manifestation of God, there was a certain apparition, outfitted with a human form.[52]

Gregory, then, seems anxious to avoid the impression that he views Jesus as gradually progressing from mere manhood to full divinity. "The man in Mary, in whom Wisdom built her own house," he writes,

---

50. Coakley, "Does 'Kenosis' Rest on a Mistake?" 257–58.
51. When Gregory refers to human nature as a lump (φύραμα), he typically alludes to Rom. 11:16: "If the first-fruit is holy, so is the lump; and if the root is holy, so are the branches." Cf. e.g. *Eun 3* (GNO 2:70, 294); *Ref Eun* (GNO 2:346, 374, 386–87); and *Cant* 13 and 14 (GNO 6:381, 391, 427). Gregory employs this imagery to characterize the relationship between Christ's individual humanity, in which the entirety of the human race is divinized *in radice*, and human nature as such, which Christ's divinity, beginning with the individual humanity of Jesus, gradually suffuses until the entirety is united to God. "The man [i.e., Jesus himself] according to Christ constitutes a kind of first-fruit of the common lump," Gregory writes, "through whom all humanity is assimilated to the divinity" (*Tunc et ipse* [GNO 3/2:14]). For further discussion of the relation between the first-fruit of Christ's individual humanity and the common lump of humanity as a whole, cf. esp. Reinhard Hübner, *Die Einheit des Leibes Christi bei Gregor von Nyssa: Untersuchungen zum Ursprung des "physischen" Erlösungslehre*, Philosophia Patrum 2 (Leiden: Brill, 1974), 95–167.
52. *Ep.* 3.16 (SC 363:136).

"though of his own nature he was of the passible lump, when the Holy Spirit came upon her, and the power of the Most High overshadowed her, he immediately became that which the overshadowing one by nature was."[53] Gregory thus explicitly rejects the notion that Jesus became more divine as his life progressed.

One ought to distinguish, moreover, between what Gregory believes occurred at the moment of Christ's conception and how the deity, in Gregory's view, transformed Christ's flesh after his ascension. When the Word became flesh, Gregory writes, he "put on our shame in the form of a servant" (Phil. 2:7).[54] This involves no association of the Word with evil, Gregory believes, because sin alone is objectively evil, and the human nature of Christ is devoid of all sin.[55] Nor does the Incarnation compromise the immutability, impassibility, etc. of Christ's divine nature, for it remains immune from the suffering of Christ's flesh. In Gregory's words, "He was poor according to the form of a servant [Phil. 2:7], but blessed according to the nature of deity."[56] Nor, furthermore, does Christ shed the poverty of the form of a servant, i.e., infirmities like liability to suffering, before his resurrection.

At his ascension, however, God, who had assumed the form of a servant in the Incarnation, "lifted it up to his own grandeur, having transformed it into the divine and undefiled nature."[57] It is then that Christ's humanity, as Gregory understands it, is "transformed into the divine and undefiled nature [so that] neither weight, nor form, nor color, nor solidity, nor softness, nor spatial limitation, nor anything else of the things that were formerly perceived endures."[58] This transmutation of Christ's humanity into an at least quasi-divine nature, according to Gregory, occurs at Jesus' ascension, not during his life. *Pace* Coakley, then, Gregory does not seem to portray Jesus' human nature as progressively assimilated to his divinity during his sojourn on earth.

53. *Ep.* 3.19 (SC 363:138).
54. *In inscriptiones Psalmorum* 2.8 (*GNO* 5:98) on LXX Ps. 92:1.
55. Cf. *Or cat* 15–16 and 28 (*GNO* 3/4:44–49 and 71–72).
56. *Inscr* 2.12 (*GNO* 5:124) on LXX Ps. 40:1.
57. *Antirrh* 25 (*GNO* 3/1:170).
58. Ibid., 42 (*GNO* 3/1:201).

Second, if Gregory did hold that God accomplished the hypostatic union by progressively infusing Jesus' human nature with qualities of the divine nature, he would seem thereby to imply that a creature, by progressing through various stages of divinization, could eventually become divine. This consequence would be highly problematic, because it would compromise divine transcendence, which Gregory is keen to uphold. For, if God is infinite, and everything other than God is finite, then the gradual accretion of characteristics that are not simply identical with the Godhead cannot conceivably render a subdivine being equal to God the Father. A sum of finite increments, be it ever so vast, cannot comprise an actual infinite.[59]

Third, a union accomplished through the suffusion of one nature with the characteristics of another would not constitute a properly hypostatic union. For the key insight communicated by the statement that Christ has two natures, but only one hypostasis, it seems, is that the Son's human nature belongs to him, because it shares the subsistence of the person of the Logos. Only thus, it seems, can Christ's human nature preserve its integrity.

For no individual nature can possess incompatible attributes. Christ's humanity, for example, cannot be both passible and impassible. If one nature suffused the other, therefore, every incompatibility between the two natures' attributes, e.g., that between the divine's omnipresence and the human's confinement to one place, would be resolved in favor of one nature or the other. This is precisely what happens in kenotic and two-minds Christologies and one of the principal reasons for Coakley's dissent from them.[60]

---

59. This truism underlies Gregory conviction that, because God is infinite, the saints may progress in their likeness to him forever. Cf. e.g. *Eun* 1 (*GNO* 1:112); *Cant* 8 (*GNO* 6:245–6); and *Vit Moys* 1.7 (SC 1:50).

60. Cf. Coakley's "Does 'Kenosis' Rest on a Mistake?" 260–62. Two-minds Christologist Thomas V. Morris, for example, asserts that, in order to reconcile one's concept of human nature with the doctrine of the Incarnation, one must eliminate from one's conception of human nature every attribute that could not conceivably characterize the divine nature (*The Logic of God Incarnate*, 62–69). Morris holds this view, because he ascribes a lone individual nature to Christ (38) and considers Christ's divinity and humanity distinct only in the sense that kind-natures such as "human" and "animal" are distinct (39–40). Between two kind-natures, as they exist in an individual nature that instantiates them both, only a conceptual distinction intervenes. No ontological disparity differentiates Socrates *qua* human, for instance, from Socrates *qua* animal. In order to avoid incoherence, therefore, Morris and other two-minds Christologists must denude

Classical Christology, by contrast, states that Christ possesses two individual natures united by their subsistence in a single hypostasis precisely in order to explain how Christ can simultaneously possess the incompatible properties scripture ascribes to him: e.g., neither sleeping nor slumbering (Ps. 121:4) and sleeping in the back of the boat (Mark 4:38; Matt. 8:24; Luke 8:23).

Conceiving of the union between Christ's human and his divine nature as a coincidence in one hypostasis rather than a direct merger of natures, moreover, is essential to conceiving of an Incarnation in which only the person of the Logos assumes human flesh. For, according to the classical conception, the entire Godhead constitutes the nature of each of the divine persons. Any nature with which the divine nature, *per impossibile*, fused itself would thus perforce be equally the nature of the Father, the Son, and the Holy Spirit. If Gregory's Christology dictated that God accomplished the union between Christ's natures by gradually imparting the Son's divine nature to his humanity until, after a long period, the two were one person, then, this Christology would jeopardize not only the doctrines of God's infinity and immutability, but also that of the Incarnation and suffering of the Word alone. If, then, as Coakley suggests, Gregory conceived of the process whereby the Word becomes flesh as "a real, but gradual, transfusion of divinity into the human,"[61] this would hardly render a revival of Gregory's Christology constructive or desirable.

III. Addressing Coakley's Concerns

It would be unfair, naturally, to conclude this critique of Coakley's proposals concerning Gregory of Nyssa's Christology without addressing the legitimate concerns she raises and proposing some alternative means of resolving them. As we noted in the introduction, Coakley recommends the retrieval of Gregory of Nyssa's Christology:

both the Godhead and humanity of essential attributes until neither possesses a single characteristic that essentially distinguishes it from the other.

61. Coakley, "Does 'Kenosis' Rest on a Mistake?" 258.

(a) in order to articulate a fundamentally classical Christology that is compatible with the biblically attested psychological, intellectual, and moral development of Jesus *qua* human being; and (b) to provoke renewed reflection on the unjustly neglected topic of the *communicatio idiomatum*.

It is the first concern, in particular, that motivates her advocacy of the third putative aspect of Gregory's Christology discussed above. One can do justice to this concern, it seems, if one disjoins the logically quite distinct notions of hypostatic union and the plenitude of habitual grace. Although medieval, Western Christologists almost universally believe that the possession of the plenitude of habitual grace by Christ's human nature follows necessarily from this nature's subsistence in the person of the eternal Word, their arguments for this conclusion are typically quite weak. Representative of scholastic reasoning on this subject are the following remarks of Thomas Aquinas:

> Grace is caused in the human person by the presence of the divinity, just as light in the air is caused by the presence of the sun. . . . The presence of God in Christ, however, is . . . by the union of the human nature with the divine person. Hence, it is understood that the habitual grace of Christ follows upon this union, as light follows the sun.[62]

Precisely why the "presence of the Godhead" must bring in its train the plenitude of habitual grace Aquinas does not explain. In his context, presumably, this is a truism. Today, by contrast, the notion that the hypostatic union of an intelligent creaturely nature with the divine Logos necessarily results in the immediate bestowal of the plenitude of created grace upon the nature assumed hardly seems obvious. Inasmuch, then, as this theologoumenon not only appears to lack warrant, but threatens the credibility of classical Christology as a whole, it seems that one can and ought to withhold assent from it and thus allow for development in Jesus' human character and psyche by less radical means than Coakley proposes.[63]

---

62. *Summa theologiae* III, q. 7, a. 13, corp. in *Opera omnia* 11 (Rome: S.C. de Propaganda Fidei, 1903), #47185.

As for the second concern that leads Coakley to advocate retrieval of Gregory's Christology, the inattention of contemporary Christologists to the doctrine of the *communicatio idiomatum*: it seems that one could more effectively increase appreciation of this doctrine by vindicating the understandings of nature, person, and their potential interrelations that Chalcedonian Christology presupposes. For advocates of two-minds and kenoticist Christologies typically regard the notion that distinct individual natures could subsist in one and the same person as untenable, if not absurd. Such persons, that is to say, almost uniformly believe with Thomas V. Morris that "no individual can have more than one individual-nature."[64]

One who holds such beliefs, however, will inevitably find even remotely orthodox doctrines of the *communicatio idiomatum* profoundly unattractive. For one cannot reasonably speak of a *communicatio* of *idiomata* between Christ's natures if Christ does not possess two individual natures, whose *idiomata* differentiate them; and one cannot justify the *communicatio* of distinct individual natures' *idiomata* if they do not subsist in a single hypostasis, a single subject of predication.

V. Conclusion

On the whole, therefore, Coakley's strategy of recalling contemporary Christology to its classical moorings by retrieving aspects of Gregory of Nyssa's Christology seems ill-conceived. The proto-Nestorian and proto-Eutychian strains in Gregory's Christology severely limit its usefulness in a post-Chalcedon environment. The notion of a progressively advancing hypostatic union that she finds in him poses much graver difficulties than it resolves; and her legitimate concerns, in any event, appear susceptible of redress by other, less radical means. This is not to say, naturally, that Coakley's work on Gregory of Nyssa lacks merit. Her work on mysticism and gender in Gregory is rightly celebrated, and her study of Gregory's image of a vinegar drop mingled

---

63. For further argumentation against the notion that the hypostatic union entails the inherence of the plenitude of created grace in Christ's human nature, cf. Edwin Chr. van Driel, "The Logic of Assumption," in *Exploring Kenotic Christology*, 265–90 at 281–89.

64. *The Logic of God Incarnate*, 38. On the same page, Morris declares this claim "a necessary truth."

with the ocean thoroughly refutes a common misreading of Gregory's analogy.

Coakley's defense of a broadly Chalcedonian Christology, moreover, evidences a commendable willingness to resist the tides of theological fashion. Her advocacy of such Christology, when purged of ill-advised appeals to Gregory of Nyssa, will, *ceteris paribus*, surely prove more persuasive, and, it is to be hoped, lead others to join her in defending an orthodox perspective on the ontology of Christ.

8

Sarah Coakley and the Prayers of the Digital Body of Christ

Matthew John Paul Tan

I became all things to all men, so that by all means I may win some.

– 1 Corinthians 9:22

Our artificial progeny will grow away from and beyond us. . . . In time their activities may become incompatible with the old Earth's continued existence.

– Hans Moravec, *Robot: Mere Machine to Transcendent Mind*

Introduction

There is a hint of familiarity behind the fantastic plots of science fiction films like *The Matrix* and *Avatar*. Such films reflect our contemporary cultural situation where humans and machines have melded into apparently seamless social complexes.[1] How is the church to respond to this context? Does the Great Commission enjoin the church to undergo its own "cyborgification"? While many accounts speak of the necessity for the church to engage cyberspace as a potential frontier for the kingdom of God, these operate off an as-yet ill-defined theological discourse on the church's relationship to cybernetics. There is also a question of whether systematic theology can make any inroad in evaluating this cultural form.

Is the Internet more than an instrument, but a powerful cultural form? To frame it in biblical terms, is cyberculture merely a "tainted thing" that Jesus enjoins the wise use of, or is it a "principality and power" against which Paul enjoins constant vigilance? If it is the latter, how are the church's identity and mission affected by its immersion in it, and can systematic theology articulate a possible answer to this problematique? Sarah Coakley's work on contemplative prayer provides an important interpretive key toward systematic theology's engagement with cyberculture. This paper will begin its answer by arguing with Graham Ward that far from a neutral space, cyberspace is a practice. Moreover, it will argue that cyberspace is a deficient practice of contemplative prayer. These parallels thus hint at an approach that does not simplistically reject cyberculture and abandon those stuck in its vortex. Indeed, because it is but a distorted practice of prayer that can be corrected, the immersion in cyberspace can be similarly redeemed.

By reference to the act of logging on, this paper will show the important overlaps that exist between the creation of the cyber-subject and Coakley's coverage of *kenosis* that creates the subject in contemplative prayer. At the same time, however, systematic theology proves important in identifying the dangers of cyberspace insofar as one's staying in cyberspace is merely a mimicry of contemplative prayer. It does not share the ends of true contemplative prayer as outlined in Sarah Coakley's work, which is the full corporeal and

---

1. Mike Featherstone and Roger Burrows, "Cultures of Technological Embodiment: An Introduction," in *Cyberspace, Cyberbodies, Cyberpunk: Cultures of Technological Embodiment*, ed. Mike Featherstone and Roger Burrows (London: Sage, 1995), 8.

spiritual redemption of creation and eventual union with the triune God. To that end, a second section will be dedicated to the identification of the cultural logic within cyberspace that creates divergences from the practice of Christian contemplative prayer. While the game may be given away prematurely, we should note here that while the latter seeks the full redemption of all creation in both spirit and body, the core of the former eschews corporeality and treats the body as "mere jelly," in the words of Hans Moravec.[2] This paper will conclude by looking at how the ecclesial body of Christ can remain "in but not of" cyberspace not by means of better codes of conduct or bureaucratic measures, but by its linkage with a site of cultural counter-logic. This paper will see how specifically sacramental ecclesial life, exemplified by the Eucharist, constitutes such a site.

Logging In and Demon(ad)ic Subjectivity?

A fair evaluation of the church's relation to cyberspace must begin by identifying areas of overlap between the ecclesial body of Christ and the cultural logic of cyberspace. To do that, one must focus on the rich political dynamics that occur in the very act of logging on, which bears unmistakable hallmarks of a cyborg subjectivity. Such an anthropology points to a form of subjectivity that de-centers the autonomous humanist subject celebrated by the Enlightenment. This section will explain why these notions of subjectivity provide important junctures with the Christian subject.

Participation

At first glance, one may notice some parallels between the Trinitarian participation of Christianity and the fissured nature of cybernetic subjectivity at the time of logging in. Graham Ward writes about our participation in a "displaced Body of Christ," in which participation in the Eucharist exposes the interrelatedness of one Christian to another,

---

2. Hans Moravec, *Mind Children: The Future of Robot and Human Intelligence* (Cambridge, MA: Harvard University Press, 1988).

and thus questions the self-sufficiency of the post-Enlightenment subject. In the context of the body of Christ, the Christian subject is mapped out onto other Christians, and one's Christian subjectivity is recognizable only insofar as it is related to other Christian subjectivities.[3] Logging into cyberspace parallels Trinitarian subjectivity insofar as "being" in cyberspace parallels the human need to be in concert with others.[4] This is put into sharper focus when considering the disposition in contemplative prayer as laid out in Coakley's *Why Three?* If prayer is understood to be more than a communication between one static monad (human) and another (God), but a dynamic process of God answering God in and through the one who prays,[5] then it follows that Christian prayer cannot be entered into solely by the will of the autonomous self-sufficient individual of the Enlightenment. That autonomous individual must be divested of any notion of sufficiency, undergo *kenosis*, an emptying of itself, in such as way as to allow God to enter and filter through the pray-er.[6]

The act of logging in to cyberspace similarly displaces the autonomous individual. One must remember that the Enlightenment undercuts any Christian subjectivity insofar as it undercuts the interdependence between one Christian subject and another. In order to "plug in," one must recognize that one has "no originary wholeness distinct from each other."[7] For the self to enter digital space, one cannot conceive of him/herself as "autonomous . . . with unambiguous boundaries."[8] Instead, the cyber subject is built on what Katherine

---

3. Graham Ward, *Cities of God* (London: Routledge, 2000), 102–6.
4. Aristotle Papanikolaou, "Person, Kenosis and Abuse: Hans Urs von Balthasar and Feminist Theologies in Conversation," *Modern Theology* 19 (2003): 49.
5. Sarah Coakley, "Why Three? Some Further Reflections on the Origins of the Doctrine of the Trinity," in *The Making and Remaking of Christian Doctrine*, ed. Sarah Coakley and David A. Pailin (Oxford: Clarendon, 1993), 37.
6. Jason Byassee, "Closer Than Kissing: Sarah Coakley's Early Work," *Anglican Theological Review* 90, no. 1 (2008): 144.
7. Udo Krautwurst, "Cyborg Anthropology and/as Endocolonisation," *Culture, Theory & Critique* 48, no. 2 (2007): 144. See also R. Rapp, "Real-Time Fetus: The Role of the Sonagram in the Age of Monitored Reproduction," in *Cyborgs and Citadels: Anthropological Interventions in Emerging Sciences and Technologies*, ed. Gary Lee Downey and Joseph Dumit (Santa Fe: School of American Research Press, 1997), 32. There Rapp very incisively mentions that "[t]echnologized bodies are eminently social, public, and contested as well as individual."
8. Katherine Hayles, *How We Became Posthuman: Virtual Bodies in Cybernetics, Literature and Informatics* (Chicago: University of Chicago Press, 1999), 290.

Hayles calls a "distributed cognition located in disparate parts that may be in only tenuous communication with one another."[9] Rather than the imposition of the subject onto cyberspace, the cyber-self is rather built up from a plethora of sites where the cyber subject is constituted not merely by its own inputs but those of others as well.[10] At the same time, the space the self occupies within cyberspace is one that is inherently fluid and its shifts are held in check by the will of the host,[11] as well as those of other users.[12] In short, the cyber-self is circumscribed by borders not of its own making. The self that emerges and the zones of operation within cyberspace are both the result of participation in the plethora of informational and infrastructural streams generated by other selves, and its contours become inevitably filtered through the lenses of these other selves. Thus, it would also be impossible "to identify a self-will that can be clearly distinguished from an other-will,"[13] since the subject arises only as it filters itself through the wills of others.

What complexifies cyber-subjectivity even further is the high degree of automation that makes cyberspace work, making it even clearer to us that cyber-selves occupy a social space wherein human agency is not the sole form of activity. Gregory Bateson, one of the early figures of cybernetic theory, remarked that individuals are so interconnected to systems of communication that "boundaries do not at all coincide with . . . either . . . the body or . . . what is popularly called 'the self.'"[14] Cyberspace operates on a series of "feedback loops" between the user and their computer with other users and other computers,[15] and the self is constituted by that interaction.[16] Cyberspace therefore

---

9. Ibid., 3–4. Cutting against the grain of this section, but nonetheless demonstrative of the section's main point, is the outing of an avatar cyber rapist called Mr. Bungles. After much investigation, it was discovered that Mr. Bungles was not a single individual but "a group of male students living in a New York University dorm." For a brief review of this case, see Chris Hables Gray, *Cyborg Citizen: Politics in the Posthuman Age* (New York: Routledge, 2002), 136–37.
10. Nishant Shah, "Material Cyborgs; Asserted Boundaries: Formulating the Cyborg as a Translator," *European Journal of English Studies* 12, no. 2 (2008): 216.
11. J. Zittrain, *The Future of the Internet and How to Stop It* (New Haven: Yale University Press, 2008), 5.
12. Ward, *Cities of God*, 231.
13. Hayles, *How We Became Posthuman*, 4.
14. Gregory Bateson, *Steps to an Ecology of Mind* (Chicago: University of Chicago Press, 2000), 319.
15. Gordon Calleja and Christian Schwager, "Rhizomatic Cyborgs: Hypertextual Considerations in a Posthuman Age," *Technoetic Arts: A Journal of Speculative Research* 2, no. 1 (2004): 6.

crystallizes the point in which "human and social reality is as much a product of machines as of human activity." "[W]e . . . grant agency to machines" insofar as our selves need to be refracted artificially, that is, cybernetically.[17] The ramifications of this latter observation will be considered in detail below. For now, it is sufficient to note that, in the same way that prayer as outlined by Coakley requires the pray-er to be emptied of self and be filled by God, the ability to be in cyberspace requires one to "be other and to move toward the other."[18]

Authority and Vulnerability

The above spoke of a need for others in order to log on to cyberspace and begin the prayer of the digital body of Christ. This second section seeks to articulate what is only implicit in the preceding one, and also tie it with another important point of Coakley's work on prayer. This section seeks to identify the parallels between the cybernetic need for Foucauldian structures of authority with Coakley's point on vulnerability as a prerequisite to prayer.

The intersection of authority with Christian subjectivity pervades the scriptures, from Jesus' instruction to occupy the lowest place, the Apostles' exercise of leadership in the early church, Paul's admonition to "submit to one another," his instruction to submit to the authority of temporal leaders, and the public acknowledgment to the lordship of the lamb in the book of Revelation. How the need for authority intersects with one's being in cyberspace becomes clear when one considers Certeau's point on place. Places do not occupy a category independent of their occupants. Rather, they are unstable and so intimately linked to their occupants that changes in their behavior similarly lead to the displacement of place.[19] In a similar way, a user

16. J. David Bolter and Richard Grusin, *Remediation: Understanding New Media* (Cambridge, MA: MIT Press, 1999).
17. Arturo Escobar, "Welcome to Cyberia: Notes on the Anthropology of Cyberculture," in *Cyberfutures: Culture and Politics on the Information Superhighway*, ed. Ziauddin Sardar and Jerome R. Ravetz (New York: New York University Press, 1996).
18. Michel de Certeau, *The Practice of Everyday Life*, trans. Steven Randall (Berkeley: University of California Press, 1984), 110.
19. Ward, *Cities of God*, 231.

within cybernetic space will increasingly be aware of their position within an "informational entity whose boundaries are not stable but shifting"[20] as *other* users move from one point to another. The shared perceptions of places by more than one user at any one time also means that any sense of stability is dependent not on the isolated volition of an individual. Rather, that individual's sense of stability hangs on the wills of others to keep it stable. In order to be able to "plug in," one requires the acceptance of the terms set by someone you have not met. In so doing the user no longer becomes the autonomous subject of the Enlightenment. Indeed, their very ability to *be* online requires a kind of cybernetic *kenosis* as it submits to a whole range of authority structures, from the host, to the electricity company, to the Internet provider, and sometimes to other users.

One can find numerous subtle ways in which the user's identity, shape, appearance, and modes and content of communication, become not only circumscribed but in some cases determined by a submission to a limited range of choices imposed by others. A cinematic trope can be seen in the movie *Cypher*. The protagonist Morgan Sullivan finds out that his life as a corporate spy for a multinational firm is a drug- and electronically induced façade. In seeking to find out his true identity, he has to follow the instructions of a stranger named Rita, who apparently knows more about this world than Sullivan and thus becomes his constant companion in the made-up worlds he navigates. A minor example is also found in the world of blogging, where one's ability to express oneself is dependent on submitting to limitations of formatting, and the length of entries has to be within the boundaries set by the host. The text, worlds, and figures are perceived in ways that are not determined by the user. In a more pronounced fashion, the appearance of one's avatar in a multi-user domain emerges from a combination of set menus, often generated by commercial interests. In a sense, one's identity is social, and it is never tailor made. There is an apparent power disparity to which the user must submit in order to plug in to cyberspace. There is thus an element of vulnerability

---

20. Hayles, *How We Became Posthuman*, 3.

insofar as the user must shed the fully determined self and assume an alternative circumscribed by others whom s/he has never met. This submission is not to be seen as the end of self-expression. Remember in *Cypher*, the vulnerability of Sullivan to the promptings of a complete stranger, Rita, was key to his realizing who he really was. Indeed, our submission into a particular power structure is what generates the knowledge necessary for self-expression.

In the same way that deference to gatekeepers to circumscribe one's identity allows articulation for the cyber-subject, Coakley reminds us that proper prayer requires a deference to a power structure in which control is ceded to God as supreme, and that this is actually necessary to enable the pray-er to acquire the knowledge categories for his or her own prayer, since those very knowledge categories emanate from an agent external to the pray-er anyway, namely God.[21] In prayer, Christ "disrupts the atomised individual [and] unseats him or her from being in command," leaving the pray-er wide open to the operations of God.[22] The power disparity inherent within the subjectivity of the pray-er is remarked on quite vividly by St. Teresa of Avila. In her *Interior Castles*, Teresa remarks that the refreshment from the divine waters, though it springs within the soul itself, it is not the product of the soul. Contrary to writers of pop-spirituality, where illumination is found from within one's own resources alone, Teresa indicates that an external agent, namely God, is responsible for the spiritual refreshment.[23] Furthermore, Teresa reminds the reader that refreshment does not come on terms set by those that are seeking refreshment. Often the soul would not even understand what it is receiving.[24] Going even further, Teresa also reminds the reader to prepare for the God that holds back the sea to let loose the springs, and actually become overwhelmed by a torrent unleashed by God.[25] Teresa leaves no room

---

21. Sarah Coakley, "Living into the Mystery of the Holy Trinity: Trinity, Prayer and Sexuality," *Anglican Theological Review* 80, no. 2 (1998): 225.
22. Graham Ward, *The Politics of Discipleship*, ed. James K. A. Smith, The Church and Postmodern Culture (Grand Rapids: Baker Academic, 2009), 280.
23. Teresa of Avila, *Interior Castles*, 4th Mansion, 2:4.
24. Ibid., 4th Mansion, 2:6.
25. Ibid., 6th Mansion, 5:3–4.

for doubt that the agenda for prayer is not set by the pray-er as such. Rather, the pray-er is rendered vulnerable because s/he enters wordless into a conversation with the triune God, where the terms are set by the triune God.[26] And like Teresa, Coakley argues that the approach to God is not dependent on the expansion of the self, but on a process of *kenosis*. The self, emptied of self, can thus be "fashioned into an extension of the redeemed, incarnate life" and in that transformation properly articulate itself.[27]

It must also be noted that the authority structure mentioned here is not an abstracted, spiritualized category. Slavoj Zizek seemed to recognize the capital inherent in the very material disciplines within Christianity, and Catholicism in particular, when he spoke of its "deceptive surface of . . . renunciation." It is deceptive because, for Zizek, Christianity's unique contribution lay in showing how the path of renunciation is the gateway to a realm of almost hedonistic pleasure.[28] In the same way, Teresa's articulation and enjoyment of the grandeur of the interior castle comes *because of*, not *in spite of*, her own deference to the very human rules, disciplines, and deprivations of the cloistered Carmelite convent. In this sense, the cybernetic subject assumes almost monastic dimensions, since the limitations brought about by the user's submission to the server and a whole array of parameters actually become the narrow gate by which one enters and articulates itself within the virtually limited realm of cyberspace.

Theology of the Anti-Body

The process of logging on to cyberspace presents a significant area of overlap because the cybernetic subject intersects with the subject of Christian contemplative prayer insofar as one's being requires the other and also requires submission to the authority of another. Here the ecclesial body of Christ dovetails into the digital body of Christ.

---

26. Byassee, "Closer Than Kissing," 144.
27. Coakley, "Mystery of the Holy Trinity," 225.
28. Slavoj Zizek, "The 'Thrilling Romance of Orthodoxy,'" in *Theology and the Political: The New Debate*, ed. Creston Davis, John Milbank, and Slavoj Zizek (Durham, NC: Duke University Press, 2005), 62–63.

As the prayer of the digital body of Christ proceeds however, we find divergences that make the coextension more and more problematic. This becomes apparent when one stops to ask the question: Is the ascent in Trinitarian prayer the same as that in the cybernetic? Coakley's reminder about the *telos* of Christian prayer is instructive here. Prayer is part of God's work of salvation and in this salvation every aspect of the person's emotions, soul *and body*, is swept up.[29] This aspect of bodily redemption is one that the salvation in the prayer of the digital body of Christ more than omits, but actively expunges.

The Cybernetic Return of Gnosticism

At one level, cyberspace repeats many threads of the old heresy of Gnosticism. It is interesting to see even within cyberculture a secular reversion toward religious experience, since technology in general does not merely refer to "items of convenience . . . but as instruments of 'deliverance.'"[30] There is within the logic of technology a desire to transcend the mundane and limited.[31] In an allusion to both New Age spirituality and the predictions of the prophet Joel, Ken Hillis spoke of the Internet's capacity to fire "the Light Within" the user and enable the user to "'see visions' when we close our eyes to the outside world."[32]

The contemporary contours of this techno-Gnosticism are articulated in the story of Kevin Warwick, professor of cybernetics at Reading University who engaged in extensive self-experimentation as part of his research. He has gone on record in regarding his being born human as "an accident of fate—a condition merely of time and place [and] something we have the power to change."[33] At the heart of his

29. Sarah Coakley, "God as Trinity: An Approach through Prayer," in *We Believe in God: A Report by the Doctrine Commission of the General Synod of the Church of England*, ed. Doctrine Commission of the General Synod of the Church of England (Wilton, CT: Morehouse-Barlow, 1987), 110.
30. David F. Noble, *The Religion of Technology: The Divinity of Man and the Spirit of Invention*, 2nd edition (New York: Penguin, 1999).
31. Elaine L. Graham, *Representations of the Post/Human: Monsters, Aliens and Others in Popular Culture* (New Brunswick, NJ: Rutgers University Press, 2002), 165.
32. Ken Hillis, "Toward the Light 'within': Optical Technologies, Spatial Metaphors and Changing Subjectivities," in *Virtual Geographies: Bodies, Space and Relations*, ed. Mike Crang, Phil Crang, and Jon May (London: Routledge, 1999).

displeasure with being human are the limitations of the biological body to the attainment of new skills and knowledge. Warwick sees the body as an accidental quantity and an impediment to the full expression and attainment of superior realities.[34] A telling example of this can be seen in his desire to eliminate language and speaking as a means of communication, opting instead for the electronic transfer of symbols and ideas, so that all manner of communication, even sexual responses (one immediately thinks of the electrode-studded-helmet-induced sexual encounter in *Demolition Man*), become instantaneously transferable between minds without aid of the mouth or hand.[35]

A similar indicator of the attitude of celebration of the transcending powers of cybernetics is Hans Moravec, a former director of robotics at Carnegie Mellon University. Moravec celebrates the wonders of technology precisely because of the hypermobility it affords to one's mind. It is important to note that Moravec goes further than Warwick in his articulation of the mind as the ultimate criterion of humanity. This is because for Moravec, the mind exists independently of its material substrate, namely the brain, hence his labeling of the ideal race as "Mind Children." The self is coterminous with the mind, a highly mobile and portable quantity whose capacities, most importantly, can only increase with the jettisoning of its biological hinges.[36] The availability of technology with increasing powers of information processing can only mean that "many of your old limitations melt away," as the mind, removed from the body can "communicate react and think a thousand times faster" than if it were attached to the brain.[37]

A third indicator that most explicitly articulates the Gnostic celebration of transcending the limitations of the human body in the cybernetic age is Ray Kurzweil. Kurzweil's *The Age of Spiritual Machines*[38]

33. Kevin Warwick, *I, Cyborg* (London: University of Reading Press, 2000). See also idem, "Cyborg 1.0," *Wired* 8.02, http://www.wired.com/wired/archive/8.02/warwick_pr.html.
34. Graham, *Representations of the Post/Human*, 171.
35. Warwick, "Cyborg 1.0."
36. Moravec, *Mind Children: The Future of Robot and Human Intelligence*, 117.
37. Ibid., 112.
38. Ray Kurzweil, *The Age of Spiritual Machines: When Computers Exceed Human Intelligence* (New York: Penguin, 1999).

speaks enthusiastically about the ability to port oneself (that is, one's mind) from one material base to another and leave its "slow carbon-based . . . machinery behind."[39] Kurzweil's celebration of the ability of humans to "transcend biology" was extended in 2005 with an update on this book. One must think of the roadside evangelist covering apocalyptic themes when one sees a book titled *The Singularity Is Near*.[40]

One may find the attitudes of Warwick, Moravec, and Kurzweil somewhat extreme. However, Katherine Hayles assures us that this desire for disembodiment is not the mere ravings of a few isolated intellectuals.[41] There is a widespread fascination with this cybernetically enabled Gnosticism that goes much further than the academy, a Gnosticism that seeks not merely the attainment of greater wisdom but also some kind of deification that comes with the acquisition of more knowledge, and more importantly the casting off of one's mortal coil as a necessary step. Indicative of these are the anecdotes within Ed Regis's *Great Mambo Chicken and the Transhuman Condition*. Regis provides a humorous coverage of real-life attempts by people to use technology for anything from individual space travel to cranial cryogenics as a path to immortality. Underneath the humor, however, Regis expresses a more serious sympathy to the visions of these experimenters to build a post-biological future for humanity. The book indicates that from the most scientific labs to the suburban backyard, there is a sense that the wider culture regards personhood as essentially "minds with bodies attached to them."[42] Because the mind is regarded as the essence of humanity and because the mind is simply a pattern of data that is not dependent on its material substrate,[43] it thus becomes possible, even desirable, to "implement the human being in alternative hardware,"[44] improve capabilities, or even live forever.

These Gnostic tendencies within attitudes to technology generally

---

39. Ibid., 129.

40. Ray Kurzweil, *The Singularity Is Near: When Humans Transcend Biology* (New York: Viking, 2005).

41. Hayles, *How We Became Posthuman*, 1.

42. Ed Regis, *Great Mambo Chicken and the Transhuman Condition: Science Slightly over the Edge* (Reading, MA: Addison-Wesley, 1990).

43. Joseph E. Davis, "If the 'Human' Is Finished, What Comes Next?: Review Essay," *Hedgehog Review* (Fall 2002): 111.

44. Regis, *Great Mambo Chicken*, 153.

are replicated in cyberspace specifically. Michael Heim asserts that more than any other technological engagement, it is "at the computer interface" that "the spirit migrates from the body . . . [and] information and images float through the Platonic mind without a ground in bodily experience."[45] The closer one gets to this Platonic ideal, the less the images in cyberspace merely remain enhanced *reflections* of reality. One must note that cyberspace is the intensification of what Guy Debord calls the "society of the spectacle," where images so saturate social space that there is a disconnect between the simulation and the tangible thing being signified, to the point where the former becomes fetishized and is afforded a higher plane of being, becoming "the tangible par excellence."[46] The projected image of the user's mind assumes a form of "hyperreality" that overwhelms actuality.[47] The cultural backdrop that most vividly indicates these aspirations of disembodiment and also fetishization of the image within cyberspace is the Wachowski brothers' *The Matrix*. In the film, Neo's fulfillment of his calling as "the One" is punctuated with a series of cybernetic enhancements, mainly through the near-instantaneous acquisition of superhuman capabilities fed through the Matrix from the tangible computer terminal on board the *Nebuchadnezzar*.[48] It is important to note that key to the activation of Neo's cybernetic enhancements, as Morpheus points out in the training sequence in the first film, is that his "mind [that] makes it real." The mind remains the sole point of interface with the Matrix. Furthermore, his messianic function, and the deployment of his superhuman abilities for most of the film, can only be carried out within the confines of the Matrix, where his mind retains only the most tenuous connection with his biological body. As a reference to the hyperreality of the Matrix, the simulation of injury or

45. Michael Heim, "The Erotic Ontology of Cyberspace," in *Cyberspace: First Steps*, ed. Michael Benedikt (Cambridge, MA: MIT Press, 1993), 75.
46. Guy Debord, *The Society of the Spectacle* (New York: Zone Books, 1994), 36.
47. Vincent J. Miller, *Consuming Religion: Christian Faith and Practice in a Consumer Culture* (New York: Continuum, 2003), 61–62.
48. As an allusion to earlier sections on the social and hierarchical nature of cyber-subjectivity, it is interesting to note Neo's ability to negotiate the Matrix only when he is plugged in to another with the technological know-how necessary to handle the work-station on board the *Nebuchadnezzar*.

death in the Matrix during a firefight results in the real-life wounding or even demise of some of the characters on board the ship.

At this juncture, some may object to the use of the cyber-fantasy of a movie as an indicator of a culture's attitudes to cyberspace. A response can be furnished at two levels. At one level, Graham Ward notes that the world in *The Matrix* is not fully dissociated from the city in the real world. Indeed, the ability of the film to come to be in the first place is dependent on the available technology that is able to replicate the simulations within the film. In short, Ward argues that the cyber city in the film is merely a conceptual skip from the cyber city in real life.[49] At another level, when speaking of representations of worlds in film, Elaine Graham does not put a neat juxtaposition between the representation of the world and worlds in real life. Indeed, Graham argues that these represented worlds actually are complicit in the *building* of worlds as they become "constituted through representational practices" such as film.[50] Going somewhere between these arguments, it is possible to argue that *The Matrix* actually makes explicit what is hidden in the cultural logic and aspirations of contemporary wired urban culture.

Indicative of these aspirations is the general cultural behavior of the player of *Second Life* or similar MMORPGs where the church wishes to extend the body of Christ. The avatar, with enhancements ranging from the fantastic (e.g., special weapons or magical powers) to the more mundane (e.g., immense wealth, intense relationships, or a successful commercial interest), is the Gnosticized self of the gamer, because the avatar's lure lies in its possession of abilities or attributes that the corporeally bounded player in real life lacks. Yet for all its endowments, the avatar is also a figure in need—of the constant gaze

---

49. Ward, *Cities of God*, 244. The tech-Gnosticism indicated above rides on the contemporary city's global capitalist social milieu, which is itself Gnostic. Indicative of this is Naomi Klein's *No Logo*, where she describes global economic players as essentially "souls" (expressly used in Klein's book) of a corporate mythology. Though these souls need to be instantiated in the products themselves, they actually desire to transcend what binds them to materiality and seek "to rid themselves" of what is "cumbersome" and "loathsomely corporeal." These impediments are manifest not just in their labor force and plants, but also their very products. See Naomi Klein, *No Logo* (New York: Picador, 1999), 22, 196.

50. Graham, *Representations of the Post/Human*, 26.

of the gamer. So long as the avatar is in play, the gamer must remain at their terminal to control and witness its every move. According to the anecdotal evidence of players of MMORPGs on *Second Skin*,[51] the ability of the gamer to live out this Gnosticized self requires ignoring of the needs of the physical body, such as proper food (if any), sleep (again, if any), calls of nature, and the carrying out of forms of employment to enable the nourishment of the body. The general attitude of the interviewees indicates a disregard of the corporeal self, as the lure of the wildest cognitive concoctions become manifested in the life of the avatar and shift the gamer's existential center of gravity.

Bodies Broken for Who and for Any

While the preceding section spoke of transference of one's being from wetware to software, one must consider also what Nishant Shah calls "reverse translation," whereby the users' investment in cyberspace reaches the point where their physical bodies are deliberately made to conform to online realities.[52] While cyberspace may not lead to an abandonment of the body for many, the machine still is "exogenously introduced . . . [and is] disrupting the operation of the . . . body."[53] The disruption here is both cultural and biological because representations within cyberspace are building a pervasive ecology that is affecting changes in the aspirations of corporeality, and thus adversely shifting attitudes to and practices on bodies as they are currently found. But before considering the biological breakdown wrought by cyberspace, attention must first be given to its cultural disruption. Graham Ward reminds us that there is no conception of the body, however biological, outside a particular social conglomeration of practices and communications.[54] As such, discussing the fate of biological bodies must first begin with the discussion of the fate of social bodies in real terrain, in particular the ecclesial body as it displaces itself into the digital body of Christ.

51. Juan Carlos Pineiro Escoriaza, *Second Skin* (2008).
52. Shah, "Material Cyborgs," 217.
53. Krautwurst, "Cyborg Anthropology," 145.
54. Ward, *Cities of God*, 91–93.

To enable this, one must return to Coakley's consideration of Christian contemplative prayer. Coakley looks at the way in which prayer, far from being a static and isolated exercise, is always geared toward the establishment of intimacy and communion,[55] and it is within social bodies that such desires become fulfilled. Cyberspace's intersection with prayer can be seen in the deep linkage between the generation of the Gnosticized self and the pervasive hunger for the establishment of cyber-sociality (demonstrated by the recent proliferation of social networking sites within cyberspace). The question thus arises on whether the digital body of Christ, while it treads on safe ground in the logging-on phase, can also fulfill a distinctly Christian communion of the ecclesial body of Christ as cybernetic prayer deepens. What will become apparent as the essay unfolds is that as social bodies as they are currently found become pulled into the orbit of cyberspace, they share the same fate as the physical body, in that their current states are found lacking. While cyberspace may have not yet led to the abandonment of these bodies, it is becoming increasingly responsible for modifying, reconfiguring, and even breaking these bodies. With this in mind, this segment would explore the ways in which bodies are being modified in cyberspace, and how its incompatibility with the body of Christ lies in an anti-sacramentality that is not averse to the fragmentation of all bodies, biological and social. To understand the fragmentary nature of cyberspace, one must first be aware of the two mutually reinforcing social institutions that serve as cyberspace's central guiding cultural tropes. Their importance lies in their responsibility for the germination and maintenance of cyberspace. One refers here respectively to the state (the Internet was created first to further military capabilities of the state) and the market (as the institution that both extends and also overwhelms the capabilities and the cultural logic of the state) respectively.[56]

---

55. Coakley, "Mystery of the Holy Trinity," 224.
56. Some may question the continued salience of the state in cybernetic innovation. However, Chris Hables Gray makes the observation that with its long-held aversion to "technological surprise," the state continues to be a major sponsor of commercial research in cybernetics, and in some

Many might regard the state as a purely administrative apparatus that harmlessly hovers over subsidiary social bodies without unreasonable interruption. In contrast to this, William Cavanaugh very compellingly outlines a brief genealogy wherein a common thread in the thought of Bodin, Hobbes, Rousseau, and Locke consisted of a primary concern for the modern concept of peace and the unity of the state. According to these thinkers, this unity was impaired by competing social compacts like the church. Peace thus became dependent on the shift of "religion" from the premodern involvement of very social and very physical disciplines, communities and practices, to an internalized and spiritualized set of beliefs that denied the church any sociality. For Cavanaugh, this development paved the way to divide the church as a political community and absorb its members into the ostensibly more unifying, and thus more peaceful, compact of state.[57] What is of interest here is that the modern state, in corporeally subordinating all social (that is, ecclesial, cultural, linguistic, etc.) bodies unto itself and naturalizing state cohesion as the primary if not sole criterion of communal harmony,[58] becomes complicit in the fragmentation of those very social bodies, and sweeps the fragments into the centrifuge of the state. The word *centrifuge* is apt here, for what intensifies the fragmentation is also the fact that what the state seeks to protect is the autonomous liberal subject which precedes any form of community, and whose integrity is sacrosanct. The compact that the state seeks is thus a series of individual monads mediated by the tenuous link of contracts administered from a distant center. The most fundamental of these contracts is that with the state, since the mechanisms of the state are in place for the sole purpose of preventing any transgression of the individual's integrity by those that the individual has established contractual relations with.[59] The sociality of

areas even conducts in own research, which sometimes overtakes those of industry. See Gray, *Cyborg Citizen*, 165.

57. William T. Cavanaugh, *Theopolitical Imagination: Discovering the Liturgy as a Political Act in an Age of Global Consumerism* (New York: T. & T. Clark, 2004), 33–42.

58. Hints of this can be seen in the writings of Jean-Jacques Rousseau, who spoke of the church as "baneful," not so much for its doctrine, but for the fact that as an embodied communion it impaired true social unity, that is, unity embodied in the nation-state. See Jean-Jacques Rousseau, *The Social Contract* (South Bend, IN: Gateway Editions, 1954), 153–62.

the state is thus a pale shadow of the sociality of other social bodies, since the primary concern is the keeping of one individual at arm's length from another in order to protect their integrity.

Market forces pick up where the state leaves off in our contemporary global consumerist context.[60] In such a context, what can be commodified and marketable becomes the basis of all aspects of non-/human existence and behavior. This is relevant for the purposes of this paper's coverage of cyberspace because commodification paves the way for social atomism on a variety of levels. Commodification preinterprets a product by conceptualizing it in isolation from the social relations that led to the emergence of that product.[61] Commodification is also the primary informing principle that led to the shift in production away from the extended family home, which reduced the significance for extended family members as sites of production and primary social site. With wider availability of goods to fill in the labor provided by the extended family, this led to the downsizing of the family to its present nuclear state as they became more independent, though in a strange twist, this soon solidified into a form of enforced isolation.[62] At a third level, the family became the training ground for consumption as the primary mode of existence, so much so that the scope of all social relations become reduced to that of the individual buyer/seller as the sole legitimate form of sociality.[63] Thus like the state the process of commodification becomes another avenue whereby the horizons of sociality are narrowed and atomized.

The forces of both state and market come to the fore in cyberspace, which is at once an exercise in atomism and commodification. As the prayer of the digital body of Christ deepens, cyberspace as it stands does not allow that body to fulfill the establishment of communal relations that are emotional, mental, and corporeal, as laid out by Coakley. This is because at one level, social bodies within cyberspace

59. Cavanaugh, *Theopolitical Imagination*, 45, 234.
60. For more on this see Kenneth Surin, "Marxism(S) and the 'Withering Away of the State,'" *Social Text* 27 (1990).
61. Miller, *Consuming Religion*, 37–38.
62. Ibid., 46–50.
63. Jeremy Gilbert, "Against the Commodification of Everything," *Cultural Studies* 22, no. 5 (2008): 562.

are made to conform to the logic of the State. Joseph Licklider and Robert Taylor, who in the late 1960s created one of the first online communities—tellingly in the U.S. Department of Defense—spoke of future communities of "geographically separated members" that are joined "not of common location but of common interest," that is, of common linkages that are purely cognitive.[64] At the same time, the primary concern of online communities tend, like their state predecessors, to center on notions of individual integrity. Viewed this way, the notion of a social compact has to proceed from a Hobbesian ontology of violence, where relationships are inherently conflictual and thus must necessarily be governed by domination and war making.[65] The extension of this logic is that protection of individual rights is predicated on its submission to the bearer of the most substantial means of violence. Social cohesion in the modern state therefore is the result of a process of violent domination of the collective over the individual. The violent underpinnings of the state as a collection of individuals mediated by contractual relations is further demonstrated by the observation of a growing number of authors, that in the absence of any shared ends the liberal state is only capable of generating a form of social integration through the deployment of war.[66] Violence then, does not become the anomaly that the state fixes, but is built into notions of community underpinned by the state.[67] Cyber communities extend the logic of the state, since one of their most central ethical issues and most readily visible operations for users involves the invocation of gatekeepers to ostracize or punish (known in some cyber circles as "toading") those that invade the integrity of an individual user. A graphic, but nonetheless demonstrative, case in point is the aforementioned cyber rape within LambdaMOO. Following the incident, a big debate swirled among the avatars within the game

---

64. Katie Hafner and Mathew Lyon, *Where Wizards Stay Up Late: The Origins of the Internet* (New York: Simon & Shuster, 1996), 44.
65. John Milbank, *Theology and Social Theory: Beyond Secular Reason* (Oxford: Blackwell, 1990), 278–325.
66. Cavanaugh, *Theopolitical Imagination*, 46.
67. This would explain Anthony Giddens's observation that the creation and maintenance of the Westphalian state that ostensibly preserves freedom has at the same time been responsible for the increase in the deployment of violence. See Anthony Giddens, *The Nation-State and Violence* (Berkeley: University of California Press, 1987), 50–51.

whereby the main concern was not so much the power to be given to the game's online comptrollers (known as "wizards") that eventually "toaded" Mr. Bungles. Rather, the driving concern for the granting of more powers to the wizards was to maintain the integrity of individual users, which became identified as the main criterion of maintaining social cohesion within the game.[68] The social body within cyberspace, like that of the state, does not resemble the human body at all. Rather, "the body that is enacted is a monstrosity of separate limbs proceeding directly out of a gigantic head."[69]

As cyberspace extends the state's dissolution of the social body into monads joined by a common threat of violence emanating from a distant center, it also extends the dissolution of biological bodies through the market's commodification of the body. Indeed, Arjun Appadurai suggests that there is a deep complicity with the state, market, and body as conceptions of body, mediated by the Internet, become defined by state intervention, which in turn become defined by patterns of consumption.[70] Because cyberspace functions as a cheap substratum that imposes little operational cost on businesses, marketing and communications no longer need to cater for a mass market. Instead, tiny niches can now be created, targeted, and catered for to the point where the primary social unit can be reduced from consumer classes to individual consumers.[71] The market gives consumption a transcendental character as the ambit of individual desires becomes widened within cyberspace to almost infinite proportions. Paradoxically, however, the more individual choice becomes celebrated, the more the particular is subsumed into a standardized (often Westernized) universal.[72] This logic is replicated in cyberspace, for as the digital becomes sublime, the divinization of self equates to the annihilation of oneself, so that it becomes absorbed into and erased by the sublime.[73] As cyber-selves come to be more

---

68. Gray, *Cyborg Citizen*, 137.

69. Cavanaugh, *Theopolitical Imagination*, 44.

70. Arjun Appadurai, *Modernity at Large* (New Delhi: Oxford University Press, 1996).

71. Miller, *Consuming Religion*, 70.

72. Cavanaugh, *Theopolitical Imagination*, 104–5. See also William Cavanaugh, *Being Consumed: Economics and Christian Desire* (Grand Rapids: Eerdmans, 2008), 60–70.

immersed in seas of images generated by powerful market players, the more the desires are tweaked toward them as ideals.[74] Through desire, the borders between the material and the cybernetic are slowly hidden from sight as the avatar becomes mapped back onto the physical body of the user, and "the original" becomes "reshaped and reconfigured to suit the translated [i.e., cybernetic] object."[75] Under such circumstances the particular embodied self becomes unworthy in the face of that digitized transcendental ideal, and is thereby cajoled into conforming to, and eventually disappearing into, that ideal. One sees the most pervasive manifestation of the breaking and disappearance of the particular so as to conform to artificially generated, standardized universals in the fashion and porn industries. The notion of "airbrushed beauty" is particularly relevant here, since it is not just the circulation but also the very *creation* of images of beauty and intimacy in both fashion and pornographic images that are facilitated by cybernetic means, as images of idealized bodies become increasingly filtered through airbrushing software and computer-generated graphic design. More than any other facet of social life, "airbrushed beauty" represents the profound digitally facilitated disconnect between the image and the real, so much so that the image *becomes* the real and overwhelms it.[76] Notions of beauty lose their consonance with what is corporeally present as exposure to such computer-generated corporeality increases. Rather they collapse into cyber-ideals. This leads to a growing sense of disappointment with what is corporeally present,[77] and thus a growing willingness to break skin (through cosmetic surgery)[78] and even bone[79] within individual bodies so that

---

73. Ward, *Cities of God*, 250.

74. Michael Budde does note that this free will now operates within a context whereby the power-balance has shifted in favor of these more powerful economic players. The free will becomes circumscribed to such a degree that freedom becomes one of choosing the options that are provided to you by the economic powers that be, and the exercise of that will serves the interests of those players. See Michael Budde, *The (Magic) Kingdom of God: Christianity and the Global Culture Industries* (Boulder, CO: Westview, 1997), 42.

75. Shah, "Material Cyborgs," 218.

76. Jean Baudrillard, *Symbolic Exchange and Death* (London: Sage, 1993), 66.

77. Maggie Wykes and Barrie Gunter, *The Media and Body Image* (London: Sage, 2005).

78. Times reporter Natasha Walter interviewed British university-aged girls and found an almost universal self-consciousness among her interviewees of their appearance in times of sexual intercourse, whereby virtually all interviewees expressed their desire to sculpt their pubic hair

such bodies could be as beautiful as their universalized cybernetic models. It is difficult to coalesce the ecclesial body of Christ (with its prayers geared toward the creation of communal bonds) with the digital body of Christ (with its form of *kenosis* equating to the dissolution of social and biological bodies).

The Eucharist as De-Centered Embodied Resistance

Given the toxic effects of the cultural logic of cyberspace mentioned in the previous sections, it is a concern that the ecclesial body of Christ should so uncritically celebrate its extension into cyberspace. Nevertheless, it is also equally naïve to categorically shun any association between the church and cyberspace. Doing so would equate to the church's abandoning of its mandate to become all things to all to win some.[80] The real question is whether the ecclesial body of Christ can graft its digital counterpart onto itself without being sucked into the latter's nihilistic center of gravity. This final section seeks to provide a brief answer. In doing so, it would not only look to the framework of prayer laid out by Sarah Coakley, but also look to other practices and the logics therein that do not negate her arguments but rather amplify them in the face of the rather powerful fragmentary vortex of cyberspace. More specifically, this section would look at sacramental praxis, in particular the celebration of the Eucharist, to

and even labia to suit pornographic images frequented by men. See Natasha Walter, "How Teenage Access to Pornography Is Killing Intimacy in Sex," *The Sunday Times* (2010), http://entertainment.timesonline.co.uk/tol/arts_and_entertainment/books/book_extracts/article6990891.ece. See also Pamela Paul, "The Porn Factor," *Time* (2004), http://www.time.com/time/2004/sex/article/the_porn_factor_in_the_01a.html.

79. Among Asian residents in Europe, America, and Asia, "European American physical features" have become so widely disseminated that they "are not only the established aesthetic ideal but are also associated with upward social mobility, respect, acceptance and self esteem." See Kathleen Kawamura and Tiffany Rice, "Body Image among Asian Americans," in *Asian American Psychology: Current Perspectives*, ed. Nita Tewari and Alvin N. Alvarez (Psychology Press, 2008), 543. Where this is most apparent is in the area of height, whereby the desire to be taller is almost seen to be a step in "psychological growth" (as one surgeon summarized the reasons for the procedure's popularity). This has led to a popular practice in Asia of surgical leg extensions where shinbones are separated just below the knee and metal plates inserted to gain on average 9-10 centimeters in height. The practice has recently been banned in China. See Hannah Beech, "High Hopes," *Time* (2001), http://www.time.com/time/world/article/0,8599,187654,00.html.

80. 1 Cor. 9:22.

provide the alternative ecclesial center of gravity to counteract that of cyberspace.

How do the sacraments provide the counterpoint to cyberspace as a practice of prayer? Sarah Coakley correctly asserts that in contemplative prayer, the Christian engages in a waiting to be swept up by God and eventually to behold the beloved.[81] A question emerges, however, when one overlays Psalm 42 to this theme, whereby the psalmist is brought into the house of God in order to see the face of God.[82] The mention of entering into the temple in order to see the face of God in the psalm leads one to ask where Christ's temple, the church, fits in the process of contemplative prayer. Is it primary or epiphenomenal to the individual's prayerful disposition? Thomas Aquinas suggests that it is the church that is the proper starting point for the beholding of God.[83] This may give rise to concerns that what is being referred to here is an institutional primacy that provides the proper anchor to the contemplative against the vortex of cyberspace. Without meaning to dismiss the importance of ecclesial institutions, it must be noted here that the vortex of cyberspace is the product of a practice, and only a counter-practice of the church can provide adequate resistance. Thomas Aquinas himself seems to suggest similarly that the practices of the sacramental life are what properly constitute the church. "The Church," Aquinas reminds us, "is . . . built up with the sacraments which flowed from the side of Christ while hanging on the Cross."[84] This theme builds on what Sarah Coakley has asserted on contemplative prayer. Prayer is properly a work of God. Going further, it is also an incorporation into an ecclesial body, which in turn emerges from a sacramental practice. In this final section, attention will be paid to the Eucharist as exemplary form of sacramental practice. While the sacramental life involves more than the Eucharist, the Eucharist more clearly than any other sacrament

---

81. Coakley, "Mystery of the Holy Trinity," 230.

82. Ps. 42:2–4.

83. Aidan Nichols, *Discovering Aquinas: An Introduction to His Life, Work and Influence* (London: Longman & Todd, 2002), 120–21.

84. Thomas Aquinas, *Summa Theologiae* IIIa, q54, a2, ad.3.

anchors the ecclesial body of Christ *vis-à-vis* cyberspace by simultaneously praying with the digital body of Christ at the logging-in phase, and providing counterpoints to the aforementioned cybernetic logics as the latter's prayer deepens.

In the Eucharist, the ecclesial body of Christ affirms the digital by affirming an interdependent subjectivity rather than an autonomous one. The pray-er in the Eucharist is not an isolated monad assembled alongside other monads. The Eucharist allows for no atomized individualism, for the offering of the Bread for the sacrifice of the mass is not that of merely one individual. Rather it is the whole people of God, brought into the body of Christ, that is offered.[85] The pray-er undergoes a *kenosis*, becoming de-centered as s/he is emptied of self and brought into a larger body of Christ.[86] This de-centering does not erase any distinctions between one pray-er and another into a monochrome unit, yet it reminds the pray-er that, in the body of Christ, his or her individual prayer is somehow articulated through the prayers of other pray-ers and that of the presbyter. At the same time, because the Eucharist is a participation of Christ's sacrifice on Calvary it also de-centers the individual pray-er because his or her prayer is but a participation in an offering of Christ by Christ (the Eastern churches explicitly state that the Eucharist is primarily a work of God, not that of the congregation).[87] No longer is agency resting solely on the pray-er, since it is the Trinitarian Godhead that ultimately articulates the prayer.

While the Eucharist that enacts the ecclesial body of Christ can affirm the digital on the point of an interdependent subjectivity, it also critiques the latter's Gnosticism. It does this because the highest instantiation of the God that transcends the material is articulated through matter, namely bread and wine. Going further, it critiques the Gnosticism of the digital body of Christ because the Bread and Wine also become the real Body and Blood of Christ in real terrain. The presence is thus not symbolic, residing only in the cognitive assent of

---

85. Ward, *Cities of God*, 153.
86. Cavanaugh, *Being Consumed*, 84.
87. See for example the Russian Orthodox *Liturgicon* (Istochnik, 2000), 27.

the believer, but also real and tangible to the bodies of those believers. Salvation is effected not *in spite* of the body. Rather the salvation of Christ is effected *through* it, by the ingestion of the body of Christ into the body of the believer, regardless of the state in which it is found. Paradoxically, it is only through the consumption of the body of Christ by the body of the recipient that the latter is able to be incorporated into the former, and thereby partake of the divinizing process.

Because the Eucharist so affirms the body, it also combats the digital body of Christ's breaking of social and physical bodies by combating its logic of subjugation of the particular by the universal, by overcoming the dichotomy of the universal and particular altogether. For in the Eucharist, the universal is not overlain over the particular; neither is the latter obliterated and absorbed into the former. Rather, the Universal is expressed *through* the particular.[88] The presence of the universal Godhead in the form of that particular bread being broken at that particular eucharistic table affirms the particular as being the key site of the unfolding of the universal.[89] In the Eucharist all elements regardless of their contours are turned toward a center as a source of unity, to form a cohesive whole.[90] Cavanaugh reminds us that this eucharistic cohesion does not mimic the modern hub-and-spoke model, because the center is located not in a single geographical locus, but in a multitude of locations wherever the Eucharist is celebrated, in a variety of rites. Furthermore, in spite of the breaking of the body of Christ for distribution among the faithful, there is at the same time no fragmentation because the faithful are not individually receiving a fragment of the body of Christ, but each individual locality becomes a receiving point of the *whole* body.[91] The particular is not merely "tolerated" or obliterated, but becomes embraced as a "figural

---

88. Daniel M. Bell Jr., "Only Jesus Saves: Towards a Theopolitical Ontology of Judgement," in *Theology and the Political: The New Debate*, ed. Creston Davis, John Milbank, and Slavoj Zizek (Durham, NC: Duke University Press, 2005), 215.

89. Cavanaugh, *Theopolitical Imagination*, 119.

90. Henri de Lubac, *The Motherhood of the Church*, trans. Sergia Englund (San Francisco: Ignatius, 1982), 174.

91. Ibid., 114.

repetition of the other differences" that in turn constitute the universal.[92]

Conclusion

Looking through the lens of Sarah Coakley's *kenotic* contemplation, and looking at cyberspace as a practice of prayer, this paper has shown some of the consonances and incongruities between the ecclesial and digital bodies of Christ. It has shown how the process of logging on provides some areas of overlap between Christian subjectivity and its cybernetic counterpart, insofar as the post-Enlightenment subject has become de-centered and exposed to a profound participation in power structures. Using that same lens, however, this paper has also shown that deep divergences begin to emerge the deeper one immerses oneself in prayer of the digital body of Christ. While the pray-er in the ecclesial body of Christ is both saved in body and soul, and enacts that salvation through embodied communion with both God and others, the digital body of Christ turns the pray-er in a direction that leads to an all-encompassing fragmentation and eventual disappearance.

In spite of these disconsonances, this paper has shown how the ecclesial can redeem the digital, through the enaction of the eucharistic liturgy. It has shown how the liturgy, far from militating against the work of Sarah Coakley, bears a cultural logic that actually could instantiate some aspects of her work on contemplative prayer. In this diagnosis and proposal of avenues of resistance, it is hoped that this paper would assist in combating the toxic effects of cyberspace without ensconcing the church in the technological dark ages. It is hoped that it also provides suggestions in enabling the church to negotiate the many areas in which one part of the body of Christ is connected to another artificially, whether through mobile telephony, social networking, or even something as mundane as bureaucracy, particularly as each of these gravitates toward cyberspace as a convenient, lost-cost operational substrate. Finally, it is also hoped

92. Bell Jr., "Only Jesus Saves," 215; Catherine Pickstock, "Liturgy, Art and Politics," *Modern Theology* 16, no. 2 (2000): 172.

that this paper will provide the basis for a more comprehensive methodology by which the digital body of Christ, anchored to the ecclesial, could fulfill its evangelical mandate in a realm to which more and more people are drawn.

9

———

Power, Sin, and Epistemic Transformation in Sarah Coakley's Theology: Reading Coakley with Foucault

Janice McRandal

Sin is hard to define. It is naïve to imagine sin with clear boundaries. And yet, in the sins we narrate against creaturely difference, there seems an inextricable relationship between sin and power. Perhaps no concept has received greater attention in postmodern discourse than that of power, and here no figure has loomed larger than Michel Foucault. Attending to the power *epistème* of modernity has enabled those concerned with difference and oppression—especially feminists —to face the full force of totalizing and normalizing discourses. However, theologically this has created problems for traditional language of divine power, and the relation between God's power and power discourses has become unclear. In this paper I wish to show that while Foucault's insights into power relations are penetrating, Christian theology needs to offer a counternarrative to the prescribed Foucauldian practices of the self. The art of living for Christians is not primarily a work exercised upon the self. Instead, the Christian tradition points to the bodily and epistemic transformation of selves through prayer and encounter with divine power—a power that is quite different from anything captured by Foucault's analysis of power relations. In her broader theological project, Sarah Coakley invokes silence as the core of a contemplative work that radically remaps the relation between power, language, and bodies. In contemplation, Coakley argues, one may "meet the ambiguous forms of worldly power in a new dimension, neither decrying them . . . nor being enslaved to them, but rather facing, embracing, resisting or deflecting them with discernment."[1]

Michel Foucault and the Limits of Power

It is perhaps time to ask a whole new set of questions about the politics of reading Foucault. How can we, for example, read his texts outside the disciplinary regimes that have so far appropriated his work? How can we let his writing find a voice, a texture and complexity outside the packaged and predictable interpretations of previous readings? How can we release him from the chains of commodified knowledges which highlight, reify and stereotype the complex folds of a thinker? How can we take his work out of the reductive introductions, the shortsighted dismissals, the obscure categories, the normalising labels and the rash generalisations? How can we begin to make his work as complex as the life of the man?[2]

Against Christian theology, Jeremy Carette's challenge is clear: "I maintain that Foucault was an atheist and that his work on religion does not sustain a traditional theological worldview."[3] Such caution is wise; Foucault himself insisted that theology should remain separate

---

1. Sarah Coakley, "Prologue: Powers and Submissions," in *Powers and Submissions: Spirituality, Philosophy and Gender*, Challenges in Contemporary Theology (Oxford: Blackwell, 2002), xix.
2. Jeremy R. Carrette, *Foucault and Religion: Spiritual Corporality and Political Spirituality* (New York: Routledge, 2000), ix.
3. Ibid., xi.

from postmodern theory, and he criticized Derrida for what he believed was an unconscious theology evident in Derrida's work.[4] And yet Foucault has been widely appropriated in Christian theology as well as in broader feminist, queer, and cultural theories. Indeed, Foucault's work is now a major strand of "postmodern theology,"[5] and it continues to challenge and stimulate thinking in areas such as Christian history, understandings of the self, human sexuality, and religious practices and belief. For feminists the influence of Foucault's work has been felt most forcefully in the areas of knowledge and power.[6] Feminist scholarship continually returns to Foucault as a means of framing the complex relationships of knowledge, power, history, and context.

In *The Order of Things*, Foucault laid out the epistemological framework from which he would later develop as his interest diverged toward theories of power and subjectivity.

> The present study is an attempt to analyse this experience [of knowledge]. I am concerned to show its developments. . . . Language as it has been spoken, creatures as they have been conceived and grouped together, and exchanges as they have been practiced; in what way, then, our culture has made manifest the existence of order, and how, to the modalities of that order, the exchanges owed their laws, the living beings their constants, the words their sequence and their representative value, what modalities of order have been recognised, posited, linked with space and time, in order to create the positive basis of knowledge as we find it in employed in grammar and philology, in natural history and biology, in the study of wealth and political economy.[7]

In seeking out this "inner law" (definitions that expose resemblances and differences necessary for "order"), Foucault was able to argue

---

4. Brian Ingraffa, *Postmodern Theory and Biblical Theology* (Cambridge: Cambridge University Press, 1995), 6ff.

5. A description made in James Bernauer and Jeremy Carrette, "Introduction: The Enduring Problem: Foucault, Theology and Culture," in *Michel Foucault and Theology: The Politics of Religious Experience*, ed. James Bernauer and Jeremy Carrette (Aldershot, UK: Ashgate, 2004), 1.

6. See Monique Deveaux, "Feminism and Empowerment: A Critical Reading of Foucault," in *Feminist Interpretations of Michel Foucault*, ed. Susan J. Hekman, *Re-Reading the Canon* (University Park: University of Pennsylvania Press, 1996), 211.

7. Michel Foucault, *The Order of Things: An Archaeology of the Human Sciences*, a translation of *Les Mots et le choses* (New York: Vintage, 1994), xxi.

for the contingency of historical sciences along with the provisional character of any given epoch's *epistème*. Foucault demonstrated this through his archaeology of not only philosophical research, but also of institutions, commercial practices, and everyday opinions. Later Foucault would remark of his approach, "I have tried to make, obviously in a rather particular style, the history not of thought in general but of all that 'contains thought' in culture, of all in which there is thought."[8] As he developed his work, the category of *epistème* was superseded by his use of *discourse* and *archive*, terms that provided Foucault with a more flexible account of nondiscursive influences, and responded to his critics who saw his work as mere theory, unable to address the "relation between knowledge and human practice."[9] After his pivotal inaugural lecture at Collège de France,[10] Foucault clarified his revised interest in the production of knowledge and the tangled web of knowledge and power. It is against the backdrop of societal systems that Foucault would explore the manufacture of discursive subjects and the prevalence of benevolent power. As Axel Honneth summarizes: "[S]ociety can thus be interpreted as a social system nourished through the twin dispositions of 'power' and 'desire' in which discourse, portrayed precisely as an omnipresent stream of linguistic events, is an object of strategic conflict."[11] Foucault would go on to expose the constant struggles between differing powers enacting their will-to-truth, and would explore the manner in which competing knowledges were contested and rejected. This leads to important conclusions about the way truth claims are used: "[T]he problem does not consist in drawing the line between that in a discourse which falls under the category of scientificity or truth, and that which comes under some other category, but in seeing historically how effects of truth are produced within discourses which in themselves are neither

8. Michel Foucault, "Interview with Raymond Bellours," in *Aesthetics, Method, and Epistemoloy*, ed. James D. Faubion, *Essential Works of Michael Foucualt, 1954-1984* (London: Penguin, 1998).

9. Michael Drolet, "Introduction," in *The Postmodernism Reader: Foundational Texts*, ed. Michael Drolet (New York: Routledge, 2004), 20.

10. Given in 1970. The lecture was titled *The Discourse on Language*.

11. Axel Honneth, *The Critique of Power: Reflective Stages in Critical Social Theory*, trans. Kenneth Baynes (Cambridge, MA: MIT Press, 1993), 151.

true nor false."[12] Foucault's analysis of power has not been without its critics. At the end of his comprehensive study of power in Foucault, Honneth, for example, argues that Foucault was mistaken to interpret societal organizations as power complexes operating in a totalitarian fashion.[13] Further, his theories of power have been judged inadequate to the complexities of late capitalism.[14] In a similar vein, Marxist feminists have been especially cautious about alliances with Foucault.[15]

However, Foucault has done more than anyone to open up a critical dialogue around the subtle interplay between power and benevolent control. The will to power—or the will to truth in Foucault—exposes not only the dominating forces of knowledge production, but also the way subjects are regulated and controlled. From within a theological framework, Foucault's critique of power helps to unmask some of the intricacies of sin in language, society, institutions, and subjects.

Moreover, because power plays such a significant role in the categorizing and subjection of *different* bodies, the work of Foucault has warranted careful attention from feminists. Several themes have emerged as special areas of interest. Foucault raises relentless questions about the creation of norms by which individuals are categorized "as either normal or pathological."[16] For Foucault, norms are produced precisely as a way of managing differences. The production of norms must therefore be interrogated on the basis of their presumed truth and their role in the management of knowledge. Foucault maintained this position until his death in 1982, stating "if we do not take up the history of the relationship between the subject and truth from the point of view of what I call, roughly, techniques, technologies, practices, et cetera, which have linked them together and established their norms, we will hardly understand what is involved in the human sciences."[17] Judith Butler has leaned heavily on Foucault's

12. Michel Foucault, *Power/Knowledge: Selected Interviews and Other Writings, 1972-1977*, ed. Colin Gordon, trans. Colin Gordon et al. (New York: Pantheon, 1980), 118.
13. Honneth, *The Critique of Power: Reflective Stages in Critical Social Theory*, 303.
14. Ibid., 202.
15. See for instance, Shahrzad Mojab, "Muslim Women and Western Feminists: The Debate on Particulars and Universals," *Monthly Review* 50, no. 7 (1988).
16. Margaret A. McLaren, "Foucault and Feminism: Power, Resistance, Freedom," in *Feminism and the Final Foucault*, ed. Dianna Taylor and Karen Vintges (Urbana: University of Illinois Press, 2004), 224.

work regarding norms in her discussion of gender. She argues that the gender norm "is a form of social power that produces the intelligible fields of subjects, and an apparatus by which the gender binary is instituted."[18] Hence Foucault's compendious studies of sexual norms (as well as the correction and punishment of the sexually abnormal[19]) have become integral to contemporary gender theory. Contained in this theory of norms is a peculiar "double bind"[20] in relation to human subjects. In what is often described as a negative (that is, one that refuses cataphatic statements) concept of the individual, Foucault's matrix of power/knowledge and normativity leads to an apparently ambivalent portrayal of the subjectivity. As John Caputo puts it, Foucault sees power as something that "produces individuals precisely in order to block individuality."[21] This does not entail the death or obliteration of the subject as is sometimes suggested,[22] but it points to a second theme of great significance to feminists, namely Foucault's concept of *discursive subjects.*

---

17. Michel Foucault, *The Hermeneutics of the Subject: Lectures at the Collège de France 1981-1982*, ed. Frédéric Gros (New York: Picador, 2001), 188.

18. Butler, *Gender Trouble: Feminism and the Subversion of Identity*, 48.

19. Foucault laid the foundations of the normalizing practices of discourse on sexuality with the inception of categories *deviant* and *pervert* in Michel Foucault, *The Will to Knowledge*, trans. Robert Hurley, vol. 1, The History of Sexuality (New York: Penguin, 1981). Notably, Foucault's challenge to modern "moral" Christian conceptions of sex, women, and erotica has been particularly unsettling. He notes "the nature of the sexual act, monogamous fidelity, homosexual relations, chastity—it would seem that men of ancient times were rather indifferent, and that none of this claimed much of their attention or constituted very serious problems as far as they were concerned. But this picture is not accurate. . . . It thus seemed to me that a whole recentering was called for. Instead of looking for basic interdictions that were hidden or manifested in the demands of sexual austerity, it was necessary to locate the areas of experience and the forms in which sexual behaviour was problematized, becoming an object of concern, an element for reflection, and a material for stylization." Foucault, *The Use of Pleasure*, trans. Robert Hurley, vol. 2, The History of Sexuality (London: Penguin, 1992), 14-15 and 23-24.

20. A phrase used in Hubert Dreyfus and Paul Rainbow, *Michel Foucault: Beyond Structuralism and Hermeneutics*, 2nd edition (Chicago: University of Chicago Press, 1983).

21. John Caputo, "Madness, Hermeneutics and the Night of Truth," in *Michel Foucault and Theology: The Politics of Religious Experience*, ed. James Bernauer and Jeremy Carrette (Aldershot, UK: Ashgate, 2004), 128.

22. For instance, feminist Nancy Harstock has consistently claimed that Foucault discounts the possibility of subjectivity: "rather than getting rid of subjectivity or notions of the subject as Foucault does and substituting his notion of the individual as an effect of power-relations, we need to engage in the historical, political, and theoretical process of constituting ourselves as subjects as well as objects of history. We need to recognize that we can be the makers of history as well as the object of those who have made history." See Nancy Hartsock, "Foucault on Power: A Theory for Women?," in *Feminism / Postmodernism*, ed. Linda J. Nicholson, *Thinking Gender* (New York: Routledge, 1990), 170, 171.

In light of Foucault's archaeological or genealogical approach to epistemology, his theory of discourse is always subject to historical specificities. Each epoch produces discourse that identifies and establishes the authority of knowledge claims. For Foucault this meant problematizing the subject to an unsettling level, a move that required a revision of whatever might generally be meant by consciousness or subjectivity. He states:

> This historical contextualisation needed to be something more than simply the relativisation of the phenomenological subject. I don't believe that the problem can be solved by historicizing the subject as posited by the phenomenologists, fabricating a subject that evolves through the course of history. One has to dispense with the constituent subject, to get rid of the subject itself, that's to say, to arrive at an analysis that can account for the constitution of the subject within a historical framework. And this is what I would call genealogy, that is, a form of history which can account for the constitution of knowledges, discourses, domains of objects etc., without having to make reference to a subject which is either transcendental in relation to the field of events or runs in its empty sameness throughout the course of history.[23]

Thus a discursive subjectivity in Foucault's account is "more than ways of thinking and producing meaning."[24] Discourse not only exercises power over the mind but also ultimately over the body in the subject produced. Further, the discursive production of subjects should not be confused with the effects of power; indeed Foucault speaks of the subject as the "very material of power, the thing through which power finds its expression."[25] Though this is the area in which Foucault has been most criticized by feminists,[26] it is also an area where his influence is felt the most acutely. In the libertine or humanist models of subjectivity that feminists have often used in the past, it was easily imagined that a woman's "self" had somehow been lost. This is clear in

---

23. Foucault, *Power/Knowledge: Selected Interviews and Other Writings, 1972-1977*, 117.
24. Chris Weedon, *Feminist Practice and Poststructuralist Theory*, 2nd edition (Oxford: Blackwell, 1997), 105.
25. Nick Mansfield, *Subjectivity: Theories of the Self from Freud to Haraway* (New York: New York University Press, 2000).
26. For instance, Rosi Braidotti argues rather vehemently against Foucault's account of subjectivity in (chapter 7 especially) Rosi Braidotti, *Nomadic Subjects: Embodiment and Sexual Differences in Contemporary Feminist Theory* (New York: Columbia University Press, 1994).

the language of recovery and retrieval, of pulling women "back" into some foundational or original mode of subjectivity.[27] Though "woman" in Foucault's account is socially constructed in discursive practices, "she none the less exists as a thinking, feeling subject and social agent, capable of resistance and innovations produced out of the clash between contradictory subject positions and practices."[28] Precisely because subjects are able to reflect on the discursive elements of knowledge production, power—which is not necessarily bad, simply ubiquitous—is always connected to resistance. Foucault's analysis of the predicament of the discursive subject, combined with his longstanding work on the way power operates through forms of disciplinary practices and self-surveillance, led him eventually to the critical theme of his later work: *practices of the self.*

Foucault was concerned to respond to claims of pessimistic nihilism in his earlier conceptions of power and the subject. His genealogical accounts fail to prescribe the kind of social remedies that liberationists had hoped for. However, in turning to the study of ethical self-formation of ancient philosophical life, Foucault conceives a "counterattack" against modern systems of power.[29] Margaret A. McLaren offers a compelling argument in favor of Foucault's practices of the self, and suggests that it is only in reading the late Foucault that one can understand the political, non-normalizing, and emancipatory character of practices of the self.[30] In his seminal address *Technologies of the Self,* Foucault gathered his thinking to date (rather loosely) around this theme:

> [W]e must understand that there are four major types of "technologies," each a matrix of practical reason: (1) technologies of production, which permit us to produce, transform, or manipulate things; (2) technologies of signs systems, which permit us to use signs, meanings, symbols, or

27. Ladelle McWhorter critiques this element of dominant feminism and suggests the popular "subject" of such feminism silences creativity and ultimately leads to a defensive conservatism. See Ladelle McWhorter, "Practicing Practicing," in *Feminism and the Final Foucault,* ed. Dianna Taylor and Karen Vintges (Urbana: University of Illinois Press, 2004), 152–56.

28. Weedon, *Feminist Practice and Poststructuralist Theory,* 121.

29. Dianna Taylor and Karen Vintges, "Introduction: Engaging the Present," in *Feminism and the Final Foucault,* ed. Dianna Taylor and Karen Vintges (Urbana: University of Illinois Press, 2004), 3.

30. McLaren, "Foucault and Feminism: Power, Resistance, Freedom."

signification; (3) technologies of power, which determine the conduct of individuals and submit them to certain ends or domination, an objectivising of the subject; (4) technologies of the self, which permit individuals to effect by their own means or with the help of others a certain number of operations on their own bodies and souls, thoughts, conduct, and way of being, so as to transform themselves.[31]

As a technology of potential resistance, "care of the self" in the ancient world was equally concerned with care of the city; the wider context of the ethical was the political. It was expected that care of one's own philosophical and ethical formation would be an act of care for the city. Not only do such practices include diet and exercise, but also writing, learning, and contemplation of oneself for purposes of purification.[32] Ultimately, Foucault looks here to the ancient practice of *askesis*; as *askesis* becomes ethos, it is, Foucault argues, "a process of becoming more subjective."[33] It is through such practices that power can be self-directed as an alternative work upon the body. This concept of practices of the self has become critical to contemporary feminist theory.[34] As a double-edged sword, Foucault's earlier concepts of power/knowledge not only provide insight into the operation of totalizing power, but also challenge the common remedial strategies of liberationist approaches.[35] As Sharon Welch comments: "How do we act after we accept Foucault's challenge and realise that there are no foolproof formulas, that all of our actions are . . . subject to error and challenge?"[36] In practices of the self, feminists find a way to imagine both resistance and transformation as a way of response to Foucault's devastating analysis of power. For Judith Butler:

---

31. Originally presented at the University of Vermont in the fall of 1982. Michel Foucault, "Technologies of the Self," in *Technologies of the Self: A Seminar with Michel Foucault*, ed. Luther H. Martin et al. (Cambridge: University of Massachusetts Press, 1988), 18.
32. Ibid., 33.
33. Ibid., 35.
34. For instance, *Feminism and the Final Foucault* is a book of fourteen essays entirely dedicated to the exploration of contemporary feminism and Foucault's ethos of self-care. See Taylor and Vintges, "Introduction: Engaging the Present."
35. See Bat-Ami Bar On, "Marginality and Epistemic Privilege," in *Feminist Epistemologies*, ed. Linda Alcoff and Elizabeth Potter, *Thinking Gender* (New York: Routledge, 1993), 93–95.
36. Sharon Welch, "'Lush Life': Foucault's Analytics of Power and Jazz," in *The Blackwell Companion to Postmodern Theology*, ed. Graham Ward, *Blackwell Companions to Religion* (Oxford: Blackwell, 2003), 86.

to intervene in the name of transformation means precisely to disrupt what has become settled knowledge and knowable reality, and to use, as it were, one's unreality to make an otherwise impossible or illegible claim. I think that when the unreal lays claim to reality, or enters its domain, something other than a simple assimilation into prevailing norms can and does take place. The norms themselves can become rattles, display their instability, and become open to resignification.[37]

Unitive Prayer and the Limits of Discourse

In Foucault's account of the practice on the self, subjective transformation is in one's own hands. To resist and offer a counterattack to totalizing powers one must exercise the types of discipline that produce alternative discourse/s and subvert the self produced by dominant systems of control. However, Christian practices offer a counternarrative, where the self is "worked on" through bodily and epistemic transformation that comes from outside of oneself. This is not one of the many powers within a social system, but is the power of divine presence. As David Tool points out, Foucault offers a possibility of resistance but it is only a contingent and provisional resistance; he cannot point to anything beyond the self that might fundamentally disrupt the rule of "principalities and powers."[38] Hence, while Foucault comes to affirm the possibility of "mysticism as revolt,"[39] he is ultimately unable to point toward the power of divine presence or the transfiguring meaning of Christian practices. At the same time, feminist attempts to consider power and empowerment have been stunted by extreme caution; efforts to exercise "power games" alert to every possibility of domination will tend to falter in the face of difference.[40] Interestingly, the renewed awareness in recent Christian scholarship of apophatic and mystical traditions has taken place in the context of sustained dialogue with poststructuralist writing. Though

---

37. Butler, *Undoing Gender*, 28.
38. David Toole, *Waiting for Godot in Sarajevo: Theological Reflections on Nihilism, Tragedy, and Apocalypse* (Boulder, CO: Westview, 1988), 269, 270.
39. For an insightful exposition of this theme, see Grace Jantzen, "Power, Gender, and Christian Mysticism," in *Orientalism and Religion: Postcolonial Theory, India and the 'Mystical East,'* ed. Richard King (London: Routledge, 1999).
40. Welch, "'Lush Life': Foucault's Analytics of Power and Jazz," 85.

theologians engaging with such traditions have, as Martin Laird observes, tried to find a way to move beyond the closed "ontotheological fists" of postmodernism, they generally do not address "the practicalities of what must happen to the discursive cognitive strategizing of the one who would encounter this God beyond all discursive knowing."[41] Christian attempts to test the limits of discourse and of power/knowledge require greater attention to embodied Christian practice, a practice that is understood not so much as a species of religious experience but as a way of life.[42]

A common theme in premodern traditions of Christian prayer was the need to quieten discourse. Martin Laird suggests that for the fourth-century monk Evagrius, the discursive mind was the stumbling block to prayer, and prayer was the "letting go of concepts."[43] In the ancient world, discourse could be overcome, and it was possible to distinguish between discursive and nondiscursive states. Here prayer functioned as a means of transcending the normal practices of thinking, speaking, and hearing. Knowing God was assumed to involve something quite outside the normal bounds of what is normally called "knowing." Mary-Jane Rubenstein makes a similar claim in relation to contemporary concerns with theological method and apophaticism. Commenting on the impasse between Derrida and Jean-Luc Marion, she suggests that ontological debate misses the point: "[T]he error of ontotheology is not using the word 'Being' to refer to the deity, but deifying being as knowledge, and, by extension, deifying the knowing subject itself." So for Rubenstein, the problem is with the objectifying epistemology behind such strategies. The self that knows God abandons all knowledge of both the self and the divine.[44]

---

41. Martin Laird, "The Open Country Whose Name Is Prayer": Apophasis, Deconstruction, and Contemplative Practice," *Modern Theology* 21, no. 1 (2005): 141.

42. Martin Laird argues that a key problem in current trends towards apophaticism is the tendency to abstract the apophatic versus cataphatic element of theological discourse, and he reminds readers that the apophatic tradition cannot be reduced to a philosophical strategy. "It is a simple life that leads to the experience of silence . . . and not merely to an apophatic style of theological thinking and writing." Ibid.

43. Ibid., 151.

44. Mary-Jane Rubenstein, "Unknow Thyself: Apophaticism, Deconstruction, and Theology after Ontotheology," *Modern Theology* 19, no. 3 (July 2003): 393.

Sarah Coakley shows in a lengthy essay that the texts of women mystics (and their bodily responses in prayer) push the boundaries of epistemology and discourse. Ironically, Coakley's essay is concerned to show that these texts, and particularly the work of Teresa of Ávila, do not quite work with the epistemic purposes contemporary philosophers have in mind.[45] Though affirming the use of what she calls epistemic "soft centres" (trust, credulity, and testimony) as bulwarks against skepticism in the postmodern context, Coakley argues that contemporary philosophers have failed to take seriously Teresa's rationality. Teresa speaks about the stages of ascent as movements away from discourse that ultimately end in the self being completely unified in its response and taken up "into God in a way that also temporarily suspends its bodily movement and its sensations."[46] Teresa describes this stage of prayer as something beyond the boundaries of discourse: "[H]ow this prayer they call union comes about and what it is, I don't know how to explain. . . . I wouldn't know the proper vocabulary."[47] In this, Coakley suggests, what contemporary philosophy often calls "reason" has gone well beyond its normal limits, into the "dark ineffable realm" of divine union.[48] Not only has discourse been silenced, but the bodily senses are also taken up into the divine life. Teresa witnesses to a self that is worked on in ways she can neither explain nor understand. And yet she "knows" that nothing will cause her peace in God to leave.[49] The normal configurations of knowledge, truth, and power have been transformed and Teresa is no longer the same self—though she could not be said to have achieved this herself through any self-directed "technology."

Though the prayer of union was originally described by Teresa as

---

45. Coakley critiques Richard Swinburne, Reformed epistemologies (Nicholas Wolterstorff and Alvin Plantinga), and William Alston for their stereotypical assumption of the feminine for justificatory purposes in analytic philosophy of religion. Sarah Coakley, "Contemporary Religious Epistemology: The Turn to 'Femininity,'" in *Analytic Theology: New Essays in the Philosophy of Religion*, ed. Oliver D. Crisp and Micheal C. Rea (Oxford: Oxford University Press, 2009).

46. Ibid., 296.

47. Teresa of Ávila, *Life*. Cited in Coakley, "Contemporary Religious Epistemology: The Turn to 'Femininity,'" 297.

48. Coakley, "Contemporary Religious Epistemology: The Turn to 'Femininity,'" 300.

49. Teresa of Ávila, *The Interior Castle Study Edition*, ed. Kieran Kavanaugh and Otilo Rodriguez, trans. Kavanaugh and Rodriguez (Washington, DC: ICS, 1976–85), 437.

occurring in sporadic encounters with the divine, by the time of writing *The Interior Castle* she could speak of a permanent union in which she experiences the tension of complete union with God at one level, and the ongoing trials and tribulations of embodied life at another. In her discursive transformation, Teresa is empowered to live her bodily existence as even her material concerns are brought into the presence of God. Thus Teresa is no longer talking about moments of religious experience, but what might be called an ontology of mystical union. Coakley writes: "[W]hatever this state of union is, it is surely this that . . . [philosophy] should be interested when it attempts to explicate the significance of 'mystical theology' for epistemology. Here we do not so much grasp or 'perceive' God, but more truly God grasps us."[50] Teresa's union with God, brought about through contemplative practices, produces a subject both seeking and finding transformation. In Foucault's terms, the self might be said to be worked upon in ways that evade discursive control. In her study of Teresa, Coakley points to an experience beyond practice and language, opening onto a very different ethos from anything envisaged in Foucault's "care of the self." In her broader theological project, Coakley evokes silence as the core of the "contemplative matrix"[51] in which the relation between power, language, and bodies is radically remapped. In contemplation, Coakley argues, one may "meet the ambiguous forms of worldly power in a new dimension, neither decrying them . . . nor being enslaved to them, but rather facing, embracing, resisting or deflecting them with discernment."[52]

If theologians work with the assumption that transformation happens at the Foucauldian level of discourse, then we will have to conclude that nothing gets through Foucault's net of power. But within Christian traditions of prayer and displacement one finds transformative possibilities in which power and discourse are

50. Coakley, "Contemporary Religious Epistemology: The Turn to 'Femininity,'" 300.
51. Part 1 of Coakley, *Powers and Submissions: Spirituality, Philosophy and Gender*, Challenges in Contemporary Theology (Oxford: Blackwell, 2002).
52. Coakley, "Prologue: Powers and Submissions," in *Powers and Submissions: Spirituality, Philosophy and Gender*, xix.

superseded through a divine power that transgresses—because it does not belong to—worldly webs of discourse or control.

The Triune Life and Divine Power

Though I have been using the language of "power" in relation to God, such talk of divine power remains problematic for most feminist theologians. As Catherine Keller argues:

> Assumed omnipotence, despite (or perhaps because of) the variety of persuasive alternatives now available, continues to dominate Christian imagination. It holds us captive to the "bad faith" of a systemic self-deception. To heal itself, theological power rhetoric requires a moral account of the character of this power and, therefore, of power itself—of the matrix of meanings we mean when we deploy power language.[53]

Keller's remarks betray the assumption that divine power is analogous to "power" as Foucault and other postmodern thinkers understand it. Lurking within the analogy is the assumption too that divine and worldly powers can only be related to one another by contrast and opposition.[54] In this way divine power becomes no more than a projection of (and continuation of the problems with) human power. And Keller's response to this knot of theological misunderstanding is a wholesale abandonment of divine omnipotence in favor of simply a *different* power, which means we are ultimately consigned to the never-ceasing struggle of one (finite) power against another.[55]

The Christian doctrinal tradition does not speak of transcendence, of creative power, of the power of re-creation, as if these belonged to a larger list of "principalities and powers." Divine power is different and does not operate on the same level as Foucauldian discursive power. Talk of divine power requires a radicalized grammar with a severe caution about analogies. Theological language about power and sin

---

53. Catherine Keller, "Power Lines," *Theology Today* 52, no. 2 (1995): 188.
54. In *God and Power*, Keller claims "the idolatry of a 'divine' finite sovereignty is exceeded only by the divinization of sovereignty itself. Historically, divine omnipotence was only achieved as a mimicry of the empire." Keller, *God and Power: Counter-Apocalyptic Journeys* (Minneapolis: Fortress Press, 2005), 51.
55. Keller, "Power Lines," 197ff.

does not simply spill over into the language of divine omnipotence. Talk of divine power is characterized by the way it makes space for the kind of transformation that one finds in contemplative traditions. In prayer, power does not dominate but creates space for the self, its body, and its future in God. In practices of prayer, women and men are invited to wait on the "presence of God." Here omnipotence is a resource that creates personal union—a union that includes (but is not confined to) the domain of discourse. Sarah Coakley shows how prayer and contemplation push us beyond the usual confines of reason and discourse. What occurs in the encounter between human beings and divine power is not a struggle for dominance or control, but what Coakley calls a "willed effacement to a gentle omnipotence."[56] Here the self lovingly receives and is lovingly received by the triune life of God.

56. Sarah Coakley, "Kenosis: Theological Meanings and Gender Connotations," in *The Work of Love*, ed. John Polkinghorne (Grand Rapids: Eerdmans, 2001), 34, 37.

10

From Evelyn Underhill to Sarah Coakley: Women Teaching Theology and the English Context

Stephen Burns

A theologian is one who prays . . .[1]

Sarah Coakley has been hailed as "one of the most influential theologians in the English-speaking world."[2] Jason Byassee elaborates with the explanation that Coakley models an integration of the

---

1. Evagrius, *Treatise on Prayer*, 61. After reading Coakley, I am cautious of taking "classics" out of context, so evoke this phrase simply as "a Christian Orthodox adage," after Janet Martin Soskice, quoted in Tina Beattie, "Vision and Vulnerability: The Significance of Sacramentality and the Woman Priest for Feminist Theology," in *Exchanges of Grace: Essays in Honour of Ann Loades*, ed. Natalie K. Watson and Stephen Burns (London, SCM, 2008), 235–49, 238.
2. Jason Byassee, "Closer Than Kissing: Sarah Coakley's Early Work," *Anglican Theological Review* (Winter 2008), online at: http://find articles.com/p/articles/mi_qa3818/is_200801/ai_n25417690/pg_10??tag etc.

theological academy and the life of faith. Since her ordination to the Anglican priesthood in 2001, her firsthand experience of liturgical presidency has entered more deeply into the pores of her work, to great effect. A woman presiding at table was not even thinkable until just recently. . . . Only more recently still are we learning the radical theological ramifications of that ecclesial decision: a close marriage between the fathers and feminism, orthodoxy and sociology, the theological academy and the prison, the rigors of Christian thought and the joys of the life of faith. That we are doing so is largely due to the work of Sarah Coakley.[3]

I affirm Byassee's sense of the vitality of Coakley's work in contemporary theology, but think it invites a number of questions. In what follows I seek to unfold some of the juxtapositions noted by Byassee, and I do so by touching on four areas, which so far as I can see collapse into each other. First, I recall Evelyn Underhill as a forebear of women theological teachers in England, and someone with special significance for Sarah Coakley herself. Second, I sketch something of the institutional history of women teaching theology in England. Third, I note some of the modes of Coakley's own theology, which she has characterized as "unsystematic systematics"; and finally I focus on one particular strand in Coakley's thinking, about women as presiders in liturgy.

I hope that by the end of these reflections, it will be clear why I think Coakley's paper on "Woman at the Altar"[4] is so important. Throughout, I have made it my concern to try to hold the content, as it were, of Coakley's thought in relation to various contexts. Sometimes I place more weight on content, though usually I place more weight on contexts, as these contexts can, it seems to me, be underestimated in more "systematic" engagements with Coakley's work—and this despite the fact that questions of context surface clearly in Coakley's own reflections on "place,"[5] not to say in the kinds of "transatlantic" comparisons she has sometimes articulated.[6] These contextual features

3. Byassee, "Closer."
4. Sarah Coakley, "The Woman at the Altar: Cosmological Disturbance or Gender Subversion?," *Anglican Theological Review* 86 (2004): 75–93.

of Coakley's work are there to be found whether or not we regard feminist theologies as contextual theologies.

Evelyn Underhill

At least according to one of her biographers, Dana Greene, Evelyn Underhill (1875–1941) was "not a theologian, but a student of human achievement and potentiality."[7] This designation of course invites questions, such as: What, and whose, criteria are being used to define a "theologian," and why? What does a person need to do or be to be counted as a "theologian" as opposed to some other kind of student? Such questions scuttle around my reflections.

Whatever we make of Greene's view, as theologian or not, Evelyn Underhill has attracted the more dazzling descriptor of "saint." In a 1988 revision of the *sanctorale* of the Episcopal Church in the United States, just forty-seven years after her death, Underhill was acclaimed—as Dana Greene notes,[8] contrary to her own designation of Underhill—as "theologian and mystic."[9] Although interest in Underhill has continually blossomed and burgeoned in the U.S., she was herself an English Anglican, and since 1997, June 15, the date of Underhill's death, has also been marked for commemoration in the Church of England's *Common Worship*, in which Underhill is designated as a "spiritual writer."[10] In various *sanctorale*, we find some other

5. Sarah Coakley, "Prayer, Place and the Poor," in *Praying for England: Priestly Presence in Contemporary Culture*, ed. Samuel Wells and Sarah Coakley (London: Continuum, 2008), 1–20.

6. Sarah Coakley, "Shaping the Field: A Transatlantic Perspective," *Fields of Faith: Theology and Religious Studies for the Twenty-first Century*, ed. David Ford, Ben Quash, and Janet Martin Soskice (Cambridge: Cambridge University Press, 2005), 39–55. The introduction to volume 1 of her forthcoming systematics engages directly in similar comparisons.

7. Dana Greene, "Introduction," in *Evelyn Underhill: Modern Guide to the Ancient Quest for the Holy*, ed. Dana Greene (New York: State University of New York Press, 1988), 1–30, 2.

8. Dana Greene, *Evelyn Underhill: Artist of the Infinite Life* (London: Darton, Longman & Todd, 1991), 174n13.

9. Compare, in the English context, Gordon Mursell's assessment of her as "the most important scholar of mysticism in the early twentieth century." Gordon Mursell, *English Spirituality: From 1700 to Today* (London: SPCK, 2001), 414. David Pfatteicher, *New Book of Common Fasts and Feasts: A Proposal for a Common Calendar of Saints* (Minneapolis: Fortress Press, 2008), 292, notes that Underhill was officially first added to the 1997 edition of the Episcopal Church in the United States of America's *Lesser Feasts and Fasts*.

10. In Australasia, the Anglican Church of New Zealand's *New Zealand Prayer Book* of 1989 had already marked June 15 as a day of commemoration for Underhill as a "mystic" and the Anglican Church of Australia's *A Prayer Book for Australia* of 1995 had marked the day for Underhill as "spiritual

descriptors to set alongside "theologian" (such as "mystic," "teacher," "spiritual writer," "person of prayer"), and these provoke more questions, such as: What has theology to do with these various practices of Christian faith, and indeed with holiness, or saintliness?

Evelyn Underhill herself is of course commemorated, as one thing or another, for a remarkable legacy that includes as more-or-less the bookends of her "spiritual writing" *Mysticism* of 1911 (although republished with various revisions, some quite significant, over time) and *Worship* of 1936. Around these major, influential, and regularly reprinted volumes are a wealth of smaller books, pamphlets, papers, and letters on what she came to call "the spiritual life," and through which it is possible to chart a number of shifts in her thinking. The first significant shift was her movement from an apparently "intellectual" interest in mysticism, that is, one not specifically associated with any particular tradition, to a decision to join the Roman Catholic Church (which she did not, because of her spouse's resistance on the one hand, and on the other hand her own sympathy for Catholic Modernism, which was condemned by Pope Pius X in the same year as her decision to join, leading her to reverse her decision). The next significant shift was from attending, for years, Roman Catholic worship while depriving herself of the sacraments, to eventually coming to make a public commitment to the Church of England, the Catholic status of which she was convinced about. As she once said in a celebrated quotation, the Church of England was "a respectable suburb of the city of God—but all the same, part of 'greater London.'"[11] And, finally, a shift from a somewhat unspecified theism to what she described as "com[ing] out strongly and self-commitingly for Traditional, Institutional, Sacramental Religion"[12]—a transition that she and others might have presumed to be a theological one.

It is interesting to begin reflections on Sarah Coakley with some

---

writer." In the 2005 *Uniting in Worship 2*, of the Uniting Church in Australia, the same day was marked for Underhill as a "person of prayer"—and her inclusion in this calendar is perhaps the first major ecumenical recognition of Underhill. Proposals for "a common calendar of saints" place her as a "teacher" (Pfatteicher, *New Book*, 291).

11. Letter to John Chapman, cited in Greene, *Artist*, 101.

12. Greene, *Artist*, 160n77.

attention to Evelyn Underhill because, in a sense, Coakley began her theology with Underhill. She has noted that her interest in the discipline she has come to teach was stirred because, as a child, she found and read and liked books of Underhill's letters—the only "religious" books in the family home: "[S]he was the very first theologian I encountered, because her work happened to be in the house."[13] And there is an obvious affinity of concern with contemplation between Underhill and Coakley, however differently they frame their thinking on this practice: both are passionately preoccupied with what Underhill, picking up an arresting phrase from John Ruysbroeck, wrote of as "the wide open gaze. The simple seeing and staring."[14] But a closer line of connection can also be traced in that the man who, after the death of Evelyn Underhill's spiritual director, Baron von Hugel, replaced him in that role, Dom John Chapman, is the "eminently practical" guide to the kind of contemplation that Coakley has made central to her own theological method.[15] And most directly, Coakley has on occasion explicitly quoted Underhill with appreciation, a notable example being her essay on "Prayer, Place and the Poor" in *Praying for England*, in which she invokes Underhill's insistence that "only a priest whose life is soaked in prayer, sacrifice and love can, by his own spirit of adoring worship, help us to apprehend [God]."[16] Coakley elaborates in her own words:

> without the daily *public* witness of a clergy engaged, manifestly and accountably, alongside their people, in the disciplined, long-haul life of prayer, of ongoing personal and often painful transformation, the Church at large runs the danger of losing its fundamental direction and meaning.[17]

13. Rupert Shortt, ed., "Sarah Coakley: Fresh Paths in Systematic Theology," in *God's Advocates: Christian Thinkers in Conversation* (Grand Rapids: Eerdmans, 2005), 67–85, 65. Notably, a chapter in Shortt's book on feminist theology is shaped in relation to Tina Beattie.
14. Underhill, "The Possibilities of Prayer," in Greene, ed., *Guide*, 147–60, 157.
15. Greene, *Artist*, 104; Sarah Coakley, *Powers and Submissions: Spirituality, Philosophy and Gender* (Oxford: Blackwell, 2002), 40–55.
16. Coakley, "Prayer, Place and the Poor," 7.
17. Ibid., 8.

Women Teaching Theology

Such references apart, it is, I think, the case that *any* woman teaching theology in England might be related to the legacy of Evelyn Underhill, in that, despite Greene's feeling that Underhill was not a theologian, Underhill was, among her formidable achievements:

- in 1893 in the first cohort of women to be admitted to study theology at Kings College, London (albeit in the "Ladies Department," and unable, as a "lady," to graduate with a degree);

- in 1923 the first woman to give lectures in theology (billed as philosophy of religion) at Oxford University[18] (albeit at the Unitarian-affiliated Manchester College, although these lectures were her own coming out for "traditional, institutional, sacramental religion");

- in 1925 the first woman formally to teach the clergy of the Church of England (at a clergy conference for the diocese of Liverpool);

- in 1927 the first woman to lead a retreat at Canterbury Cathedral;

- also in 1927 the first woman to be made a fellow of Kings College, London; and

- in 1938 the first woman working in a theological area to be recipient of an honorary degree from Aberdeen University.

She was of course not ordained, though women in free church traditions in England were being ordained by the late 1910s,[19] while the first woman to be ordained anywhere as an Anglican priest was also—just—in Underhill's lifetime: Florence Li Tim-Oi in Hong Kong, in 1940. In fact, for her own part, Underhill opposed the ordination of

---

18. I think this is also true of Cambridge, Durham, St. Andrews, and other long-established British universities.

19. Julia Pitman, "A History of the Presidency of Women: Snapshots from the Movement for Women's Ordination in America, Britain and Australia," in *Presiding Like a Woman*, ed. Nicola Slee and Stephen Burns (London: SPCK, 2010), 67–78, 68, notes that Constance Coltmann was ordained in English Congregationalism in 1917. On the same page, we find a point that relates to comments I make later: "In Britain . . . the movement for women's ordination was firmly embedded in the wider desire for equality for women."

women as priests.[20] This notwithstanding, the key point here is that "Evelyn Underhill had no qualifications and no institutional position such as a job in a church or university which might have been hers had she been a man,"[21] yet through "best-selling" books, leadership of retreats, and an extensive ministry of spiritual direction, she gained enormous influence. Coakley herself describes Underhill as a "powerful lay woman."[22] Indeed, Underhill is commonly regarded as having given unmatched momentum to the retreat movement and singularly important advocacy of the necessity of being accompanied by and accountable to a so-called soul-friend. Of the twentieth-century saints in the *Common Worship* calendar, she is the only "spiritual writer" (however, there are two male bishops, Westcott and Temple, deemed "teachers of the faith").

This notwithstanding, we can hold Underhill's remarkable achievements and "firsts" in mind as we reflect upon accolades bestowed upon Sarah Coakley, who is taking some firsts of her own. Most obviously, Coakley is the first woman in a chair in "divinity" (Regius or Norris-Hulme, as opposed to in biblical studies[23]) at Cambridge, having been appointed to that position in 2008 after fifteen years at Harvard as the Edward Mallinckrodt Jr. Professor of Divinity. By the time she left the U.K. in 1993—to anticipate a point on which I want to touch later in my reflections, on the cusp of the ordination of women to the priesthood in the Church of England—she had held posts in both Lancaster and Oxford, and she found herself being appointed to "full" professor at a time when there had been only two such appointments to women in theology (as theologians, in Greene's sense, or otherwise) in English universities.

In fact, the first woman appointed to a professorship in theology

---

20. Greene, *Artist*, 100. Her argument was that this move would weaken the Church of England's relationship to the Roman Catholic Church. In 1907—the same year as Underhill decided not to join the Catholic Church—a papal bull, *Apostolicae Curae*, declared Anglican orders invalid.

21. Ann Loades, *Evelyn Underhill* (London: Fount, 1997), 1. Note that these are the very first words of Loades's book.

22. Coakley, *Powers and Submissions*, 41.

23. In Cambridge, Morna Hooker already held a professorship in New Testament, and in Birmingham, Frances Young held the Cadbury Chair in theology, with her own work focused on biblical studies while spanning into patristics. Both Young and Hooker are Methodists.

in the U.K. happened in 1989, and since then there have been several developments. A very bare sketch, taking in only those also made full professor, might look something like this:

- in 1989, Bristol appointed Ursula King as professor of religious studies;

- in 1993, Mary Grey was appointed by Southampton as professor of contemporary theology;[24]

- in 1995, Ann Loades was appointed as professor of divinity in Durham;

- in 1996, Grace Jantzen became professorial research fellow in Manchester, the university at which Elaine Graham was appointed as professor of pastoral and social theology in 1998;

- in 2002, Lisa Isherwood was made professor of feminist liberation theologies (in the plural) at the college of St. Mark and St. John, Plymouth, later moving to a chair with the same title in Winchester,[25] where she was joined by Elizabeth Stuart as professor of theology;[26]

- in 2008 Linda Woodhead was made professor of religious studies in Lancaster (where Coakley started her teaching career);[27]

- also in 2008 Tina Beattie became professor in Catholic theology at Roehampton;[28]

- and finally, in 2008, Janet Martin Soskice was appointed to a professorship in philosophical theology at Cambridge.[29]

---

24. Grey came from a previous post as only the second occupant of the first chair in feminist theology in Europe, at Nijmegen. She went on to other posts in pastoral theology at Bristol and Lampeter, and is currently associated with Twickenham University.
25. Beyond her place of daily work, Isherwood was also the founding member of the publishing arm of the British and Irish School of Feminist Theology, the journal *Feminist Theology*, which has been in print since 1992.
26. Interestingly, in 2007, Stuart became archbishop of the Open Episcopal Church, related to the Liberal Catholic Church, in the U.K. (although she has now left this ecclesial role).
27. Like Coakley and Loades, Woodhead has been a member of the Church of England's Doctrine Commission.
28. So far as I know, Beattie is the first woman in this sketch to have had another woman in the sketch as doctoral supervisor—in Beattie's case, King.

In order to seek carefully to identify Coakley's distinctive contribution in such company, awareness of these persons' public ecclesial commitments and academic writings as well as their institutional affiliations is important. And at the very least a number of points should be made clear. Firstly, none of these women were specifically appointed to a post in *systematic* theology. Such posts are in any case quite rare in English universities. These professors came to their positions, however named, through various routes in religious studies (for example, King, Woodhead), pastoral theology (for example, Graham, Grey), contextual theology (for example, Isherwood, if we take contextual to embrace "feminist liberation/ist"), or philosophy of religion (for example, Jantzen, Loades, Soskice). Indeed, it is the case that in certain respects systematic theology has been closed off as an area open to women teachers in English institutions, and this situation becomes clearer if we take just one example as illustrative of wider dynamics. When Ann Loades went to Durham as an undergraduate in 1957, it was not possible for her then even to study systematics, as this was at that time reserved to ordinands in the Church of England (a situation that did not change until the 1970s).[30] Then, although Durham has a teaching post (the Van Mildert chair) closely associated with systematics, this chair is tied to a dual-role as cathedral canon, so it has not until very recently been possible for a woman to teach systematics in the most senior post in the field at that institution. Women entered the order of priests in the Church of England in only 1994.

This leads to the second point, which is that none of the women I have named are Anglican priests. Yet one woman who has been a professor of theology in an English university *is* an Anglican priest, and has not yet been named: Marilyn McCord Adams, an American, was ordained a priest in the Episcopal Church in the United States, and from 2004 to 2009 a canon of Christchurch, Oxford, in the Regius chair

---

29. Soskice is also only the second female president of the Society for the Study of Theology, after Loades.
30. David Brown, "Biographical Epilogue," in *Exchanges of Grace: Essays in Honour of Ann Loades*, ed. Natalie K. Watson and Stephen Burns (London: SCM, 2008), 271–75, 271.

there (a post that also ties teaching to cathedral clerical duties—Oxford and Durham having the only two remaining such positions).[31]

Third, although Isherwood is the only one to have the descriptor in her position title, all of the women named in the various theological areas would, in one way or another, be associated with feminist perspectives. Yet there is, as even passing acquaintance with their work will suggest, a variety of styles and approaches to feminist theology among them. They make evident that there is no one kind of feminist theology—that is, feminist theology in the singular as opposed to "feminist theologies" (which Isherwood's title recognizes). Within the evident plurality of these women's convictions, however, and despite the tail end of Byassee's claims about Coakley, we should note, in fairness to them, that a number of the women professors of theology in whose company I have placed Coakley are, like Coakley, deeply engaged with the so-called "classical" sources of Christian tradition,[32] although they might well at the same time remind us that "'obedience' . . . has never been understood to be a cardinal (let alone theological) virtue in [that] Christian tradition,"[33] with obvious implications for how they engage the tradition. Even so, many, if not all, of them would concur with Ursula King's suggestion that "Christianity still possesses great reservoirs of hope and large scriptural, historical and spiritual resources for empowering women to seek liberation and justice."[34]

In light of this quotation from King, however, we might in turn observe that Coakley has been notably more reluctant than most of these other women explicitly to relate her feminist agenda to the language of advocacy, or a call for gender-justice. The closest thing

---

31. Like Soskice, Loades, and Jantzen, Adams has a background in philosophy of religion.
32. I mean this point to nuance Byassee's assessment of Coakley's "marriage" of "the fathers and feminism."
33. Ann Loades, "The Nativity in Recent British Poetry," in *New Perspectives on the Nativity*, ed. Jeremy Corley (London: Continuum, 2009), 148–64, 160, and Ann Loades, "Mary: Bone of Contention," in *From the Margins 2: Women of the New Testament and Their Afterlives*, ed. Christine E. Joynes and Christopher Rowland (Sheffield: Sheffield Phoenix, 2009), 53–66, 58—the latter essay concluding with an argument for "fully humanly inclusive" ministry, which can be mapped onto discussion at the end of this paper.
34. Ursula King, "Feminist Theologies in Contemporary Contexts: A Provisional Assessment," in *Is There a Future for Feminist Theology?*, ed. Deborah F. Sawyer and Dianne M. Collier (Sheffield: Sheffield Academic, 1999), 100–114, 113.

that I can find to any such a statement by Coakley is her comment—in which at the key point of the parallel she uses the voice of another —that:

> It is worth asking . . . what "feminism" and "feminist theology" stand for in generic terms. This is a surprisingly difficult question to answer simply. Minimally, we can say, following Janet Radcliffe Richards, that (secular) feminism works to alleviate the manifest social disadvantages of women, since "there are excellent reasons for thinking that *women suffer from systematic and social injustice because of their sex.*" But under that voluminous feminist umbrella, a variety of schools of thought can shelter, and feminist theology, in echoing and complexifying those schools with religious themes has proved equally multifarious.[35]

And in relation to the various kinds of feminism espoused by Coakley's peers, we should, I think, also note an important comment made by Janet Martin Soskice (in an essay under Ann Loades's simple editorial heading, "God loves women"), which may well speak for more than Soskice alone:

> Despite cowardly tendencies to trundle back to the ontological argument, or science and religion, or some other safe topic, I feel a certain obligation to write on the topics of women and the Church, and women and ethics, [because] one day I feel God might ask of me, "You were there. You saw it. What have you done for these ones that I love . . ."[36]

Fourth, from a range of feminist perspectives, it is crucial, especially when suggesting the barest historical sketch, to remember not only to "focus on roles that have been noted by a male audience, but [to] take into account the presence of women in the church as worshippers and as readers of spiritual works that were to a large extent not written

---

35. Sarah Coakley, "Feminist Theology," in *Modern Christian Thought: Volume 2: The Twentieth Century,* ed. James Livingston and Francis Schüssler Fiorenza with Sarah Coakley and James H. Evans Jr. (Englewood Cliffs, NJ: Prentice Hall, 1999) 417–42, 418. Note in anticipation of discussion later in this essay that alongside Elizabeth Schüssler Fiorenza and Rosemary Radford Ruether, Coakley discusses the work of "French feminist" philosopher Luce Irigaray. But compare Janet Martin Soskice's uncompromising assertion that "[s]exism is not something that hurts women's feelings, sexism kills millions and millions of girls and women each year," with reasons given for it: "Just Women's Problems," in *Spiritual Classics from the Late Twentieth Century,* ed. Ann Loades (London: Church House Publishing, 1995), 55–58, 55.

36. Janet Martin Soskice, "Women's Problems," in Ann Loades, ed., *Spiritual Classics from the Late Twentieth Century,* 47–54, 54.

with their presence in mind."[37] This can be both to recall Underhill (and not least her work providing texts for women and men to read), and to introduce the very important point that there are many other women teaching theology in England besides the ones I have named,[38] in places other than universities, including in roles that involve teaching clergy or trainee clergy—and their work should by no means be underestimated. This is of course apart from women presiding in old-line churches as well as in circles of "women-Church" (in which I can find no trace of Coakley's involvement). Depending on the male (or female) audience, such things may or may not be noticed. And "women-Church" especially, with bodies like the British and Irish School of Feminist Theology, has been a crucial context for the development of feminist theological perspectives and personages, especially in a wider environment that has more-or-less openly, to greater-or-lesser extent institutionally, barred or blocked women not only from teaching the Christian tradition as systematic theologians, but also from representing the Christian community as women priests. For some of the feminist theologians just mentioned, as well as others, my opening questions about what counts as theology and Christian tradition resurface insistently at this point. So far as I can see, it is not without good reasons that they are suspicious about any use of speech that sets "theological" against other supposedly "secular" perspectives. To my mind, the institutional back-story of women's teaching roles, about which I have hinted, sets in serious question any easy divisions between constructs of theological or sacred and secular arenas.[39]

---

37. Natalie K. Watson, *Feminist Theology* (Grand Rapids: Eerdmans, 2002), 21.
38. Indeed, we might note that a pioneer alongside Underhill, Dorothy L. Sayers, declined an honorary doctorate from Lambeth Palace because she did not wish her influence to be diminished by being perceived narrowly as a "theologian." (See Ann Loades, "The Vitality of Tradition: Austin Farrer and His Friends," in *Captured by the Crucified: The Practical Theology of Austin Farrer*, ed. David Hein and Edward Hugh Henderson (London: Continuum, 2004), 15–46, 29–30 and Ann Loades, "Dorothy L. Sayers: War and Redepemption," in *C. S. Lewis and His Friends: Faith and the Power of the Imagination*, ed. David Hein and Edward Henderson (London: SPCK, 2011), 53–70. Not all women have, like Sayers, had a wide audience outside both the church and academy, but something in the spirit of Sayers's reserve has nevertheless "stuck," perhaps as a conscious decampment from the "master's house."
39. I think I understand some of Coakley's reasons for this, but I am reluctant to follow her in this practice. And I mean this point to nuance Byassee's juxtaposition of "orthodoxy and sociology."

Nevertheless, the point toward which I am pressing is that Sarah Coakley is the first woman priest *in the orders of the Church of England* to be appointed to a professorship in theology in an English university. Notably, however, Coakley went to Harvard on the cusp of the first priestings of women in England, and was ordained herself—in England, while at the same time then being based in the U.S.—later in 2001. Whether deliberately or by happenchance, by relocating for a time to the USA and by seeking ordination only after the whitest heat of debate about women priests, she may have side-stepped some of the constraints facing other women theological teachers in the Church of England. For it is striking how many female English Anglican theologians have remained defiantly lay. So, as Nicola Slee puts it in her "Letter to the Church," "Brother Church . . . I will work with you/ but I will not work for you."[40] This has been the case even amidst moves, such as the workings of the Maude Royden Society,[41] intent on bringing lay and ordained Anglican women together.[42] At the same time, it is perfectly clear that, as Tina Beattie names the problem, women who have been ordained priests have "often [been] reluctant to identify themselves with feminism or to challenge patriarchal hierarchies and clerical norms in case it further compromised their already precarious standing in the Church of England."[43] All this is to suggest that, quite apart from Sarah Coakley's undoubted native talent, there are complex issues at play in assessment of her significance.

If we take what may at first seem like a tangential point—tangential because Coakley herself makes it about what she calls the "explosive and unresolved [issue] of homosexuality . . . hav[ing] to be painfully debated and played out precisely in the context of the Church,"[44] we

---

40. Nicola Slee, *Praying Like a Woman* (London: SPCK, 2004), 31.

41. Maude Royden founded the Movement for the Ordination of Women in 1929 and became the first English woman to gain a doctorate in divinity, in 1930.

42. It remains another question just how feminist an elitist and exclusive, seemingly invite-only, society, such as the Maude Royden Society, might be.

43. Beattie, "Vision and Vulnerability," 235–49, 247.

44. She continues: "[T]he Church's anguished (and often unedifying) division nonetheless 'represents' a wider cultural *aporia* [and so] cannot be hurried or quickly foreclosed: it is a painful process, unsolvable by false bids for power or fast attempts to capture the moral high ground" (Coakley, "Prayer, Place and the Poor," 4).

can, I think, turn this statement back as a lens to reflect on the public significance of the position in which Coakley now finds herself *as a woman priest* in an English university theological professorship: she represents a breakthrough in wider cultural, but especially churchly *aporia* about women's leadership.[45] It is notable that Anglican women only came to be appointed to professorships in England in close proximity to the first ordinations of women as priests (1994, with Loades given a chair in 1995 at a university at which Anglican ordinands are among those who study in the university). The issues here are complicated, *com-plicatio*,[46] and Coakley is a particular folding together of different issues that are larger than her considerable personal gifts. In any case, she now finds herself in the thick of these dynamics. And it might be that Coakley, while spurning "false bids for power," has nevertheless quite consciously been engaged in tactics as to how the two roles could be folded into one. (I wish more people, women and men, would take up this concern.)

On the heels of Coakley's achievement, we need also to observe that there is another "first" yet to be gained when a woman is appointed to a senior university role such as her own *directly* from the orders of the Church of England.

Unsystematic Systematics

In moving from reflections on the contexts of Coakley's significance to a greater emphasis on the contents of Coakley's thinking, we might recall my opening comments about my foci collapsing into one another. For while all of the women I have named above are identified in one way or another with feminist theologies, Coakley has been widely lauded as a *systematic* theologian and has emphatically retained the descriptor of "systematic theologian" for herself.

45. Compare the view of previous moderator of the United Reformed Church, David Cornick, who has already made a point related to Coakley's with reference to the significance of the Church of England's struggles to appoint women to the episcopate. See http://www.churchtimes.co.uk/content.asp?id=87984.
46. See Pamela Cooper-White, "Com|plicated Women: Multiplicity and Relationality Across Gender and Culture," *Women Out of Order: Risking Change and Creating Care in a Multicultural World*, ed. Jeanne Stevenson-Moessner and Teresa Snorton (Minneapolis: Fortress Press, 2009), 7–21, 9.

The first volume of Coakley's systematics, *God, Sexuality and the Self: An Essay 'On the Trinity'* is based on her Hulsean Lectures delivered in 1992, has been heralded since at least 1996,[47] and has taken time for what I find the delightful reason that Coakley has, she once said, been busy in the parish during her summer holidays. What has emerged in the meantime has nevertheless been very substantial, in different senses, but it has also in a certain way been piecemeal. What we have of Professor Coakley's work is a version of her doctoral thesis; and after that numerous contributions to collections of essays and journals; several edited volumes with introductions as well as other contributions to such collections (some of which themselves started out as special editions of journals); work on commissions; and, perhaps most interestingly, her part in the almost uncategorizable collection *Swallowing a Fishbone? Feminist Theologians Debate Christianity*, in which, as Peter Selby suggests, we are invited to "eavesdrop on [a] vibrant conversation" in a form "much better than the standard 'collection of essays,'" "hear[ing] the debate happen" as contributors present their own particular essays, then respond to each other's before each in turn offering an afterword (and all this after the preface has been shared by two of the six feminist theologians whose voices are collected in the book).[48]

The *Swallowing a Fishbone?* project—in the words of one of the contributors, a "difficult and protracted" one, an "arduous, even torturous, venture,"[49] nevertheless—remains in my view an apex of feminist process in British publishing, a publishing stream that, according to Heather Walton, began significantly in 1983[50] (note, several years before any British or British-based women became professors), with SCM Press's publication of two books written in the

47. Daphne Hampson, ed., *Swallowing a Fishbone? Feminist Theologians Debate Christianity* (London: SPCK, 1996), viii.
48. One of the contributors even suggests that the feminist process of this book could have been improved by sharing the editorial load. Coakley's main chapter in *Swallowing a Fishbone?* is included in *Powers and Submissions*, but arguably there loses something of the "vibrant conversation" with other participants in the original debate.
49. Nicola Slee, "Response," in *Swallowing a Fishbone?*, ed. Hampson, 129–34, 129.
50. Heather Walton, "You Have to Say What You Cannot Speak: Feminist Reflections upon Public Theology," *International Journal of Public Theology* 4 (2010): 21–36, 26n12.

U.S. by Roman Catholics: Elizabeth Schüssler Fiorenza's *In Memory of Her* and Rosemary Radford Ruether's *Sexism and God-talk*, the latter being a systematic theology. The piecemeal and collaborative[51] nature of what has emerged of Sarah Coakley's work is not just akin to, but a part of, the way in which many feminist theologians have worked, even as Coakley has repeatedly included critique of older, earlier, or other feminists for lack of philosophical acuity.[52]

This notwithstanding, what Coakley has called the "unsystematic systematics"[53] on which she has embarked embraces what has often-times been more readily identified by (what are sometimes intended as denigrating) labels such as "contextual," "pastoral," and "liturgical," quite apart from the study of "spirituality," which also melds into the so-called fourth area of the theological curriculum.[54] Hence, Coakley has spoken of her fourfold project as an attempt to construct a *théologie totale*.[55] In any case, whatever "fresh paths in systematic theology"[56] she is forging, as I have already stated, some of her concerns and methods are not entirely unfamiliar ground in Christian feminist thinking in Britain, even if Coakley brings a particular kind of heft to the common concern. Perhaps her particular approach is best identified as a two-way critique, not only of (at least first-wave) feminism for lack of theoretical sharpness but also firmly calling (analytic) philosophy, and any systematic theology that might turn to it, into "critical play" with gender-sensitive perspectives.[57]

---

51. Also noted by Byassee, "Closer."
52. For example, Sarah Coakley, "Feminism," in *A Companion to Philosophy of Religion*, 2nd edition, ed. Charles Taliaferro, Paul Draper, and Philip L. Quinn (Oxford: Blackwell, 2010), 688–94, 688. (The second edition has not updated references to works referred to as being published "this decade" [693], so that there is a mismatch between the content of the essay and the references.) Alongside Coakley's charge, however, recall Janet Martin Soskice's reflection (which is "this decade") that "[f]eminist theology is sometimes attacked by others in feminist fields as a theoretical backwater. If this is true, it may be part of the price paid for keeping an ear to the ground. . . . Feminism in theology may lack the theoretical frameworks of some of its sister subjects, but its prospect for reaching millions of lives, including those of the world's poorest women, is immense," in *Feminism and Theology*, ed. Janet Martin Soskice and Diana Lipton (Oxford: Oxford University Press, 2003), 7–8.
53. Sarah Coakley, "Is There a Future for the Systematic Task? On Gender, Contemplation and the Systematic Task," *Criterion* 47 (2009): 2–11, 7.
54. Elaine Graham and Nicola Slee might well be regarded as leading this field.
55. Coakley, "Is There a Future . . . ?," 4.
56. Shortt, "Fresh Paths."

This notwithstanding, it is clear that for Sarah Coakley publishing in piecemeal ways has not detracted from deep continuities emerging across the breadth of her work. As Byassee indicates, these continuities include Coakley's ongoing attention to feminist perspectives, her respect for "classical" Christian sources, and her reflection on her own immersion in contemplative prayer. Despite my suspicion that Byassee might betray a certain ignorance of other feminist theologians and their achievements, I strongly concur that Sarah Coakley is groundbreaking, and add that this is, in part, because of her *symbolic* status. For as a systematician, or unsystematic systematician, or whatever, she is a female priest and as such she is a particular kind of "a gathering place for wider meaning."[58]

Woman at the Altar

This brings me to Coakley's own reflections on her role as priest, in particular as presiding celebrant when the church makes Eucharist. In her more recent work, interest in contemplation yields to, or at least comes to be complemented by, concern with the dynamics of sacramental celebration, liturgical presidency, and the pastoral care that accompanies the task of presidency.[59] Some of Coakley's reflection on this role remains as promise—it is, I note, to be the focus of the last chapter of the first volume of her systematics—but it has at least been anticipated in an essay forthcoming in *The New Asceticism* and published already in *Anglican Theological Review*, "The Woman at the Altar: Cosmological Disturbance or Gender Subversion?" In this essay,

---

57. Coakley, "Feminism," 693—and perhaps by extension other "inclusive"/human optics: she mentions children and "illiterates," 693.

58. Gordon W. Lathrop, *The Pastor: A Spirituality* (Minneapolis: Fortress Press, 2006), 5.

59. When we look around her earlier works, we can find some reflection on the *sursum corda* in *We Believe in God* (London: Church House Publishing, 1991), 114–15 (Coakley writes anonymously in this commission paper), some comments on ideas of the Trinity shaped by the church year, alongside reflections on "classic" baptismal formula, in "Why Three? Some Further Reflections on the Origins of the Doctrine of the Trinity," in *The Making and Remaking of Christian Doctrine: Essays in Honour of Maurice Wiles*, ed. Sarah Coakley and David A. Pailin (Oxford: Clarendon, 1993), 29–53, a sense of her being somewhat underwhelmed by her liturgical experience of gospel proclamation in *Fishbone* (149)—and also keen interest in corporate glossalia, *We Believe in the Holy Spirit* (London: Church House Publishing, 1991), 17–36 (again, anonymously for the Doctrine Commission of the Church of England).

Coakley concerns herself with what she calls the "mysterious liminality of priestly enactment,"[60] in a way that engages, on the one hand, more than "mere consideration of the liturgical text and rubric" but also "the more nebulous but intuitive category of ritual performance"[61] and, on the other hand, contest with the arguments of "eminent conservatives" in the Roman Catholic tradition who are opposed to the ordination of women. These opponents include Hans Urs von Balthasar. In Balthasar's case, his opposition is on the basis of an understanding of nuptial imagery of "the bride of Christ" applied to the church. Notoriously, Balthasar has argued that the Eucharist is "the fruitful outpouring of divine love," a vision interpreted by Tina Beattie as a

> metaphysical consummation of homosexual love, a marriage between men and God in which the male body is both the masculine bridegroom and the feminine bride, masculine God and the feminine creature, the masculine Christ and the feminine Church.[62]

Coakley turns her discussion to issues of how the priest may mediate nuptial relationship between Christ and the church by means of posture.[63] Without wanting to overlook the nuances of Coakley's argument, I think she can be summarized as follows. She notes that, in the parish of Littlemore, where she spent her summer vacations, because the stone altar was fixed to the east wall, she faced east to voice eucharistic prayer. She had, she says, "expected to find this offensive as a feminist,"[64] but "oddly . . . I found it impinged on the gender implications of the rite with surprisingly positive effect."[65] The east-facing position for presidential prayer underscores for her the

---

60. Coakley, "Woman," 93.
61. Ibid., 78.
62. Tina Beattie, *God's Mother, Eve's Advocate: A Marian Narrative of Women's Salvation* (London: Continuum, 2002), 80, drawing the quotation from Sarah Coakley, "Creaturehood Before God: Male and Female," *Theology* 93 (1990): 343–53, 349. Coakley's essay is reprinted in *Powers and Submissions.*
63. She is particularly interested in postures in relation to what Graham Hughes calls "liturgical direction": Graham Hughes, *Worship as Meaning: A Liturgical Theology for Late Modernity* (Cambridge: Cambridge University Press, 2005). See more below.
64. Coakley, "Woman," 78–79.
65. Ibid., 79.

priest's "inherently fluid gender role as beater of the liminal bounds between the divine and the human,"[66] oriented with the assembly for prayer, turning to face the assembly for dialogue. Challenging current liturgical consensus, Coakley suggests that

> [w]hen I am struck, fixed behind the altar west-facing throughout, I also contribute unwittingly to a gender fixing that blocks the play of liminality those [east-facing] movements conveyed.[67]

Significantly, while articulating her autobiographical account of presiding, Coakley also suggests that east-facing celebration for both priest and people together can be gender-subverting whether the presiding celebrant is female or male. Or at least it may be if that presidency can be conceived in terms of

> subtly kenotic dispossession, a rendering of oneself prayerfully diaphanous to the fluidity of the *proto*-erotic dimensions of the divine nuptial enactment that one is "representing."[68]

The feminist force of her argument is that the woman at the altar is

> not just . . . dressing up as a man dressing up as a woman (though sartorial details are certainly significant in this "play"), but rather that the gender fluidity that the male priest has always enjoyed *qua* liturgically liminal can no longer be a means of "*leaving everything else* as it is."

Apart from anything else, we see here a powerful extension of some of her writing on contemplative prayer, now being carried into common worship,[69] not to say at least an implicit demand for justice.

Here, Coakley might, I think, fruitfully be brought into conversation with two liturgical theologians of the Uniting Church, Graham Hughes

---

66. Ibid., 76.
67. Ibid., 89.
68. Ibid., 92.
69. Asserting the communal dimension of liturgy is itself an important ally of the feminist charge that contemplative prayer has required too little "love and attention" to embodied others. Janet Martin Soskice, *The Kindness of God: Metaphor, Gender and Religious Language* (Oxford: Oxford University Press, 2007), 14. Soskice's argument is particularly about childcare, itself a focus of Coakley's argument in her contribution to the collection on constructs of "analytic theology": "Dark Contemplation and Epistemic Transformation: The Analytic Theologian Re-Meets Teresa of Avila," in *Analytic Theology: New Essays in the Philosophy of Theology*, ed. Oliver D. Crisp and Michael C. Rae (Oxford: Oxford University Press, 2009), 280–312.

and Anita Monro. Both write from a tradition that ordains women as ministers of the word,[70] as well as permitting lay men and women to preside in sacramental celebration. And while Hughes's published work is not explicitly gender-sensitive, Anita Monro's work most certainly is acutely astute in this respect.[71] Hughes is interested in the "iconicity" of the presiding celebrant in her or his liturgical direction, facing, or facing away from, others in Christian assembly. Albeit while suggesting that "none of us, I imagine, is going to relinquish the 'basilican' position in which the leader stands behind the table,"[72] he nevertheless asks questions that can be brought to Coakley's thoughts:

> Is Christ supposed to speak from the people's side, as mediator? Or is Christ the second person of the Godhead who speaks God's grace and favour to the people? Is Christ God's Word? If a leader understands herself or himself as occupying a role as *in persona Christi*, is that then acting from God's side, the people's side, or somewhere between them?[73]

These strike me as good questions and ones that can be imagined stretching across gaps in denominationally flavored terminology as well as differences in polity. Hughes also makes a number of suggestions about how liturgical direction might work in aspects of liturgical celebration other than eucharistic prayer, as well as offering creative ideas about how the whole assembly, and not just the presiding celebrant, might be engaged in movements that broaden the focus away from the presider alone. So Hughes suggests collective entrance into celebration space, and congregational dance,[74] for instance; but his key theological point is to underscore that the assembly itself is "the basic symbol."[75] This is a collective turn that Coakley's theology has not yet made, or witnessed to in print.

In light of Hughes's questions, Coakley's reflections on presidency

---

70. "Minister of the Word" is ecumenically equivalent to priest, though the UCA opted against the language of presbyter.
71. Manifest in Anita Monro, *Resurrecting Erotic Transgression: Subjecting Ambiguity in Theology* (London: Equinox, 2006).
72. Hughes, *Worship*, 164. Note: It is precisely this position that Coakley has relinquished.
73. Hughes, *Worship*, 162.
74. Ibid., 159.
75. Gordon W. Lathrop, *Holy People: A Liturgical Ecclesiology* (Minneapolis: Fortress Press, 1999), 23, quoted by Hughes, *Worship*, 156.

also invite connection to the sense that centripetal liturgical space may manifest the "feminist consciousness" of the liturgical movement,[76] which, like at least some feminists, has advocated for "church in the round."[77] This arrangement entails an inevitable reframing of practical questions about how and when the priest faces the assembly. Moreover, centripetal space potentially reconfigures at least any visual depictions of immanent divine presence and transcendent otherness. It also beckons feminist attention toward a potentially full (perhaps as yet only partly imagined) repertoire of gesture,[78] and one that attends to different women's sense of being differently physically able or constrained from men. With respect to the former, there are the like of the "timbre, resonance, pitch and cadence" of the voice to think about;[79] with respect to the latter, pregnant woman may not be prostrate,[80] while postures of blessing that involve leaving breasts and belly exposed may feel like either empowering embrace or extreme vulnerability.[81]

To this conversation, I bring, in conclusion, another voice to the table: that of Anita Monro in her discussion of her "phronetic dramaturgy" of women's presidency in liturgy.[82] Both Coakley and Monro are readers of the so-called "French feminists," and like Coakley's, Monro's argument is complex. Yet Monro suggests—in a different way from Coakley—a challenge of female leadership at Eucharist. Building closely on Julia Kristeva's philosophical constructions, the force of Anita Monro's analysis of the gendered dynamics of eucharistic presidency is that in whatever way presiders of

---

76. See Gail Ramshaw, "Christian Worship from a Feminist Perspective," in *Worship Today: Understanding, Practice, Ecumenical Implications*, ed. Thomas Best and Dagmar Heller (Geneva: World Council of Churches, 2004), 208–13, 212.

77. Note Letty Russell, *Church in the Round: Feminist Interpretation of the Church* (Louisville: Westminster John Knox, 1993).

78. Such questions are the burden of Stephen Burns, "'Four in a Vestment': Liturgical Gesture for Christian Assembly," in *Presiding Like a Woman*, ed. Slee and Burns, 9–18.

79. Lucy Winkett, "'Why Is That Priest Singing in a Woman's Voice?'" in *Presiding Like a Woman*, ed. Slee and Burns, 95–102.

80. Ali Green, *A Theology of Women's Priesthood* (London: SPCK, 2009), 143.

81. Andrea Bieler and David Plüss, "In This Moment of Utter Vulnerability: Tracing Gender in Presiding," in *Presiding Like a Woman*, 113–23, 113–14.

82. Anita Monro, "'And Ain't I a Woman?': The Phronetic Dramaturgy of Feeding the Family," in *Presiding Like a Woman*, ed. Slee and Burns, 124–33.

different sexes might be reconfigured in the act of presidency, female presiders enter, and open, new symbolic space, such that "the stark and messy reality of incarnation is confronted" in an intense way.[83] Questions of liturgical direction are not a part of Monro's reflections, but rather, through a philosophical skein, the emergence of the possibility that Christ and the church ("the body of Christ") can both be re-gendered under female leadership: the woman at the altar "is provider for the family" and in her care "Christ feeds her people with her very self at her own hand."[84] Monro's depiction of "[t]he feminine body (Church) [being] fed with the feminine body (Eucharist) by the feminine body (presider)"[85] is both a counterpoint to the Balthasarian imagery that Coakley contests as well as at least a partial ally of, and partial question-mark against, Coakley's own position. The meaning-making process by which Monro understands what Coakley calls "gender subversion" to occur unfolds as

> the body of the woman (because woman and body are not so easily separated) juxtaposed with the body of Christ (the Eucharist) raises issues about its gender. The body of the woman juxtaposed against the body of Christ, the Church, blurs the boundaries between presider and participant. The bodies merge, and the illusion of singular, autonomous, separate complete subjectivity is exposed.[86]

If nuptial imagery is central for Coakley, sacrificial images are key for Monro. And while the sexual resonance of *jouissance* is part of Monro's depiction, it underscores the ambiguous and messy "union" effected by eucharistic action, and certainly not the kind of stability that Balthasar supposes and that Coakley wants in her own way to

---

83. Monro, "Feeding the Family," 125.
84. Ibid., 129.
85. Ibid., 129. Monro's argument can also be allied to Ali Green, "Being and Becoming: How the Woman Presider Enriches Our Sacred Symbols," in *Presiding Like a Woman*, ed. Slee and Burns, 103–12. Green notes that the woman at the altar may amplify associations of nurture, "inhabiting what has historically been the mother's domain: not only giving birth and nurturing, but teaching the young, preparing food, laying the table, feeding the family, clearing up, caring for the sick and frail" (108) but also that the female presider brings to the altar an embodied experience of blood, different from men's, which can contest "women's age-old exclusion from sacred ritual, particularly sacrifice" (107)—points that are argued at length in Ali Green, *A Theology of Women's Priesthood.*
86. Monro, "Feeding the Family," 129.

unravel. The space between Coakley and Monro opens up in terms that can also be related to Hughes's more communal emphasis, for whereas Coakley emphasizes the role of the female presiding celebrant, Monro offers a stronger consciousness of the "female" christic community, itself merged with Christa.

While it is not to be supposed that Coakley would necessarily assent to such a view—let alone that Evelyn Underhill would—it can be asserted that all of these issues in sacramental celebration are matters for "public witness," to put alongside Coakley's stress on the public witness of prayer.

Author Biographies

Myles Werntz is Assistant Professor of Biblical and Theological Studies at Palm Beach Atlantic University. He is the author of *Bodies of Peace: Nonviolence, Ecclesiology, Witness* (Fortress, 2014).

Benjamin Myers is lecturer in systematic theology at Charles Sturt University's School of Theology in Sydney. His books include *Christ the Stranger: The Theology of Rowan Williams* and *Milton's Theology of Freedom*. He is generally a very nice person even though he sometimes misses deadlines and infuriates his poor hapless editors.

Dennis W. Jowers (PhD, Edinburgh) is Professor of Theology & Apologetics at Faith Evangelical College & Seminary in Tacoma, Washington. He has authored, co-authored, and/or edited four books, including *Four Views on Divine Providence* (Zondervan, 2011) and *Reasons for Our Hope: An Introduction to Christian Apologetics* (B & H, 2011).

Nicola Hoggard-Creegan is a Visiting Scholar (theologian) at St John's Theological College in Auckland. She is interested in and has written in areas of systematics, and on the boundary between theology and the natural sciences, especially evolutionary biology and ecology. She is the author of *Animal Suffering and the Problem of Evil* (OUP, 2013) and she is currently working on a book on free will.

Brandy Daniels is a Ph.D. candidate in theological studies and a fellow in the theology and practice program at Vanderbilt University, with a minor in Ethics & Society and a certificate in Women's & Gender Studies. She has an M.Div. and an A.M. in Comparative Literature and African-American Studies from Duke University. Her research interests center around questions of theological anthropology at the intersections of systematics, critical theory, and ethics. Her dissertation, "Who is the 'We?' Formation and Theological Method in a Queer Time and Space," explores the relationship between spiritual formation and theological method by placing theological analyses of time and space (eschatology and anthropology) in conversation with queer theoretical reflections on these themes (queer temporality and antisociality).

Eugene F. Rogers Jr. is is the professor of religious studies and program faculty in women's and gender studies at University of North Carolina in Greensboro. He is author or editor of six books and over thirty-five articles and translations and is currently at work on a book about Christian uses of blood-language called *The Analogy of Blood.*

Annette Pierdziwol is a Research Associate at the Institute for Ethics and Society at the University of Notre Dame Australia's Sydney campus. She was awarded her PhD in Philosophy from the University of Sydney in 2010. Her research focuses on the concepts of moral responsibility and conscience, as well as approaches to moral cultivation in the history of philosophy.

Prior to her appointment at the IES, Annette held a postdoctoral research fellowship at the Institute for Advanced Studies in the Humanities at the University of Edinburgh. She has lectured in Philosophy at the University of Sydney and the University of New South Wales, coordinating units on topics in moral philosophy, history of philosophy and philosophy of religion.

Matthew Tan is the Felice and Magradel Zaccari Lecturer in Theology and Philosophy at Campion College, a Catholic liberal arts college in the west of Sydney. He had previously served as Visiting Assistant Professor in Catholic Studies and a Research Fellow at the Centre for World Catholicism and Intercultural Theology at DePaul University in Chicago. He is the author of *Justice, Unity & the Hidden Christ: the Theopolitical Complex of the Social Justice Approach to Ecumenism in Vatican II.*

Stephen Burns is Stewart Distinguished Lecturer in Liturgical and Practical Theology, Co-ordinator of Ministry Formation and Associate Dean at Trinity College Theological School, University of Divinity, Melbourne, Australia. He is a priest in the orders of the Church of England. His publications include: *Exchanges of Grace: Essays in Honour of Ann Loades* (co-editor with Natalie Watson, SCM Press, 2008), *Presiding Like a Woman* (co-editor with Nicola Slee, SPCK, 2010) and *Public Theology and the Challenge of Feminism* (co-editor with Anita Monro, Routledge, 2014) as well as *Worship in Context* (Epworth Press, 2006), *Christian Worship: Postcolonial Perspectives* (co-author with Michael N. Jagessar, Equinox/Routledge, 2011), *Worship and Ministry* (Mosaic Press, 2012) and *Pastoral Theology for Public Ministry* (Seabury Press, 2015).

Janice McRandal is Lecturer in Systematic Theology and Coordinator of Research and Continuing Education at Trinity College Queensland (Charles Sturt University). Her research is focused on the relationship between systematic theology and feminist theology / gender theory / race theory / post-colonial studies. She is the author of *Difference, Doctrine, and Discourse: A Contribution to Feminist Systematic Theology* (Minneapolis: Fortress Press, February 2015).

Published Work by Sarah Coakley

1. Books, Edited Collections, and Special Journal Issues

Christ without Absolutes: A Study of the Christology of Ernst Troeltsch (Oxford: Oxford University Press, hbk, 1988; pbk, 1994).

The Making and Remaking of Christian Doctrine: Essays in Honour of Maurice Wiles, co-ed. with David A. Pailin (Oxford: Oxford University Press, hbk, 1993).

Religion and the Body, ed. with introduction (Cambridge: Cambridge University Press, hbk, 1997; pbk, 2000).

    Romanian trans., Bucharest, Univers, 2003.

Powers and Submissions: Spirituality, Philosophy and Gender (Oxford: Blackwell, hbk and pbk, 2002) (*Gesammelte Schriften*, vol. 1).

    Chinese trans., Beijing: China Renmin University Press, 2006.

    German trans., Gütersloher, 2007.

    ch. 9 Swedish trans. in *Postmodern Teologi: En Introduktion*, eds. Ola Sigurdson and Jayne Svenungsson (Stockholm: Verbum, 2006), 240–58.

Re-thinking Gregory of Nyssa, ed. with introduction (Oxford: Blackwell, pbk, 2003) (originally a special issue of *Modern Theology* 18, 4, 2002).

The God of Nicaea: Disputed Questions in Patristic Trinitarianism, ed. with introduction, a special issue of *Harvard Theological Review* 100, 2, 2007.

Pain and its Transformations: The Interface of Biology and Culture, co-ed. with Kay Kaufman Shelemay (Cambridge, MA: Harvard University Press, hbk, 2007).

Praying for England: Priestly Presence in Contemporary Culture, co-ed. with Samuel Wells with introduction (London: Continuum, pbk, 2008).

Re-thinking Dionysius the Areopagite, co-ed. with Charles M. Stang, with introduction (Oxford: Wiley-Blackwell, pbk, 2009) (originally a special issue of *Modern Theology* 24, 4, 2008).

The Spiritual Senses: Perceiving God in Western Christianity, co-ed. with Paul L. Gavrilyuk, with introduction (Cambridge: Cambridge University Press, hbk, 2012).

    Polish trans., 2013.

Sacrifice Regained: Reconsidering the Rationality of Religious Belief, inaugural lecture as Norris-Hulse Professor of Divinity (Cambridge: Cambridge University Press, pbk, 2012).

Fear and Friendship: Anglicans Engaging with Islam, co-ed. with Frances Ward (London: Continuum, pbk, 2012).

Sacrifice Regained: Evolution, Cooperation and God, the 2012 Gifford Lectures at Aberdeen University, at http://www.abdn.ac.uk/gifford/about/ (forthcoming with Oxford, Oxford: Oxford University Press, pbk with Grand Rapids, MI: Eerdmans, 2016).

Faith, Rationality and the Passions, ed. with introduction and postscript (Oxford: Wiley-Blackwell, pbk, 2012) (originally special issues of *Faith and Philosophy* 28, 1, 2011 and *Modern Theology* 27, 2, 2011).

Evolution, Games and God: The Principle of Cooperation, co-ed. with Martin A. Nowak (Cambridge, MA: Harvard University Press, April, 2013).

    Korean trans., 2015.

God, Sexuality and the Self: An Essay 'On the Trinity' (Cambridge: Cambridge University Press, hbk and pbk, 2013) (vol. 1 of a 4-vol. systematic theology).

The New Asceticism: Sexuality, Gender and the Quest for God (London: Continuum, pbk, 2015).

Spiritual Healing: Science, Meaning and Discernment, ed. with introduction, afterword and chapter (Grand Rapids, MI: Eerdmans, 2015).

2. Parts of Books

English trans. of Trutz Rendtorff and Friedrich Wilhelm Graf, 'Ernst Troeltsch' in eds. Ninian Smart, John Clayton, Patrick Sherry and Steven T. Katz, *Nineteenth Century Religious Thought in the West*, vol. III (Cambridge: Cambridge University Press, 1985), 305-32.

'Christologie „auf Treibsand"? Zur Aktualität von Troeltschs Christusdeutung', in eds. Horst Renz and Friedrich Wilhelm Graf, *Troeltsch-Studien*, iv. *Umstrittene Moderne. Die Zukunft der Neuzeit im Urteil der Epoche Ernst Troeltschs* (Gütersloh, Gerd Mohn, 1987), 338-51.

'God as Trinity: An Approach through Prayer', in Doctrine Commission of the Church of England, *We Believe in God* (London: Church House Publishing, 1987), 104-21.

'"Femininity" and the Holy Spirit?', in ed. Monica Furlong, *Mirror to the Church: Reflections on Sexism* (London: S.P.C.K., 1988), 124-35.

'Charismatic Experience: Praying "In the Spirit"', in Doctrine Commission of the Church of England, *We Believe in the Holy Spirit* (London: Church House Publishing, 1991), 17-36.

'Mariology and "Romantic Feminism": A Critique', in ed. Teresa Elwes, *Women's Voices: Essays in Contemporary Feminist Theology* (London: HarperCollins, 1992), 97-110.

'Visions of the Self in Late Medieval Christianity: Some Cross-Disciplinary Reflections', in ed. Michael McGhee, *Philosophy, Religion and the Spiritual Life*, Royal Institute of Philosophy Supplements (Cambridge: Cambridge University Press, 1992), 89-103.

'Why Three? Some Further Reflections on the Doctrine of the Trinity', in eds. Coakley and Pailin, *Making and Remaking* [see above, under 1.], 29-56

'Is the Resurrection an "Historical" Event? Some Muddles and Mysteries', in ed. Paul D. L. Avis, *The Resurrection of Jesus Christ* (London: D.L.T., 1993), 85-115.

'*Kenōsis* and Subversion: On the Repression of "Vulnerability" in Christian Feminist Writing', in ed. Daphne Hampson, *Swallowing a Fishbone? Feminist Theologians Debate Christianity* (London: S.P.C.K., 1996), 82-111.

'Introduction: Religion and the Body', in ed. Coakley, *Religion and the Body* [see above, under 1.], 1-12.

'Feminism', in eds. Charles Taliaferro, Paul Draper and Philip L. Quinn, *A Companion to Philosophy of Religion* (Oxford: Blackwell, 1997), 601-6 (excerpted in eds. Michael Peterson, William Hasker, Bruce Reichenbach and David Basinger, *Philosophy of Religion: Selected Readings* (Oxford: Oxford University Press, 2nd edn, 2001), 366-67).

'Response' to William Alston, in eds. Stephen T. Davis, Daniel Kendall, S.J., and Gerald O'Collins, S.J., *The Resurrection* (Oxford: Oxford University Press, 1997), 184-90.

'"Persons" in the "Social" Doctrine of the Trinity: A Critique of Current Analytic Discussion', in eds. Stephen T. Davis, Daniel Kendall, S.J. and Gerald O'Collins, S.J., *The Trinity: An Interdisciplinary Symposium on the Doctrine of the Trinity* (Oxford: Oxford University Press, 1999), 123-44.

'Feminist Theology' in James C. Livingston and Francis Schüssler Fiorenza with Sarah Coakley and James H. Evans, Jr., *Modern Christian Thought* (rev. edn), vol. II: *The Twentieth Century* (Upper Saddle River, NJ: Prentice Hall, 2000), 417-42 (reprinted by Augsburg Fortress, 2006; Korean trans., Seoul, Eunsung; Chinese trans., Nanjing, Yilin).

'*Kenosis*: Theological Meanings and Gender Connotations', in ed. John Polkinghorne, *The Work of Love: Creation as Kenosis* (Grand Rapids, MI: Eerdmans, 2001), 192-210.

'Deepening "Practices": Perspectives from Ascetical and Mystical Theology', in eds. Miroslav Volf and Dorothy C. Bass, *Practicing Theology: Beliefs and Practices in Christian Life* (Grand Rapids, MI: Eerdmans, 2001), 78-93.

'What Does Chalcedon Solve and What Does it Not? Some Reflections on the Status and Meaning of the Chalcedonian "Definition"', in eds. Stephen T. Davis, Daniel Kendall, S.J. and Gerald O'Collins, S.J., *The Incarnation: An Interdisciplinary Symposium on the Incarnation of the Son of God* (Oxford: Oxford University Press, 2002), 143-63.

'Re-thinking Gregory of Nyssa: Introduction—Gender, Trinitarian Analogies, and the Pedagogy of *The Song*', in ed. Coakley, *Re-thinking Gregory of Nyssa* [see above, under 1.], 1-13 (originally in *Modern Theology* 18, 2002, 431-43).

'The Resurrection: The Grammar of "Raised"', in eds. D. Z. Phillips and Mario von der Ruhr, *Biblical Concepts and Our World* (Basingstoke, Palgrave, 2004), 169-89.

'Response to Trutz Rendtorff', in eds. Slavica Jakelić and Lori Pearson, *The Future of the Study of Religion: Proceedings of Conference 2000* (Leiden: Brill, 2004), 315-20.

'Feminism and Analytic Philosophy of Religion', in ed. William J. Wainwright, *The Oxford Handbook of Philosophy of Religion* (New York: Oxford University Press, 2005), 494-525.

'Shaping the Field: A Transatlantic Perspective', in eds. David F. Ford, Ben Quash and Janet Martin Soskice, *Fields of Faith: Theology and Religious Studies for the Twenty-first Century* (a Festschrift for Nicholas Lash) (Cambridge: Cambridge University Press, 2005), 39–55.

'The Trinity and Gender Reconsidered', in eds. Miroslav Volf and Michael Welker, *God's Life in Trinity* (a Festschrift for Jürgen Moltmann) (Minneapolis, MN: Fortress, 2006), 133–42.

'Does Kenosis Rest on a Mistake? Three Kenotic Models in Patristic Exegesis', in ed. C. Stephen Evans, *Exploring Kenotic Christology: The Self-Emptying of God* (Oxford: Oxford University Press, 2006), 246–64, pbk edn Vancouver BC, Regent College Publishing, 2009.

'Beyond Libertarianism and Repression: The Quest for an Anglican Theological Ascetics', in ed. Terry Brown, *Other Voices, Other Worlds: The Global Church Speaks Out on Homosexuality* (London: D.L.T., 2006), 331–8.

'Critical Response to Mark Lewis Taylor', in eds. Jonathan Rothchild, Matthew Myer Boulton and Kevin Jung, *Doing Justice to Mercy: Religion, Law and Criminal Justice* (Charlottesville, VA: University of Virginia Press, 2007), 174–80.

'The Identity of the Risen Jesus: Finding Jesus Christ in the Poor', in eds. Beverly Roberts Gaventa and Richard B. Hays, *Seeking the Identity of Jesus: A Pilgrimage* (Grand Rapids MI, Eerdmans, 2008), 301–19 (reprinted with minor alterations in eds. Terrence Merrigan and Frederik Glorieux, '*Godhead Here in Hiding': Incarnation and the History of Human Suffering* (Leiden: Peeters, 2011), 309–27).

'Introduction: Prayer, Place and the Poor', in eds. Wells and Coakley, *Praying for England* [see above, under 1.], 1–20 (partially excerpted as 'The Vicar at Prayer: An English Reflection on Ministry', *The Christian Century*, 1 July 2008, 28–33).

'"Mingling" in Gregory of Nyssa's Christology: A Reconsideration', in eds. Andreas Schuele and Günter Thomas, *Who is Jesus Christ for Us Today? Pathways to Contemporary Christology* (a Festschrift for Michael Welker) (Louisville, KY: Westminster/John Knox, 2009), 72–84.

'On Clouds and Veils: Divine Presence and "Feminine" Secrets in Revelation and Nature', in ed. John W. Bowker, *Knowing the Unknowable: Science and Religions on God and the Universe* (London: Tauris, 2009), 123–59.

'Dark Contemplation and Epistemic Transformation: The Analytic Theologian Re-Meets Teresa of Avila', in eds. Oliver D. Crisp and Michael C. Rea, *Analytic Theology: New Essays in the Philosophy of Theology* (Oxford: Oxford University Press, 2009), 280–312.

'Providence and the Evolutionary Phenomenon of "Cooperation": A Systematic Proposal', in eds. Francesca Aran Murphy and Philip G. Ziegler, *The Providence of God: Deus Habet Consilium* (Edinburgh: T&T Clark, 2009), 181–95.

'Afterword: "Relational Ontology", Trinity, and Science', in ed. John Polkinghorne, *The Trinity and an Entangled World: Relationality in Physical Science and Theology* (Grand Rapids, MI: Eerdmans, 2010), 184–99.

'In Defense of Sacrifice: Gender, Selfhood, and the Binding of Isaac', in eds. Linda Martín Alcoff and John D. Caputo, *Feminism, Sexuality and the Return of Religion* (Bloomington, IN: Indiana University Press, 2011), 17–38 (and contributor to 'Concluding Roundtable: Feminism, Sexuality, and the Deconstruction of "Religion"', 160–84).

'On the Fearfulness of Forgiveness: Psalm 130:4 and its Theological Implications', in eds. Andreas Andreopoulos, Augustine Casiday and Carol Harrison, *Meditations of the Heart: The Psalms in Early Christian Thought and Practice* (Turnhout, Brepols, 2011), 33–51.

'Gregory of Nyssa', in eds. Paul L. Gavrilyuk and Coakley, *The Spiritual Senses: Perceiving God in Western Christianity* (Cambridge: Cambridge University Press, 2012), 36–55.

'Natural Theology and the Flat Plane Fallacy', in ed. Andrew Robinson, *Darwinism and Natural Theology: Evolving Perspectives* (Newcastle, Cambridge Scholars, 2012), 96–100.

'Eastern "Mystical Theology" or Western "Nouvelle Théologie"? On the Comparative Reception of Dionysius the Areopagite in Lossky and de Lubac', in *Orthodox Constructions of the West*, eds. George E. Demacopoulos and Aristotle Papanikolaou (New York: Fordham University Press, 2013), 125–141.

'Beyond "Belief": Liturgy and the Cognitive Apprehension of God', in *The*

Vocation of Theology Today, eds. Tom Greggs, Rachel Muers and Simeon Zahl (Eugene, OR: Wipf & Stock, 2013), 130-45.

3. Articles in Journals

'Theology and Cultural Relativism—What is the Problem?', *Neue Zeitschrift für systematische Theologie und Religionsphilosophie* 21, 1979, 223-43.

'Can God be Experienced as Trinity?', *The Modern Churchman* 28, 1986, 11-23.

'Traditions of Spiritual Guidance: Dom John Chapman O.S.B. (1865-1933)', *The Way* 30, 1990, 243-57.

'Creaturehood before God, Male and Female', *Theology* 93, 1990, 343-53 (reprinted in ed. Robin Gill, *Readings in Modern Theology*, London, S.P.C.K., 1995).

'Gender and Knowledge in Western Philosophy: The "Man of Reason" and the "Feminine" "Other" in Enlightenment and Romantic Thought', in eds. Elisabeth Schüssler Fiorenza and Anne E. Carr, *The Special Nature of Women* (*Concilium* 1991/6), London: S.C.M., 1991, 75-83.

'"Batter My Heart..."?', *Harvard Divinity Bulletin* 23, 3/4, 1994, 12-17.

'"Batter my heart ..."? On Sexuality, Spirituality, and the Christian Doctrine of the Trinity', *Graven Images* 2, 1995, 74-83 (reprinted in ed. Gary Gilbert, *The Papers of the Henry Luce III Fellows in Theology*, Atlanta, GA: Scholars Press, 1996, 49-68).

'Making Pentecost out of Babel', *Harvard Divinity Bulletin* 25, 4, 1996, 6.

'Living into the Mystery of the Holy Trinity: Trinity, Prayer, and Sexuality', *The Anglican Theological Review* 80, 1998, 223-32 (also in slightly revised form as 'The Trinity, Prayer and Sexuality: A Neglected Nexus in the Fathers and Beyond', *Centro Pro Unione* 58, 2000, 13-17; and anthologized in shortened form in eds. Janet Martin Soskice and Diana Lipton, *Feminism and Theology* (Oxford: Oxford University Press, 2003), 258-67).

'The Eschatological Body: Gender, Transformation and God', *Modern Theology* 16, 2000, 61-73 'Lay and Ordained Ministries: Some Theological Reflections', *Sewanee Theological Journal* 43, 2000, 207-13.

'Climax or Incoherence? The Place of Christology in Thomas's *Summa Theologiae*', *Providence* 8, 2003, 60-69.

'The Woman at the Altar: Cosmological Disturbance or Gender Fluidity?', *The*

Anglican Theological Review 86, 2004, 75-93 (75-9 and 87-93 excerpted in *Disability in the Christian Tradition: A Reader*, eds Brian Brock and John Swinton (Grand Rapids, MI: Eerdmans, 2012)).

'Pleasure Principles: Toward a Contemporary Theology of Desire', *Harvard Divinity Bulletin* 33, 2, 2005, 20-33.

'Theological Scholarship as Religious Vocation', *Christian Higher Education* 5, 2006, 55-68.

'"In persona Christi": Gender, Priesthood and the Nuptial Metaphor', *Svensk Teologisk Kvartalskrift* 82, 2006, 145-54 [lecture delivered on the occasion of the receipt of the degree Theologiae Doctricem Honoris Causa, University of Lund].

'Introduction: Disputed Questions in Patristic Trinitarianism', in ed. Sarah Coakley, *The God of Nicaea: Disputed Questions in Patristic Trinitarianism*, special guest-edited issue of *Harvard Theological Review* 100, 2007, 125-38.

'Why Gift? Gift, Gender, and Trinitarian Relations in Milbank and Tanner', *Scottish Journal of Theology* 16, 2008, 224-35.

'Introduction: Re-Thinking Dionysius the Areopagite', *Modern Theology* 24, 2008, 531-40.

'Is there a Future for Gender and Theology? On Gender, Contemplation, and the Systematic Task', 'Pain and its Transformations: A Discussion' and 'Brief Responses to my Interlocutors', *Svensk Teologisk Kvartalskrift* 85, 2009, 52-61, 81-4 and 90-2, an issue devoted to discussion of Coakley's work, with the first article also in *Criterion* 47/1, 2009, 2-11.

'A Response from Sarah Coakley [at a theological colloquy on same-sex relationships and the nature of marriage]', *The Anglican Theological Review* 93, 2011, 111-13.

'Introduction: Faith, Rationality and the Passions' and 'Postscript: What (If Anything) can the Sciences tell Philosophy and Theology about Faith, Rationality and the Passions?', *Modern Theology* 27, 2011, 217-25 and 357-61.

'Response to John Hare', *Studies in Christian Ethics* 25, 2, 2012, 255-60.

David G. Rand, Anna Dreber, Omar S. Haque, Rob Kane, Martin A. Nowak, and Sarah Coakley, 'Religious Motivations for Cooperation: An Experimental Investigation Using Explicit Primes', *Social Science Research Network* 2012, at http://papers.ssrn.com/sol3/papers.cfm?abstract_id=2123243. In slightly revised form, the same paper is in *Religion, Brain and Behavior*, 2013 http://dx.doi.org/10.1080/2153599X.2013.775664.

'Evolution, Cooperation and Ethics: Some Methodological and Philosophical Hurdles', *Studies in Christian Ethics* 26, 2013, 135-39.

'Prayer, Politics and the Trinity: Vying Models of Authority in 3rd-4th Century Debates on Prayer and "Orthodoxy" ', *The Scottish Journal of Theology* 66, 2013, 379-99.

'Why Analytic Theology is Not a Club', *Journal of the American Academy of Religion* 81, 2013, 601-08.

'Introduction: Ethics, Theology and the Contemporary Conundrum of State Punishment', *Studies in Christian Ethics* 27, 2014, 253-57.

Forthcoming:

The Oxford Handbook to the Reception History of Christian Theology, co-ed. with Richard Cross (Oxford: Oxford University Press, 2016).

The Broken Body: Israel, Christ and Fragmentation (Oxford: Wiley-Blackwell, 2016) (*Gesammelte Schriften*, vol. 2).

Knowing Darkly: An Essay 'On the Contemplative Life' (Cambridge: Cambridge University Press, 2016) (vol. 2 of 4-vol. systematic theology).

4. Reviews

Review of ed. John Powell Clayton, *Ernst Troeltsch and the Future of Theology* (Cambridge: Cambridge University Press, 1976) in *The Heythrop Journal* 18, 1977, 327–28.

Review of eds. Robert Morgan and Martin Pye, *Ernst Troeltsch: Writings on Theology and Religion* (London: Duckworth, 1977) in *The Times Literary Supplement*, 12 May 1978, 529.

Review of ed. B.A. Gerrish, *Tradition and the Modern World: Reformed Theology in the Nineteenth Century* (Chicago: University of Chicago Press, 1978) in *The Expository Times* 91, 1979, 60.

Reviews of Brian Hebblethwaite, *The Problems of Theology* (Cambridge: Cambridge University Press, 1980) and George Newlands, *Theology of the Love of God* (London, Collins, 1980) in *The Times Literary Supplement*, 31 October 1980, 1243.

Review of Jürgen Moltmann, *The Church in the Power of the Spirit* (London: S.C.M., 1977) in *Scripture Bulletin* 10, 1980, 48.

Review of John Ferguson, *Jesus in the Tide of Time: An Historical Study* (London: Routledge & Kegan Paul, 1980) in *Religion* 11, 1981, 199–200.

Review of Mary Clare, S.L.G., *Encountering the Depths* (London: D.L.T., 1981) and Donald Nicholl, *Holiness* (London: D.L.T., 1981) in *The Times Literary Supplement*, 24 July 1981, 854.

Review of William J. Abraham, *Divine Revelation and the Limits of Historical Criticism* (Oxford: Oxford University Press, 1982) in *The Modern Churchman* 25, 1983, 60–62.

Review of eds. George Every, Richard Harries and Kallistos Ware, *Seasons of the Spirit* (London: S.P.C.K., 1984) in *Religion Today* 2, 3, October 1985, 14.

Review of A.M. Allchin, *Ann Griffiths: The Furnace and the Fountain* (Cardiff, Wales: University of Wales Press, 1987) in *Literature and Theology* 2, 1988, 269–70.

Review of ed. Ursula King, *Women in the World's Religions, Past and Present* (New York: Paragon House, 1989) in *World Religions in Education*, 1989, 13–14.

Review of Daphne Hampson, *Theology and Feminism* (Oxford: Blackwell, 1990) in *Theology* 94, 1991, 132–33.

Review of Nicholas Lash, *Believing Three Ways in One God: A Reading of the Apostles' Creed* (London: S.C.M., 1992) in *Modern Theology* 11, 1995, 262–64.

Review of ed. Alvin F. Kimel, Jr., *Speaking the Christian God: The Holy Trinity and the Challenge of Feminism* (Grand Rapids, MI: Eerdmans, 1992) in *Journal of Theological Studies* 47, 1996, 389–94.

Review of ed. Robert Morgan, *The Religion of the Incarnation: Anglican Essays in Commemoration of 'Lux Mundi'* (Bristol: Classical Press 1989) in *The Heythrop Journal* 38, 1997, 328–29.

Review of Leonardo Boff, *The Maternal Face of God: The Feminine and its Religious Expressions* (London: Collins, 1989), in *The Heythrop Journal* 42, 2001, 102–24.

Review of Gavin D'Costa, *Sexing the Trinity: Gender, Culture and the Divine* (London: S.C.M., 2000), in *Theology and Sexuality* 11, 2005, 91–94.

Reviews of Edward O. Wilson, *The Creation: A Meeting of Science and Religion* (New York, Norton, 2006), and of O. Gingerich, *God's Universe* (Cambridge, MA:

Belknap/Harvard University Press, 2006), in 'Twin Passions: Two Scientists Explore Science and Religion', *Harvard Magazine*, May/June 2007, 22-26.

Review of Eugene F. Rogers, *After the Spirit: A Constructive Pheumatology from Resources Outside the Modern West* (Grand Rapids, MI: Eerdmans, 2005), in *Journal of the American Academy of Religion* 75, 2007, 429-32.

5. Other Items

'The Doctrine of God and the Challenges of "Feminist" Theology: An Iconographical Approach' (an address with 22 slides for the Lambeth Conference, July 1988; distributed in a print-run of 1,000 to the Anglican bishops and others at the Conference and available in video form from Church House, London).

'Lay and Ordained Ministry: Some Theological Reflections' (an address to the Discernment for Ministries Conference, Episcopal Diocese of Massachusetts, 11 January 1997; distributed in the Diocese with the booklet *The Ordination Process for the Diocese of Massachusetts*).

(with Peter Machinist), 'Morning Prayers at Harvard', *Harvard Divinity Bulletin* 24, 4, 1995, 10-11.

'The Silent Prayer Group at Harvard Divinity School', *The Anglican Catholic* 13, Winter 2001-2, 36-42 (also lightly revised as 'The Deepening Life of a Silent Prayer Group', *Harvard Divinity Bulletin* 30, 4, Spring 2002, 23-4).

'Easier Said than Defined', *Commonweal* (special Easter issue 'Christology: What It Is and Why It's Important), 22 March 2002, 17.

'Jail Break: Meditation as a Subversive Activity', *The Christian Century*, 29 June 2004, 18-21.

'Is Cooperation Evolution's Clue to God's Existence?', *The Church Times*, 21 November 2008, 16-17 (reprinted as 'Evolution and Sacrifice: Cooperation as a Scientific Principle' in *The Christian Century*, 20 October 2009; Swedish trans. in *Signum* 7, 2009, 4-10).

'Foreword' to Aref Ali Nayed, *Growing Ecologies of Peace, Compassion and Blessing: A Muslim Response to 'A Muscat Manifesto'*, Dubai, Kalam Research & Media, 2010, 5.

'5 Picks: Essential Theology Books of the Past 25 Years', *The Christian Century*,

19 October 2010, 35 'Prayer as Crucible: How My Mind has Changed', *The Christian Century*, 22 March 2011, 32-40.

'Prayer as Crucible: How My Mind has Changed', *The Christian Century*, 22 March 2011, 32-40.

Holy Week Sermons 2011, Little St Mary's, Cambridge, 2011.

'Has the Church of England finally lost its reason? Women bishops and the collapse of Anglican theology', *ABC Religion and Ethics* website, 23 November, 2012.

The Cross and the Transformation of Desire: The Drama of Love and Betrayal (Cambridge: Grove Books S 128, 2014).

6. Feature Articles by Others

'Sarah Coakley', in Sian Griffiths, *Beyond the Glass Ceiling: Forty Women Whose Ideas Shape the Modern World* (Manchester University Press, 1996), 36-43.

Mark Oppenheimer, 'Prayerful Vulnerability: Sarah Coakley Reconstructs Feminism', *The Christian Century*, 28 June 2003, 25-31.

Sam Allis, 'Bridging the Abyss [the gulf between religion and medicine]', *Boston Sunday Globe*, 17 October 2004, A2.

'Sarah Coakley: Fresh Paths in Systematic Theology', in Rupert Shortt, *God's Advocates: Christian Thinkers in Conversation* (London, D.L.T., 2005), 67-85.

Jason Byassee, 'Closer than Kissing: Sarah Coakley's Early Work', *The Anglican Theological Review* 90 (2008), 139-55.

Jason Byassee, 'Sarah Coakley: Living Prayer and Leadership', for Faith & Leadership website, Duke University, 18 August 2009, at http://www.faithandleadership.com/qa/sarah-coakley-living-   prayer-and-leadership.

'Sarah Coakley: A Symposium', *Svensk Teologisk Kvartalskrift* 85, 2 (2009), ed. Gösta Hallonsten, includes contributions by Antje Jackelén, Philip Geister, Anne-Louise Eriksson, Jonna Bornemark and Jayne Svenungsson.

Janice Rees, "Sarah Coakley: Systematic Theology and the Future of Feminism". In *Pacifica* 24:3 (2011), 300-314.

Stephen Wilson, 'Sarah Coakley Discusses *Waiting on God*', *Cambridge Alumni Magazine (CAM)* 65 (Lent 2012), 43.

Sarah Coakley and Sue-Jeanne Koh, 'Prayer as Divine Propulsion: An Interview with Sarah Coakley, Part I', *TheOtherJournal.com* December 20, 2012, and 'Part II', *TheOtherJournal.com* December 27, 2012.

Matthew Reisz, 'Giving but not yielding', feature article on Sarah Coakley, *Times Higher Education*, 8 August, 2013, 38-41.